Lecture Notes in Computer Sc

Commenced Publication in 1973
Founding and Former Series Editors:
Gerhard Goos, Juris Hartmanis, and Jan van Leeuw

Stefano Spaccapietra
Elisa Bertino   Sushil Jajodia
Roger King   Dennis McLeod
Maria E. Orlowska   Leon Strous (Eds.)

Journal on
Data
Semantics II

 Springer

Volume Editors

Stefano Spaccapietra
E-mail: stefano.spaccapietra@epfl.ch

Elisa Bertino
E-mail: bertino@cs.purdue.edu

Sushil Jajodia
E-mail: jajodia@gmu.edu

Roger King
E-mail: roger@cs.colorado.edu

Dennis McLeod
E-mail: mcleod@usc.edu

Maria E. Orlowska
E-mail: maria@itee.uq.edu.au

Leon Strous
E-mail: strous@iae.nl

Library of Congress Control Number: 2004117338

CR Subject Classification (1998): H.2, H.3, I.2, H.4, C.2

ISSN 0302-9743
ISBN 3-540-24208-2 Springer Berlin Heidelberg New York

Springer is a part of Springer Science+Business Media

springeronline.com

© Springer-Verlag Berlin Heidelberg 2005
Printed in Germany

Typesetting: Camera-ready by author, data conversion by Boller Mediendesign
Printed on acid-free paper   SPIN: 11371861   06/3142   5 4 3 2 1 0

The LNCS Journal on Data Semantics

Computerized information handling has changed its focus from centralized data management systems to decentralized data exchange facilities. Modern distribution channels, such as high-speed Internet networks and wireless communication infrastructures, provide reliable technical support for data distribution and data access, materializing the new popular idea that data may be available to anybody, anywhere, anytime. However, providing huge amounts of data on request often turns into a counterproductive service, making the data useless because of poor relevance or inappropriate levels of detail. Semantic knowledge is the essential missing piece that allows the delivery of information that matches user requirements. Semantic agreement, in particular, is essential to meaningful data exchange.

Semantic issues have long been open issues in data and knowledge management. However, the boom in semantically poor technologies, such as the Web and XML, has prompted a renewed interest in semantics. Conferences on the Semantic Web, for instance, attract crowds of participants, while ontologies on its own has become a hot and popular topic in the database and artificial intelligence communities.

Springer's LNCS Journal on Data Semantics aims at providing a highly visible dissemination channel for the most remarkable work that in one way or another addresses research and development on issues related to the semantics of data. The target domain ranges from theories supporting the formal definition of semantic content to innovative domain-specific applications of semantic knowledge. This publication channel should be of highest interest to researchers and advanced practitioners working on the Semantic Web, interoperability, mobile information services, data warehousing, knowledge representation and reasoning, conceptual database modeling, ontologies, and artificial intelligence.

Topics of relevance to this journal include:

- semantic interoperability, semantic mediators
- ontologies
- ontology, schema and data integration, reconciliation and alignment
- multiple representations, alternative representations
- knowledge representation and reasoning
- conceptualization and representation
- multimodel and multiparadigm approaches
- mappings, transformations, reverse engineering
- metadata
- conceptual data modeling
- integrity description and handling
- evolution and change
- Web semantics and semistructured data
- semantic caching

- data warehousing and semantic data mining
- spatial, temporal, multimedia and multimodal semantics
- semantics in data visualization
- semantic services for mobile users
- supporting tools
- applications of semantic-driven approaches

These topics are to be understood as specifically related to semantic issues. Contributions submitted to the journal and dealing with semantics of data will be considered even if they are not within the topics in the list.

While the physical appearance of the journal issues looks like the books from the well-known Springer LNCS series, the mode of operation is that of a journal. Contributions can be freely submitted by authors and are reviewed by the Editorial Board. Contributions may also be invited, and nevertheless carefully reviewed, as in the case of issues that contain extended versions of best papers from major conferences addressing data semantics issues. Special issues, focusing on a specific topic, are coordinated by guest editors once the proposal for a special issue is accepted by the Editorial Board. Finally, it is also possible that a journal issue be devoted to a single text.

The journal published its first volume in 2003. This is the second volume, and it will be followed by three volumes to appear in 2005.

The Editorial Board comprises one Editor-in-Chief (with overall responsibility) and several members. The editor-in-chief has a four-year mandate to run the journal. Members of the board have three-year mandates. Mandates are renewable. More members may be added to the Editorial Board as appropriate

We are happy to welcome you into our readership and authorship, and hope we will share this privileged contact for a long time.

Stefano Spaccapietra
Editor-in-Chief

JoDS Volume 2 – Guest Editorial

Conferences provide researchers with the fastest way to disseminate their ideas and results to a selected community of other researchers in the same domain. Conferences, however, must enforce limitations in the sizes of the written contributions as well as in the time allocated for the on-site presentations of the contributions. They also have limited audiences, although some publishers such as Springer have a dissemination scheme that brings conference proceedings to much wider audiences than just the actual participants at the conferences.

Publication of an extended version of a conference paper is a much appreciated opportunity for researchers to widely disseminate a significantly improved presentation of their work, where they can develop the appropriate motivations, reasoning, results and comparative analysis. To foster dissemination of the best ideas and results, the Journal on Data Semantics (JoDS) pursues a policy that includes annually publishing extended versions of the best papers from selected conferences whose scope encompasses or intersects the scope of the journal.

The selection for this issue comprises the International Conference on Ontologies, Databases and Applications of Semantics (ODBASE), the International Conference on Cooperative Information Systems (COOPIS), and the IFIP TC11 WG11.5 Working Conference on Integrity and Internal Control in Information Systems (IICIS). Papers from these conferences were selected based on their quality, relevance, and significance, and the viability of extending their results. All extended papers were subject to a stringent review process and the authors were required to respond to all concerns expressed by the reviewers before papers were accepted.

Four papers, showing consistently high reviews from the program committee, were selected among those presented at the *Ontologies, Databases and Applications of Semantics (ODBase)* conference, held in Catania, Italy, November 4–6, 2003. Three of the papers have to do with the construction and maintenance of ontologies and structured taxonomies. *Incrementally Maintaining Materializations of Ontologies Stored in Logic Databases* (by Raphael Volz, Steffen Staab, and Boris Motik) presents a method for propagating changes made to an ontology; the technique is broadly applicable, as it is compatible with any ontology language that can be translated into Datalog programs. *Ontology Translation on the Semantic Web* (by Dejing Dou, Drew McDermott, and Peishen Qi) addresses the highly important problem of resolving terminology differences between related ontologies; the technique manages syntactic as well as semantic translations. *Compound Term Composition Algebra: the Semantics* (by Yannis Tzitzikas, Anastasia Analyti, and Nicolas Spyratos) presents an elegant, formal algebra for specifying the valid compound terms in a taxonomy.

The fourth paper, *Dynamic Pattern Mining: an Incremental Data Clustering Approach* (by Seokkyung Chung and Dennis McLeod) addresses one of the central problems facing users of data mines – the incremental maintenance of a data mine that is constantly updated. The paper deals specifically with services that provide integrated access to news articles; the method described in the paper is simple yet semantically powerful and quite efficient.

The volume continues with two papers that are comprehensive descriptions of the topics of the two top-rated papers that appeared in the *CoopIS* portion of the proceedings of the conference triad *On the Move to Meaningful Internet Systems*, November 2003. The first paper, *A Knowledge Network Approach for Implementing Active Virtual Marketplaces*, by Minsoo Lee, Stanley Su, and Herman Lam, presents a network approach for implementing virtual marketplaces: bringing buyers and sellers cooperatively together. The paper focuses on an infrastructure that enables sharing of knowledge over the Web and thus effectively supports the formation of virtual marketplaces on the Web. The concept of an active virtual marketplace is realized using this infrastructure by allowing buyers and sellers to specify their knowledge in the form of events, triggers, and rules. The knowledge network can actively distribute and process these knowledge elements to help buyers and sellers to locate and interact with each other.

The second paper, *Stream Integration Techniques for Grid Monitoring*, by Andy Cooke, Alasdair Gray, and Werner Nutt, focuses on a technique for providing information about the status of a cooperative computation grid by utilizing database integration techniques. This novel approach provides an infrastructure for publishing and querying grid monitoring data. Emphasis is placed on the use of the technique for distributed sets of data streams, which provide information about the changes over time of a data source. The concepts and mechanisms devised can also be applied more generally where there is a need for publishing and querying information in a distributed manner.

Finally, the volume contains two papers originally presented at the *6th IFIP TC 11 WG 11.5 Working Conference on Integrity and Internal Control in Information Systems*, which was held November 13–14, 2003 in Lausanne, Switzerland. Traditionally, access controls have been used to limit the availability of data to users; however, they do not protect unauthorized disclosure of sensitive information from careless or malicious insiders with authorized access to the system. The first paper *Information Release Control: a Learning-Based Architecture*, by Claudio Bettini, X. Sean Wang, and Sushil Jajodia, explores the information release control paradigm, which is based on checking data when they are being released across organizational boundaries. Rather than relying simply on source/destination addresses, as in current firewall systems, or on simple "dirty word" matching as in current filtering software, the checking process analyzes the semantics of the released data. This paper formalizes this process and presents the architecture of a system that incorporates a module for learning release constraints.

Nowadays, surveillance devices such as video cameras and microphones have become commonplace in our society. The second paper, *Enforcing Semantics-Aware Security in Multimedia Surveillance*, by Naren Kodali, Csilla Farkas, and Duminda Wijesekera, considers the surveillance data flowing at secured facilities such as airports, nuclear power plants, and national laboratories. Typically, different parts of such facilities have different degrees of sensitivity. Likewise, human guards are categorized according to their rights of access to various locations within the facilities. The main security requirement is that the guards can view data gathered from locations whose sensitivity is consistent with their access rights. This paper shows how to model the surveillance requirements using the synchronized multimedia integration language (SMIL) with appropriate multilevel security enhancements.

Guest Editors

ODBASE	Roger (Buzz) King, University of Colorado at Boulder, USA
	Maria Orlowska, University of Queensland, Australia
COOPIS	Elisa Bertino, Purdue University, USA
	Dennis McLeod, University of Southern California, Los Angeles, USA
IICIS	Sushil Jajodia, George Mason University, USA
	Leon Strous, De Nederlandsche Bank, The Netherlands

We are pleased to express our gratitude to the reviewers, who invested much of their time in careful analysis and evaluation of the submissions:

Dave Abel, CSIRO, Australia
Karl Aberer, École Polytechnique Fédérale de Lausanne, Switzerland
John Carlis, University of Minnesota, USA
Tiziana Catarci, University of Rome, Italy
Brian Cooper, Georgia Institute of Technology, USA
Guido Governatori, University of Queensland, Australia
Michael Kifer, Stonybrook State University of New York, USA
Dik Lee, University of Science and Technology, Hong Kong, China
Qing Li, City University of Hong Kong, Hong Kong, China
Leo Mark, Georgia Institute of Technology, USA
Ravi Mukkamala, Old Dominion University, USA
Erich Neuhold, Darmstadt University of Technology, Germany
Brajendra Panda, University of Arkansas, Fayetteville, USA
Evagelia Pitoura, University of Ioannina, Greece
Amit Sheth, University of Georgia, USA
Antonio Si, Oracle, USA
Steffen Staab, University of Koblenz-Landau, Germany
Sean Wang, University of Vermont, USA
Chao Yao, George Mason University, USA
Roger Zimmermann, University of Southern California, USA

JoDS Editorial Board[1]

---

[1] The late Yahiko Kambayashi (Kyoto University, Japan) was a member of the JoDS Editorial Board.

Table of Contents

Incrementally Maintaining Materializations of Ontologies Stored in Logic Databases

Raphael Volz[1,2], Steffen Staab[1], and Boris Motik[2]

[1] Institute AIFB, University of Karlsruhe, Germany
`lastname@aifb.uni-karlsruhe.de`
[2] FZI, University of Karlsruhe, Germany
`volz@fzi.de`

Abstract. This article presents a technique to incrementally maintain materializations of ontological entailments. Materialization consists in precomputing and storing a set of implicit entailments, such that frequent and/or crucial queries to the ontology can be solved more efficiently. The central problem that arises with materialization is its maintenance when axioms change, viz. the process of propagating changes in explicit axioms to the stored implicit entailments.

When considering rule-enabled ontology languages that are operationalized in logic databases, we can distinguish two types of changes. Changes to the ontology will typically manifest themselves in changes to the rules of the logic program, whereas changes to facts will typically lead to changes in the extensions of logical predicates. The incremental maintenance of the latter type of changes has been studied extensively in the deductive database context and we apply the technique proposed in [30] for our purpose. The former type of changes has, however, not been tackled before.

In this article we elaborate on our previous papers [32, 33], which extend the approach of [30] to deal with changes in the logic program. Our approach is not limited to a particular ontology language but can be generally applied to arbitrary ontology languages that can be translated to Datalog programs, i.e. such as O-Telos, F-Logic [16] RDF(S), or Description Logic Programs [34].

1 Introduction

Germane to the idea of the Semantic Web are the capabilities to assert facts and to derive new facts from the asserted facts using the semantics specified by an ontology. Both current building blocks of the Semantic Web, RDF [13] and OWL [21], define how to assert facts and specify how new facts should be derived from stated facts.

The necessary derivation of entailed information from asserted information is usually achieved at the time clients issue queries to inference engines such as logic databases. Situations where queries are frequent or the procedure to derive entailed information is time consuming and complex typically lead to low performance. Materialization can be used to increase the performance at

S. Spaccapietra et al. (Eds.): Journal on Data Semantics II, LNCS 3360, pp. 1–34, 2004.

query time by making entailed information explicit upfront. Thereby, the re-computation of entailed information for every single query is avoided.

Materialization has been applied successfully in many applications where reading access to data is predominant. For example, data warehouses usually apply materialization techniques to make *online* analytical processing possible. Similarly, most Web portals maintain cached web pages to offer fast access to dynamically generated web pages.

We conjecture that reading access to ontologies is predominant in the Semantic Web and other ontology-based applications, hence materialization seems to be a promising technique for fast processing of queries on ontologies.

Materialization is particularly promising for the currently predominant approach of aggregating distributed information into a central knowledge base (cf. [8, 14, 31, 20]). For example, the OntoWeb[3] Semantic portal [28] employs a *syndicator* (cf. Figure 1), which regularly visits sites specified by community members and transfers the detected updates into a central knowledge base in a batch process. Hence, the knowledge base remains unchanged between updates for longer periods of time.

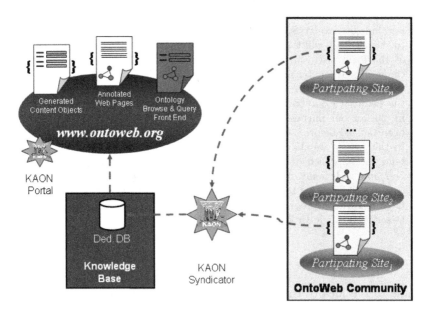

Fig. 1. OntoWeb Architecture

The OntoWeb portal, however, provides answers to queries issued on the knowledge base whenever visitors browse the portal content. This is due to the fact that most queries are hard-coded into the definition of dynamic Web pages,

---

[3] http://www.ontoweb.org/.

which are generated for every request. In applications such as OntoWeb, materialization turns out to be a sine qua non.[4]

Central to materialization approaches is the issue of maintaining a materialization when changes occur. This issue can be handled by simply recomputing the whole materialization. However, as the computation of the materialization is often complex and time consuming, it is desirable to apply more efficient techniques in practice, i.e. to *incrementally* maintain a materialization.

1.1 Contribution

We present a technique for the incremental maintenance of materialized ontologies. Our technique can be applied to a wide range of ontology languages, namely those that can be axiomatized by a set of rules[5].

The challenge that has not been tackled before comes from the fact that updates of ontology definitions are equivalent to the updates and new definitions of rules, whereas existing maintenance techniques only address the update of ground facts.

To cope with changing rules, our solution extends a declarative algorithm for the incremental maintenance of views [30] that was developed in the deductive database context. We show the feasibility of our solution in a performance evaluation.

1.2 Organization

The remainder of the article is organized as follows: Section 2 reviews how current Web ontology languages such as RDF(S) and OWL interplay with rules. Section 3 presents the underlying principles which are applied to achieve incremental maintenance of a materialization. Section 4 recapitulates the incremental maintenance algorithm presented in [30] , presents a novel modular rewriting algorithm based on generator functions and shows how this algorithm deals with changes to facts. Section 5 extends this algorithm to deal with changing rules as they result from changes in the ontology. Section 6 sketches how the developed techniques can be applied in implementations of RDF rule languages. Section 7 describes our prototypical implementation. Section 8 performs a performance analysis and shows the benefits of our approach. Section 10 summarizes our contribution and discusses further uses.

2 Web Ontology Languages and Logic Databases

In the brief history of the Semantic Web, most applications, e.g. [7], have implemented the logical entailment supported by ontology languages either directly

---

[4] Even though in OntoWeb, due to the unavailability of the solution developed in this article, the problem was approached by caching the Web pages through a proxy server.

[5] The underlying rule language used for our approach is Datalog with stratified negation.

using Logic Programming techniques, e.g. [4, 25], or by relying on (available) logic databases[6] [22, 27]. Furthermore, a large expressive fragment of the recently standardized Web Ontology Language (OWL) can be implemented in logic databases [34].

2.1 Axiomatization of Ontology Languages

Systems like SilRi [7], CWM[7], Euler [25], JTP[8] or Triple [27] and Concept-Base [15] implement the semantics of a particular ontology language via a static axiomatization, i.e. a set of rules. For example, Figure 2 presents the Datalog axiomatization of the RDF vocabulary description language (RDFS) [5]. This axiomatization implements the semantics of RDF specified by the RDF model theory [13] (without datatype entailments and support for stronger iff semantics of domain and ranges). The ontology and associated data is stored in a single ternary predicate t, i.e. the extension of t stores all triples that constitute a particular RDF graph.

t(P,a,rdf:Property)	:- t(S,P,O).	*rdf1*
t(S,a,C)	:- t(P,domain,C), t(S,P,O).	*rdfs2*
t(O,a,C)	:- t(P,range,C), t(S,P,O).	*rdfs3*
t(S,a,Resource)	:- t(S,P,O).	*rdfs4a*
t(O,a,Resource)	:- t(S,P,O).	*rdfs4b*
t(P,subPropertyOf,R)	:- t(Q,subPropertyOf,R), t(P,subPropertyOf,Q).	*rdfs5a*
t(S,R,0)	:- t(P,subPropertyOf,R), t(S,P,O).	*rdfs6*
t(C,a,Class)	:- t(C,subClassOf,Resource).	*rdfs7*
t(A,subClassOf,C)	:- t(B,subClassOf,C), t(A,subClassOf,B).	*rdfs8*
t(S,a;B)	:- t(S,a,A), t(A,subClassOf,B).	*rdfs9*
t(X,subPropertyOf,member)	:- t(X,a,ContainerMembershipProperty).	*rdfs10*
t(X,subClassOf,Literal)	:- t(X,a,Datatype).	*rdfs11*
t(Resource,subClassOf,Y)	:- t(X,domain,Y), t(rdf:type,subPropertyOf,X).	*rdfs12*

Fig. 2. Static Datalog rules for implementing RDF(S)

2.2 Dynamic Rule Sets

The set of rules is typically not immutable. With the advent of higher layers of the Semantic Web stack, i.e. the rule layer, users can create their own rules.

---

[6] We use the term logic database over the older term deductive databases since the later is very closely associated with Datalog, a particular Logic Programming language that is frequently used in logic databases. Modern logic databases such as XSB [26] and CORAL [24] support more expressive Logic Programming languages that include function symbols and nested expressions. Furthermore, several lectures, e.g. http://user.it.uu.se/v̆oronkorov/ddb.htm nowadays use this term.

[7] http://www.w3.org/2000/10/swap/doc/cwm

[8] http://ksl.stanford.edu/software/jtp/

Hence, we are facing a scenario where not only base facts can change but also the set of rules. This requires the ability to maintain a materialization in this situation.

Besides support for a rule layer, the ability to maintain a materialization under changing rule sets is also required for approaches where the semantics of the ontology language is not captured via a static set of rules but instead compiled into a set of rules. Such an approach is for example required by Description Logic Programs (DLP) [34], where OWL ontologies are translated to logic programs.

2.2.1 Semantic Web Rule Layer We now briefly present some languages for the specification of Semantic Web rules that may be compiled into the paradigm we use. The Rule Markup Initiative[9] aims to develop a canonical Web language for rules called RuleML. RuleML covers the entire rule spectrum and spans from derivation rules to transformation rules to reaction rules. It has a well-defined Datalog subset, which can be enforced using XML schemas, and for which we can employ the materialization techniques developed within this paper. The reader may note, that materialization is not an issue for many other aspects found in RuleML, e.g. transformation rules or reaction rules.

In parallel to the RuleML iniative, Notation3 (N3)[10] has emerged as a human-readable language for RDF/XML. Its aim is to optimize expression of data and logic in the same language and has become a serious alternative since many systems that support inference on RDF data, e.g. cwm[11], Euler (cf. http://www.agfa.com/w3c/euler/), Jena2 (cf. http://www.hpl.hp.com/semweb/jena.htm), support it. The rule language supported by N3 is an extension of Datalog with existential quantifiers in rule heads. Hence, the materialization techniques developed within this paper can be applied to the subset of all N3 programs which do not make use of existential quantification in the head.

2.2.2 Description Logic Programs (DLP) Both of the above mentioned approaches allow the definition of rules but are not integrated with the ontology layer in the Semantic Web architecture. Description Logic Programs [34] aim to integrate rules with the ontology layer by compiling ontology definitions into a logic program which can later be extended with additional rules. This approach can deal with an expressive subset of the standardized Web ontology language OWL (i.e. OWL without existential quantification, negation and disjunction in rule heads).

OWL classes are represented in the logic database as unary predicates and OWL properties is represented as binary predicates. Classes may be constructed using various constructors (cf. Table 1). The OWL T-Box may consist of class inclusion axioms and class equivalence axioms, which are mapped to logical

---

[9] cf. http://www.ruleml.org/

[10] cf. http://www.w3.org/DesignIssues/Notation3.html

[11] cf. http://www.w3.org/2000/10/swap/doc/cwm

OWL Abstract Syntax	Logic Database
`Class` $(A$ partial $D_1 \ldots D_n)$	$\bigcup_{i \in [1,n]} \varphi_{\mathcal{LP}}(A \sqsubseteq D_i)$
`Class` $(A$ complete $D_1 \ldots D_n)$	$\bigcup_{i \in [1,n]} \varphi_{\mathcal{LP}}(A \equiv D_i)$
`EquivalentClasses` $(D_1 \ldots D_n)$	$\bigcup_{i \in [1,n]} \varphi_{\mathcal{LP}}(D_1 \equiv D_i)$
`SubClassOf` $(D_1 D_2)$	$\varphi_{\mathcal{LP}}(D_1 \sqsubseteq D_2)$
$\varphi_{\mathcal{LP}}(C \equiv D)$	$\begin{cases} \varphi_{\mathcal{LP}}(C \sqsubseteq D) \\ \varphi_{\mathcal{LP}}(D \sqsubseteq C) \end{cases}$
$\varphi_{\mathcal{LP}}(C \sqsubseteq D)$	$\varphi_{\mathcal{LP}}^R(D,x)\text{:-}\varphi_{\mathcal{LP}}^L(C,x).$
$\varphi_{\mathcal{LP}}^R(A,x)\text{:-}B.$	$A(x)\text{:-}B.$
$\varphi_{\mathcal{LP}}^R(\exists R.\{i\}, x)\text{:-}B.$	$R(x,i)\text{:-}B.$
$\varphi_{\mathcal{LP}}^R(C \sqcap D, x)\text{:-}B.$	$\begin{cases} \varphi_{\mathcal{LP}}^R(C,x)\text{:-}B. \\ \varphi_{\mathcal{LP}}^R(D,x)\text{:-}B. \end{cases}$
$\varphi_{\mathcal{LP}}^R(\forall R.C, x)\text{:-}B.$	$\varphi_{\mathcal{LP}}^R(C,y_i)\text{:-}R(x,y_i),B.$
$H\text{:-}\varphi_{\mathcal{LP}}^L(\exists R.\{i\}, x), B.$	$H\text{:-}R(x,i),B.$
$H\text{:-}\varphi_{\mathcal{LP}}^L(A, x), B.$	$H\text{:-}A(x),B.$
$H\text{:-}\varphi_{\mathcal{LP}}^L((\exists R.C), x), B.$	$H\text{:-}R(x,y_i),C(y_i),B.$
$H\text{:-}\varphi_{\mathcal{LP}}^L((C \sqcap D), x), B.$	$H\text{:-}\varphi_{\mathcal{LP}}^L(C,x),\varphi_{\mathcal{LP}}^L(C,x),B.$
$H\text{:-}\varphi_{\mathcal{LP}}^L((C \sqcup D), x), B.$	$\begin{cases} H\text{:-}\varphi_{\mathcal{LP}}^L(C,x),B. \\ H\text{:-}\varphi_{\mathcal{LP}}^L(D,x),B. \end{cases}$

Table 1. DLP representation of OWL classes in logic databases

implications, i.e. rules[12]. Similarly, the T-Box may also consist of inclusion and equivalence axioms between properties. Properties may have inverses and may be defined to be symmetric and transitive (cf. Table 2).

Example 1. The following example OWL fragment declares Wine to be potable liquids who are made by Wineries:

$$\text{Wine} \sqsubseteq \text{PotableLiquid} \sqcap \forall \text{hasMaker.Winery}$$

This will be translated to the following set of rules:

PotableLiquid(X) :- Wine(X).
Winery(Y) :- Wine(X), hasMaker(X,Y).

We can easily see that a change to the class and property structure of an ontology will result in a change of the compiled rules. Again, it is necessary to be able to maintain a materialization in case of such a change.

An OWL A-Box, i.e. individuals and property fillers, are represented as facts in the logic database, where individuals i instantiating a class C and fillers (a, b) of a property P are simple facts of the form $C(i)$ and $P(a,b)$.

---

[12] Equivalence is decomposed into two inverse inclusion axioms

OWL Abstract Syntax	Logic Database
`ObjectProperty` $(P$	
super(Q_1) ... super(Q_n)	$\bigcup_{i\in[1,n]}\{Q_i(x,y)\text{:-}P(x,y).\}$
domain(C_1)	$C_1(x)\text{:-}P(x,y).$
...	...
domain(C_n)	$C_n(x)\text{:-}P(x,y).$
range(R_1)	$R_1(y)\text{:-}P(x,y).$
...	...
range(R_n)	$R_n(y)\text{:-}P(x,y).$
inverseOf(Q)	$P(x,y)\text{:-}Q(y,x).$
	$Q(x,y)\text{:-}P(y,x).$
Symmetric	$P(x,y)\text{:-}P(y,x).$
Transitive	$P(x,z)\text{:-}P(x,y),P(y,z).$
$)$	
`EquivalentProperties` $(P_1 \dots P_n)$	$\bigcup_{i\in[1,n]}\{P_1(x,y)\text{:-}P_i(x,y).P_i(x,y)\text{:-}P_1(x,y).\}$
`SubPropertyOf` $(P\ Q)$	$Q(x,y)\text{:-}P(x,y).$

Table 2. DLP Representation of OWL properties in logic databases

2.3 Differentiating Between Asserted and Entailed Information

The fundamental requirement for our approach to maintenance is the ability to distinguish entailed information from asserted information. This ability is required in order to propagate changes. The requirement also commonly arises in many ontology-based applications [2], which often need to differentiate between asserted information and information that has been derived by making use of TBox axioms, e.g. one could prevent users from updating entailed information [3].

To achieve this differentiation, all TBox axioms are translated into rules between purely intensional predicates C_{idb}, P_{idb}. ABox assertions, however, are stored in dedicated extensional predicates C_{edb}, P_{edb}. The connection between the intensional and the extensional database is made using simple rules that derive the initial (asserted) extension of the intensional predicates:

$$C_{idb}(x)\text{:-}C_{edb}(x).$$
$$P_{idb}(x,y)\text{:-}P_{edb}(x,y).$$

3 Maintenance Principles

This section discusses how the two main kinds of updates that have been mentioned in the introduction of the chapter, viz. updates to facts and rules, affect the materialization of an example knowledge base. Based on this discussion, we identify the main assumptions that underly the approaches for incremental maintenance presented in the subsequent sections.

As an example, we use the genealogical relationships between the different (more prominent) members of the Bach family. The relevant subset of the ABox is presented in Figure 3.

3.1   Updates to Facts

Since we expect that the historic data about the Bach family members in our knowledge base is unlikely to change, we choose to materialize the closure of the transitive ancestorOf property to speed up query processing. Figure 3 depicts an excerpt of the family tree of the Bach family, where the left-hand side of Figure 3 depicts the asserted property fillers. The right-hand side of the Figure depicts the transitive closure of the ancestorOf graph. We will now consider how updates, which we consider as deletions and insertions only, will affect the materialization (cf.lower part of Figure 3).

3.1.1   Deletions Let us assume that we have to revoke an asserted property filler, since a historian finds out that *Johann Sebastian* was not the father of *Wilhelm Friedemann*. Clearly, this has consequences to our materialization. For example, *Johann Ambrosius* is no longer an ancestor of *Wilhelm Friedemann*. However, *Johannes* is still an ancestor of *Wilhelm Friedemann*, since not only *Johann Sebastian* but also his cousin and first wife *Maria Barbara* are descendants of *Johannes*.

If we maintain the materialization of the graph depicted in Figure 3 ourselves, a natural and straightforward approach proceeds in two steps. In order to delete links that do not hold any longer, we first mark all links that could have potentially been derived using the link leading from *Wilhelm Friedemann* to the nodes in the graph that possibly interact with the deleted link, viz. are also connected with *Johann Sebastian*. As the second step, we check whether the deletion mark is correct by reconsidering whether the respective link could be derived on some other way by combining the links supported by the updated source graph. If a mark is determined to be correct, we can delete the appropriate link in our source graph.

This two staged principle for deletion is common to most approaches for the incremental maintenance of materializations [11, 30, 12] and is applied by the approach presented in Section 4.

3.1.2   Insertions Now assume that we assert that *Johann Sebastian* is the ancestor of another *Johann Christian*. Clearly, we can manually derive in the example graph that *Johann Christian* must be linked with the nodes that can possibly interact with the new link, viz. are also connected with *Johann Sebastian* in the updated source graph. All new links discovered in this way have to be added to the materialization.

3.2   Updates to Rules

A typical source of updates in Web ontologies is the change of TBox axioms, since ontologies have to evolve with their applications and react to changing

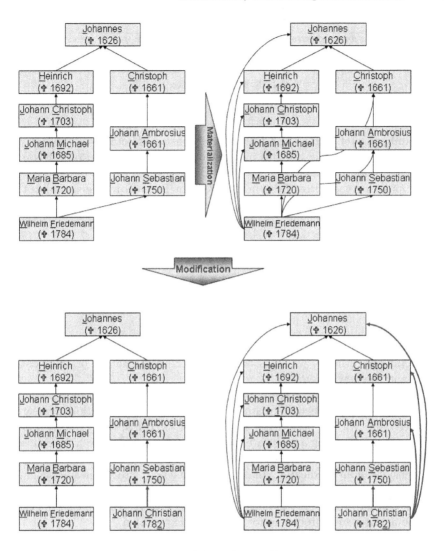

Fig. 3. Bach Family Tree Excerpt

application requirements [19, 20]. Similarly, the advent of a rule layer in the Semantic Web will lead to changing rules. In the case of DLP, both situations, changing TBox axioms and changing rules, are actually equivalent since they manifest both themselves as changes to the logic program $\mathcal{LP}$.

Let's assume that our TBox states that the transitive ancestorOf property is a specialization of the inDynasty property (which is not necessarily transitive), i.e. $\mathcal{T} = \{T_0, T_1\}$ (cf. Table 3). Let's additionally assume that our ABox only contains property fillers for ANCESTOROF, e.g. the tuples $\{(h, jc1), (j, h), (j, c) \ldots\}$, where each constant is the abbreviation for the name of an individual in the

Axiom	OWL	DLP
T_0	SubPropertyOf (ANCESTOROF INDYNASTY)	INDYNASTY(x, y) :− ANCESTOROF(x, y)
T_1	ObjectProperty (ANCESTOROF Transitive)	ANCESTOROF(x, y) :− ANCESTOROF(x, z), ANCESTOROF(z, y).

Table 3. Example TBox $\mathcal{T}$

Bach family tree (cf. Figure 3). Clearly, the extension of both ANCESTOROF and INDYNASTY are equivalent in this particular knowledge base, since INDYNASTY has no own property fillers.

Manipulating the TBox $\mathcal{T}$ by deleting axiom T_0 leads to the situation that the extension of INDYNASTY is empty, since the derivations supported by the respective axiom are no longer supported.

Now assume that we add a new axiom T_2 to the old $\mathcal{T}$, i.e. $\mathcal{T} = \mathcal{T} \cup \{T_2\}$, that states that the property INDYNASTY is symmetric:

Axiom	OWL	DLP
T_2	ObjectProperty (INDYNASTY Symmetric)	INDYNASTY(x, y):−INDYNASTY(y, x).

Apparently, the new extension of INDYNASTY will now contain the tuple $(jc1, c)$ (among others), which is derived by the combination of the existing axioms and the new axiom.

Unlike the change of facts, we do not only have an interaction of particular (inserted or deleted) facts with existing facts, but also the interaction of (inserted or deleted) rules with all other rules. In particular, we can observe that we need to consider all rules defining a predicate to determine the extension of the predicate.

The approach to maintenance presented in Section 5 will therefore recompute the extensions of all predicates, which are redefined, i.e. are the head of changed rules. We will, however, reuse the mechanisms of propagating the resulting fact changes to other predicates (and possibly back to the predicate in case of cycles) from the maintenance procedure for facts (cf. next section).

4   Maintaining Changing Facts

This section presents the maintenance of a materialization when facts change, viz. new tuples are added or removed from the extension of a predicate.

4.1   Approach

We reuse the declarative variant [30] of the delete and re-derive (DRed) algorithm proposed in [11]. DRed takes the three steps illustrated in Section 3.1 to incrementally maintain the materialization of an intensional database predicate:

1. *Overestimation of deletion:* Overestimates deletions by computing all direct consequences of a deletion.

2. *Rederivation:* Prunes those estimated deletions for which alternative derivations (via some other facts in the program) exist.
3. *Insertion:* Adds the new derivations that are consequences of insertions to extensional predicates.

The declarative version[13] of DRed maintains the materialization of a given predicate by means of a maintenance program. The maintenance program is rewritten from the original program using several rewriting patterns.

The goal of the rewriting is the provision of a pair of maintenance predicates P^+ and P^- for every materialized predicate P, such that the extensions of P^+ and P^- contain the changes that are needed to maintain P after the maintenance program is evaluated on a given set of extensional insertions P^{Ins} and deletions P^{Del}.

The maintenance process is carried out as follows: First, we *setup* maintenance, i.e. the maintenance program is created for a given source program and the initial materialization of intensional predicates is computed.

Whenever extensional changes occur, the actual maintenance is carried out. In this step, we first put insertions (deletions) to an extensional predicate P_{edb} into the extension of the predicate P_{edb}^{Ins} (P_{edb}^{Del}). We then evaluate the maintenance program. For every intensional predicate P_{idb}, the required incremental changes, viz. insertions and deletions, can be found in the extension of P_{idb}^+ and P_{idb}^-. We use these changes to update the materialization of the intensional predicate P and update P_{edb} with the explicit changes P_{edb}^{Ins} and P_{edb}^{Del}, while the extensions of the later predicates are deleted.

4.2 Maintenance Rewritings

The maintenance of an intensional predicate P is achieved via seven maintenance predicates :

1. P itself contains the (old) materialization.
2. P^{Del} receives so-called deletion candidates, which are the aforementioned overestimation of facts that ought to be deleted from the materialization. For extensional predicates, P^{Del} contains explicitly what should be removed from the materialization.
3. P^{Ins} contains the facts that ought to be inserted into the materialization. For extensional predicates, P^{Ins} contains the explicit insertions that were asserted by the user.
4. P^{Red} receives those facts that are marked for deletion but have alternative derivations.

---

[13] The benefit of reusing the declarative version of DRed with respect to the original (procedural) version is that it allows us to reuse generic logic databases for the evaluation of the maintenance program. This also motivates why we did not use the optimized version provided in [30], since the optimization requires logic databases to evaluate the maintenance program using the supplementary magic set technique, which is not used in all logic databases (e.g. XSB [26]).

5. P^{New} describes the new state of the materialization after updates.
6. P^+ receives the net insertions required to maintain the materialization of P.
7. P^- receives the net deletions required to maintain the materialization of P.

New Materialization For every intensional predicate P, P^{New} captures the new materialization, which is constituted of all old data that has not been deleted (N_1). Additionally, it contains re-derived data (N_2) and inserted data (N_3):

$$(N_1) \quad P^{New} \colon\text{-} P, \mathbf{not}\, P^{Del}.$$
$$(N_2) \quad P^{New} \colon\text{-} P^{Red}.$$
$$(N_3) \quad P^{New} \colon\text{-} P^{Ins}.$$

For every extensional database predicate P, we only instantiate the rules (N_1 and N_3) to define an auxiliary predicate P^{New}. P^{New} is used in the rewritings for insertions and re-derivation of dependent intensional predicates.

Differentials The following differentials P^+ and P^- compute positive and negative deltas, i.e. the changes that are necessary to incrementally maintain the stored materialization of an intensional predicate P:

$$P^+ \colon\text{-} P^{Ins}, \mathbf{not}\, P.$$
$$P^- \colon\text{-} P^{Del}, \mathbf{not}\, P^{Ins}, \mathbf{not}\, P^{Red}.$$

Deletion Candidates The deletion candidates P^{Del} are constituted by all possible combinations between deleted facts of a given body predicate and the remaining body predicates. Therefore, n deletion rules are created for every rule with n conjuncts in the body:

$$(D_i) \colon \quad P^{Del} \colon\text{-} R_1, \dots, R_{i-1}, R_i^{Del}, R_{i+1}, \dots, R_n.$$

If R_i is an extensional predicate, R_i^{Del} contains those facts that are explicitly deleted from R_i. Otherwise, R_i^{Del} contains the aforementioned overestimation.

Re-derivations The re-derivations P^{Red} are computed by joining the new states of all body predicates with the deletion candidates:

$$(R) \colon \quad P^{Red} \colon\text{-} P^{Del}, R_1^{New}, \dots, R_n^{New}.$$

Insertions Insertions P^{Ins} for intensional predicates P are calculated by ordinary semi-naive rewriting, i.e. by constructing rules (I_i) that join the insertions into a body predicate with the new materializations of all other body predicates:

$$(I_i) \colon P^{Ins} \quad \colon\text{-} \quad R_1^{New}, \dots, R_{i-1}^{New}, R_i^{Ins}, R_{i+1}^{New}, \dots, R_n^{New}.$$

If R_i is an extensional predicate, R_i^{Ins} contains those facts that are explicitly inserted into R_i.

4.3   Maintenance Programs

A logic program $\mathcal{LP}$ consists of a finite set of rules of the form $H:\text{-}B_1,\ldots,B_n.$, where $H, B_i \in \mathbf{P}$. We call $\mathbf{P}$ the set of predicates used in $\mathcal{LP}$. Without loss of generality we assume that $\mathbf{P}$ can be partioned into two disjoint sets of intensional and extensional predicates, i.e. $\mathbf{P} = \mathbf{P}_{idb} \cup \mathbf{P}_{edb}$ and $\mathbf{P}_{idb} \cap \mathbf{P}_{edb} = \emptyset$. A maintenance program is generated from a program $\mathcal{LP}$ through the application of generator functions (cf. Table 4).

Generator	Parameter	Rewriting Result
	Predicate	
θ_{idb}	$P \in \mathbf{P}_{idb}$	$\theta_{idb}^{New}(P) \cup \theta_{idb}^{Ins}(P) \cup \theta_{idb}^{Del}(P) \cup \theta_{idb}^{Red}(P)$
θ_{idb}^{New}	$P \in \mathbf{P}_{idb}$	$\{\theta_1^{New}(P)\} \cup \{\theta_2^{New}(P)\} \cup \{\theta_3^{New}(P)\}$
θ_{edb}^{New}	$P \in \mathbf{P}_{edb}$	$\{\theta_1^{New}(P)\} \cup \{\theta_3^{New}(P)\}$
θ_1^{New}	$P \in \mathbf{P}$	$P^{New}:\text{-}P, \mathbf{not}\, P^{Del}.$
θ_2^{New}	$P \in \mathbf{P}_{idb}$	$P^{New}:\text{-}P^{Red}.$
θ_3^{New}	$P \in \mathbf{P}$	$P^{New}:\text{-}P^{Ins}.$
θ_{idb}^{+}	$P \in \mathbf{P}_{idb}$	$P^{+}:\text{-}P^{Ins}, \mathbf{not}\, P.$
θ_{idb}^{-}	$P \in \mathbf{P}_{idb}$	$P^{-}:\text{-}P^{Del}, \mathbf{not}\, P^{Ins}, \mathbf{not}\, P^{Red}.$
θ_{idb}^{Ins}	$P \in \mathbf{P}_{idb}$	$\{\cup \theta^{Ins}(r)|\forall r \in rules(P)\}$
θ_{idb}^{Del}	$P \in \mathbf{P}_{idb}$	$\{\cup \theta^{Del}(r)|\forall r \in rules(P)\}$
θ_{idb}^{Red}	$P \in \mathbf{P}_{idb}$	$\{\theta^{Red}(r)|\forall r \in rules(P)\}$
	Rule	
θ	$H:\text{-}B_1,\ldots,B_n.$	$\{\theta^{Red}\} \cup \theta^{Del} \cup \theta^{Ins}$
θ^{Red}	$H:\text{-}B_1,\ldots,B_n.$	$H^{Red}:\text{-}H^{Del}, B_1^{New},\ldots,B_n^{New}.$
θ^{Del}	$H:\text{-}B_1,\ldots,B_n.$	$\{H^{Del}:\text{-}B_1,\ldots,B_{i-1}, B_i^{Del}, B_{i+1},\ldots,B_n.\}$
θ^{Ins}	$H:\text{-}B_1,\ldots,B_n.$	$\{H^{Ins}:\text{-}B_1^{New},\ldots,B_{i-1}^{New}, B_i^{Ins}, B_{i+1}^{New},\ldots,B_n^{New}.\}$

Table 4. Rewriting Functions (derived from [30])

Definition 1 (Maintenance Program). *A maintenance program $\mathcal{LP}_M$ of a logic program $\mathcal{LP}$ is a set of maintenance rules such that:*

1. $\forall P \in \mathbf{P}_{idb} : \theta_{idb}(P) \in \mathcal{LP}_M$
2. $\forall P \in \mathbf{P}_{edb} : \theta_{edb}^{New}(P) \in \mathcal{LP}_M$

The θ_{idb} and θ_{edb}^{New} rewriting functions themselves call other rewriting functions presented in Table 4. For example, the function $\theta : R \to \mathbf{MR}$ rewrites a rule $R \in \mathcal{LP}$ into a set of maintenance rules $\mathbf{MR}$ by instantiating rewriting patterns for deletion θ^{Del}, insertion θ^{Ins} and rederivation θ^{Red}. By definition, θ maps every rule with n body literals into $2 * n + 1$ maintenance rules.

The reader may note that the rewriting makes use of two auxiliary functions:

- $head : \mathcal{LP} \to \mathbf{P}_{idb}$ maps a rule to its rule head.
- $rules : \mathbf{P}_{idb} \to \mathbf{R}$ maps rule heads to a set of rules $\mathbf{R}$, such that:

$$\forall P \in \mathbf{P}_{idb} : rules(P) = \{R \in \mathbf{R}|head(R) = P\}$$

Example 2 (Maintenance Rewritings). Let us return to the Bach family tree example established in Section 3.1 and consider all edges between the different individuals depicted in Figure 3 as fillers of the transitive property ANCESTOROF.

Let us consider the following logic program $\mathcal{LP}$, which generated from a simple ontology containing one single (transitive) property called ANCESTOROF. The second rule implements the differentiation between asserted and entailed information, that was described in Section 2.3:

$$(R_1) \text{ ANCESTOROF}(x, z)\text{:-}\text{ANCESTOROF}(x, y), \text{ANCESTOROF}(y, z).$$
$$(R_2) \text{ ANCESTOROF}(x, y)\text{:-}\text{ANCESTOROF}_{edb}(x, y).$$

In the following we will use the abbreviation A for ANCESTOROF.

Since $\mathcal{LP}$ includes one intensional predicate A and one extensional predicate A_{edb}, the generation of the maintenance program $\mathcal{LP}_M$ only involves to apply θ_{idb} to A and θ_{edb}^{New} to A_{edb}:

$$
\begin{aligned}
\theta_{edb}^{New}(A_{edb}) = \ & \{A_{edb}^{New}(x,y)\text{:-}A_{edb}(x,y), \mathbf{not}\,A_{edb}^{Del}(x,y). & (\theta_1^{New}(A_{edb})) \\
& A_{edb}^{New}(x,y)\text{:-}A_{edb}^{Ins}(x,y).\} & (\theta_3^{New}(A_{edb})) \\
\theta_{idb}(A) = \ & \{A^{Del}(x,y)\text{:-}A_{edb}^{Del}(x,y). & (\theta^{Del}(R_2)) \\
& A^{Red}(x,y)\text{:-}A^{Del}(x,y), A_{edb}^{New}(x,y). & (\theta^{Red}(R_2)) \\
& A^{Ins}(x,y)\text{:-}A_{edb}^{Ins}(x,y). & (\theta^{Ins}(R_2)) \\
& A^{New}(x,y)\text{:-}A(x,y), \mathbf{not}\,A^{Del}(x,y). & (\theta_1^{New}(A)) \\
& A^{New}(x,y)\text{:-}A^{Red}(x,y). & (\theta_2^{New}(A)) \\
& A^{New}(x,y)\text{:-}A^{Ins}(x,y). & (\theta_3^{New}(A)) \\
& A^{Del}(x,z)\text{:-}A^{Del}(x,y), A(y,z). & (\theta^{Del}(R_1)) \\
& A^{Del}(x,z)\text{:-}A(x,y), A^{Del}(y,z). & (\theta^{Del}(R_1)) \\
& A^{Red}(x,z)\text{:-}A^{Del}(x,z), A^{New}(x,y), A^{New}(y,z). & (\theta^{Red}(R_1)) \\
& A^{Ins}(x,z)\text{:-}A^{Ins}(x,y), A^{New}(y,z). & (\theta^{Ins}(R_1)) \\
& A^{Ins}(x,z)\text{:-}A^{New}(x,y), A^{Ins}(y,z).\} & (\theta^{Ins}(R_1)) \\
\mathcal{LP}_M = \ & \theta_{idb}(A) \cup \theta_{edb}^{New}(A_{edb})
\end{aligned}
$$

The invocation of the θ_{edb}^{New} generator on A_{edb} initiates the invocation of the $(\theta_1^{New}(A_{edb}))$ and $(\theta_3^{New}(A_{edb}))$ generators and collects their results. Similarly, the invocation of the θ_{idb} generator on A leads to the invocation of *rules* on A to retrieve the rules R_1, R_2 and the invocation of $\theta_1^{New}, \ldots, \theta^{Ins}(R_1)$.

4.4   Size of Maintenance Programs

As we can see from example 2 the size of the maintenance program $\mathcal{LP}_M$ is substantially larger than the original program $\mathcal{LP}$.

4.4.1   OWL (DLP) Maintenance Programs

The structure of the rules that are generated by translating OWL axioms into a logic program allows us to observe that the rewriting of each OWL inclusion axiom creates the following number of maintenance rules:

$$|\theta(\phi_{\mathcal{LP}}(C \sqsubseteq D))| \qquad\qquad = 3$$
$$|\theta(\phi_{\mathcal{LP}}(C_1 \sqcap \ldots \sqcap C_n \sqsubseteq D))| = 2 * n + 1$$
$$|\theta(\phi_{\mathcal{LP}}(C \sqsubseteq D_1 \sqcap \ldots \sqcap D_n))| = n * |\theta(\phi_{\mathcal{LP}}(C \sqsubseteq D_i))|$$
$$|\theta(\phi_{\mathcal{LP}}(D_1 \sqcup \ldots \sqcup D_n \sqsubseteq E))| = n * |\theta(\phi_{\mathcal{LP}}(D_i \sqsubseteq E))|$$
$$|\theta(\phi_{\mathcal{LP}}(C \sqsubseteq \forall R.D))| \qquad = |\theta(\phi_{\mathcal{LP}}(\exists R.C \sqsubseteq D))| = 5$$

OWL object property transitivity is translated to five maintenance rules by applying θ to $\phi_{\mathcal{LP}}$. All other DL property axioms are translated to three maintenance rules by applying θ to $\phi_{\mathcal{LP}}$. θ is applied to all atomic classes and properties in $\mathcal{KB}_0^{DLP}$ as well as the auxiliary classes that are created by the structural transformation which is carried out during the preprocessing step.

4.4.2 RDF(S) Maintenance Programs

Since the 12 static Datalog rules for the single predicate-based axiomatization of RDF(S) (cf. Table 2) contain 19 body predicates, the application of θ leads to the generation of 60 rules, namely 19 insertion rules, 19 deletion rules, 12 re-derivation rules, 5 maintenance rules for t^{New}, t^+ and t^-, as well as 5 further rules to differentiate between entailments and assertions.

4.5 Evaluating Maintenance Programs

[29] show that the evaluation of the maintenance rules is a sound and complete procedure for computing the differentials between two database states when extensional update operations occur.

During the evaluation it is necessary to access the old state of a predicate. Bottom-up approaches to evaluation therefore require that all intensional relations involved in the computation are completely materialized.

The maintenance rules for capturing the new database state contain negated predicates to express the algebraic set difference operation. Hence, even though the original rules are pure Datalog (without negation), a program with negation is generated. The rewriting transformation keeps the property of stratifiability, since newly introduced predicates do not occur in cycles with other negations. Hence, it is guaranteed that predicates can be partitioned into strata such that no two predicates in one stratum depend negatively on each other, i.e. predicates only occur negatively in rules that define predicates of a higher stratum. The evaluation can then proceed, as usual, stratum-by-stratum starting with the extensional predicates themselves.

Example 3 (Evaluating Maintenance Programs). The direct links between members of the Bach family in Figure 3 constitute the extension of A_{edb}, where we abbreviate the names of each individual by the first letters of their forenames:

$$A_{edb} = \{(j, h), (j, c), (h, jc1), (jc1, jm), (jm, mb), (mb, wf), (js, wf), (ja, js), (c, ja)\}$$

Using the maintenance rewriting the materialization of A changes to A^{New} as follows, if $A^{Ins} = (js, jc2)$ is inserted and $A^{Del} = (js, wf)$ is deleted:

$$A_{edb}^{Ins} = \{(jc, jc2)\}$$
$$A_{edb}^{Del} = \{(js, wf)\}$$
$$A_{edb}^{New} = A_{edb} \cup A_{edb}^{Ins} \setminus A_{edb}^{Del}$$
$$A^{Ins} = \{(js, jc2), (ja, jc2), (c, jc2), (j, jc2)\}$$
$$A^{Del} = \{(js, wf), (ja, wf), (c, wf), (j, wf)\}$$
$$A^{Red} = \{(j, wf)\}$$
$$A^{New} = (A \setminus A^{Del} \cup A^{Ins} \cup A^{Red})$$
$$= A \cup \{(js, jc2), (ja, jc2), (c, jc2), (j, jc2)\} \setminus \{(js, wf), (ja, wf), (c, wf)\}$$
$$A^{-} = \{(js, wf), (ja, wf), (c, wf)\}$$
$$A^{+} = \{(js, jc2), (ja, jc2), (c, jc2), (j, jc2)\}$$

Since all maintenance rules of a given predicate have to be evaluated, an axiomatization of RDF(S) based on a single ternary predicate leads to complete re-computation in case of updates. We sketch an optimization for this case in Section 6 which should result in more efficient evaluation for the single predicate axiomatization.

5   Maintaining Changing Rules

This section presents the maintenance of a materialization if the definition of rules changes, i.e. rules that define a predicate are added or removed in the source program. We introduce two simple extensions to the rewriting-based approach presented in the previous section. Firstly, the materialization of predicates has to be maintained in the case of changes. Secondly, the maintenance programs have to be maintained such that additional rewritings are introduced for new rules and irrelevant rewritings are removed for deleted rules.

5.1   Approach

We illustrated in Section 3.2 that every change in the rule set might cause changes in the extension of an intensional predicate P, with the consequence that the materialization of intensional predicates has to be updated. However, unlike in the case of changing extensions, both auxiliary predicates which capture the differences which are used to update the materialization of some predicate $P \in \mathbf{P}_{idb}$, i.e. P^{+} and P^{-} have empty extensions since no actual facts change.

Obviously, we can categorize the intensional predicates that are affected by a change in rules into two sets: *(I)* predicates that are directly affected, i.e. occur in the head of changed rules and *(II)* predicates that are indirectly affected, i.e. by depending on directly affected predicates through the rules in the program.

Our solution uses the existing maintenance rewriting for facts to propagate updates to the *indirectly affected* predicates. To achieve this, the maintenance computation for *directly affected* predicates is integrated into the maintenance program by redefining the auxiliary predicates that are used to propagate changes between predicates, i.e. P^{New}, P^{Ins} and P^{Del}.

5.2 Maintenance Rewriting

Let $\delta^+(\delta^-)$ be the set of rules which are inserted (deleted) from the logic program $\mathcal{LP}$. The reader may recall from the previous section that the function $head : \mathcal{LP} \rightarrow P_{idb}$ maps a rule to its rule head, and the function $rules : P_{idb} \rightarrow \mathcal{LP}$ maps rule heads to rules.

Definition 2 (Directly affected predicate). *An intensional predicate $p \in P_{idb}$ is a directly affected predicate, if $p \in \{head(r)|r \in \delta^+ \cup \delta^-\}$.*

Generator	Parameter	Rewriting Result
	Predicate	
ϑ	$P \in \mathbf{P}_{idb}$	$\{\vartheta_{idb}^{Ins}(P)\} \cup \{\vartheta_{idb}^{Del}(P)\} \cup \{\vartheta_{idb}^{New}(P)\}$
ϑ_{idb}^{Ins}	$P \in \mathbf{P}_{idb}$	$P^{Ins}\!:\!-P^{New}.$
ϑ_{idb}^{Del}	$P \in \mathbf{P}_{idb}$	$P^{Del}\!:\!-P.$
ϑ_{idb}^{New}	$P \in \mathbf{P}_{idb}$	$\{\vartheta^{New}(r)|\forall r \in rules(P)\}$
	Rule	
ϑ^{New}	$H\!:\!-B_1,\dots,B_n.$	$H^{New}\!:\!-B_1^{New},\dots,B_n^{New}.$

Table 5. Rewriting Functions ϑ

The rule structure of the maintenance program $\mathcal{LP}_M$ is modified for all directly affected predicates. For these predicates all maintenance rules are substituted by maintenance rules generated using the ϑ rewriting function (cf. Table 5). ϑ is instantiated for every directly affected predicate P and the following is done:

1. The existing rules defining P^{New} in the maintenance program $\mathcal{LP}_M$ are deleted;
2. New rules axiomatize P^{New} using the (new) rule set that defines P in the updated original program. These rules are slightly adapted, such that references to any predicate P are altered to P^{New}, by instantiating the following rewriting pattern for all rules $R \in rules(P)$:

$$P^{New}\!:\!-R_1^{New},\dots,R_n^{New}.$$

The rewrite pattern simply states that the new state of the predicate P follows directly from the combination of the new states of the predicates R_i in the body of of all rules defining P in the changed source program.

3. All maintenance rules for calculating the insertions and deletions to P have to be removed from the maintenance program and are replaced by the following two static rules.

$$P^{Ins}\!:\!-P^{New}.$$
$$P^{Del}\!:\!-P.$$

The role of P^{Ins}, P^{Del}, P^{New} is exactly the same as in the rewriting for facts, i.e. they propagate changes to dependent predicates. While P^{Ins} propagates the new state of a predicate as an insertion to all dependent predicates, P^{Del} propagates the old state of a predicate as a deletion to all dependent predicates. Figure 4 shows how the information flow in the maintenance program changes with respect to the rewriting of a rule $H(x):\text{-}B(x).$ from the maintenance rewriting for fact changes *(a)* to the maintenance for rule changes *(b)*. The arrows to (from) nodes depict that the respective predicate possibly uses (is used by) some other predicate in the maintenance program.

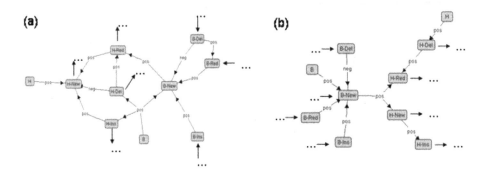

Fig. 4. Information Flow in Maintenance Programs: (a) Maintenance for Facts; (b) Maintenance for Rules

5.3   Evaluating Maintenance Programs

The evaluation of maintenance programs is now carried out in three steps:

1. Update the maintenance rewriting $\mathcal{LP}_M$ of $\mathcal{LP}$ to incorporate the set of rules that are added (δ^+) or removed (δ^-).
2. Evaluate the maintenance program $\mathcal{LP}_M$ and incrementally maintain all materialized predicates.
3. Maintain the maintenance rewriting $\mathcal{LP}_M$ by changing rewritings back to the rewriting for facts.

Step 1. Step 1 is implemented by Algorithm 5.1. This algorithm has three functions. Firstly, it replaces all maintenance rewritings for directly affected predicates with the new maintenance rewritings. Secondly, it alters the source program $\mathcal{LP}$ such that the set of updated rules is incorporated into $\mathcal{LP}$. Thirdly, it maintains auxiliary rewriting rules, viz. generates rules for previously unknown intensional predicates and removes those rules if an intensional predicate no longer occurs in the source program.

Require:
δ^+ Set of inserted rules
δ^- Set of deleted rules
$\mathcal{LP}_M$ Maintenance program
Ensure:
Updated maintenance program $\mathcal{LP}_M$

removeMR $= \emptyset$ // *Collects maintenance rules to be removed*
addMR $= \emptyset$ // *Collects maintenance rules to be added*
affectedPred $= \emptyset$ // *Collects all affected predicates*
 // *Add new rewriting rules for added rules*
for all $r \in (\delta^+ \setminus \delta^-)$ **do**
   addMR $= \{\theta^{Red}(r)\}\cup$ addMR
   $p = \text{head}(\, r\,)$
   affectedPred $= \{p\} \cup$ affectedPred
    // *First rule defining a predicate ?*
   if $p \notin \{head(r) \mid r \in \mathcal{LP}\}$ **then**
      addMR $= \theta_{idb}^+(p) \cup \theta_{idb}^-(p)\cup$ addMR   // *Need new auxiliary predicates*
   end if
   $\mathcal{LP} = \mathcal{LP} \cup r$
end for
 // *Add new rewriting rules for deleted rules*
for all $r \in (\delta^- \setminus \delta^+)$ **do**
   $p = \text{head}(\, r\,)$
   affectedPred $= p \cup$ affectedPred
    // *Last rule defining a predicate ?*
   if $rules(p) \setminus \{r\} = \emptyset$ **then**
      removeMR $= \theta_{idb}^+(p) \cup \theta_{idb}^-(p) \cup \theta_{idb}^{Red}(p)\cup$ removeMR
   end if
   $\mathcal{LP} = \mathcal{LP} \setminus r$
end for
 // *Replace rewriting rules for affected predicates*
for all $p \in$ affectedPred **do**
   addMR $= \vartheta_{idb}^{New}(p) \cup \vartheta_{idb}^{Ins}(p) \cup \vartheta_{idb}^{Del}(p)\cup$ addMR
   removeMR $= \theta_{idb}^{New}(p) \cup \theta_{idb}^{Ins}(p) \cup \theta_{idb}^{Del}(p)\cup$ removeMR
end for
$\mathcal{LP}_M = (\mathcal{LP}_M \cup \text{addMR}\,)\setminus$ removeMR

Algorithm 5.1: Updating Rules (Pre-Evaluation Algorithm)

Example 4 (Maintenance Rewritings for New Rule). Let us return to the maintenance program $\mathcal{LP}_M$ established in Example 2 and consider that rule R_3 is inserted into $\mathcal{LP} = \{R_1, R_2\}$, i.e. the new $\mathcal{LP}$ consists of the following rules after the application of Algorithm 5.1:

(R_1) ANCESTOROF(x, z):-ANCESTOROF(x, y), ANCESTOROF(y, z).
(R_2) ANCESTOROF(x, z):-ANCESTOROF$_{edb}(x, y)$.
(R_3) INDYNASTY(x, y):-ANCESTOROF(x, y).

Since $\delta^+ = R_3$ and $\delta^- = \emptyset$ and none of the previously existing intensional axioms is directly affected, the algorithm does not remove any rewriting rules from the maintenance program $\mathcal{LP}_M$ in this example. We have, however, to add the new maintenance rules for the directly affected predicate INDYNASTY, which we will abbreviate as I in the following. The algorithm augments $\mathcal{LP}_M$ with the rules generated by the following calls to rewriting generators (in this order):

$$
\begin{aligned}
\theta^{Red}(R_3) &= I^{Red}(x,y)\text{:-}I^{Del}(x,y), \text{ANCESTOROF}^{New}(x,y). \\
\theta^+_{idb}(I) &= I^+(x,y)\text{:-}I^{Ins}(x,y), \mathbf{not} I(x,y). \\
\theta^-_{idb}(I) &= I^-(x,y)\text{:-}I^{Del}(x,y), \mathbf{not} I^{Ins}(x,y), \mathbf{not} I^{Red}(x,y). \\
\vartheta^{New}(I) &= I^{New}(x,y)\text{:-}\text{ANCESTOROF}^{New}(x,y). \\
\vartheta^{Ins}(I) &= I^{Ins}(x,y)\text{:-}I^{New}(x,y). \\
\vartheta^{Del}(I) &= I^{Del}(x,y)\text{:-}I(x,y).
\end{aligned}
$$

The new state of I is now directly derived from the new state of A, which is calculated as part of the maintenance program. Hence, we can obtain the first materialization I just by evaluating the maintenance program.

Step 2. Step 2 evaluates the maintenance program as presented in Section 4.

Require:
    δ^+ Set of inserted rules
    δ^- Set of deleted rules
    $\mathcal{LP}$ Original logic program
    $\mathcal{LP}_M$ Maintenance program
Ensure:
    Updated logic program $\mathcal{LP}$
    Updated maintenance program $\mathcal{LP}_M$

    removeMR $= \emptyset$
    addMR $= \emptyset$
    affectedPred $= \emptyset$
    for all $r \in (\delta^+ \setminus \delta^-)$ **do**
       affectedPred $= head(r) \cup$ affectedPred
    end for
    for all $r \in (\delta^- \setminus \delta^+)$ **do**
       $p = head(\ r\ )$
       if $rules(p) \neq \emptyset$ **then**
          affectedPred $= p \cup$ affectedPred
       end if
    end for
    for all $p \in$ affectedPred **do**
       removeMR $= \vartheta^{New}_{idb}(p) \cup \vartheta^{Ins}_{idb}(p) \cup \vartheta^{Del}_{idb}(p) \cup$ removeMR
       addMR $= \theta^{New}_{idb}(p) \cup \theta^{Ins}_{idb}(p) \cup \theta^{Del}_{idb}(p) \cup$ addMR
    end for
    $LP_M = LP_M \cup$ addMR $\setminus$ removeMR

Algorithm 5.2: Updating Rules (Post-Evaluation Algorithm)

Step 3 Step 3 is implemented by Algorithm 5.2. It essentially only undoes our special maintenance rewriting, i.e. it replaces the maintenance rewritings that have been generated by Algorithm 5.1 for directly affected predicates with the normal maintenance rewritings for facts.

Example 5 (Maintenance Rewritings for New Rule). Algorithm 5.2 would remove the following maintenance rules from the maintenance program $\mathcal{LP}_M$:

$$\vartheta^{New}(I) = I^{New}(x,y)\colon\!-\textsc{ancestorof}^{New}(x,y).$$
$$\vartheta^{Ins}(I) = I^{Ins}(x,y)\colon\!-I^{New}(x,y).$$
$$\vartheta^{Del}(I) = I^{Del}(x,y)\colon\!-I(x,y).$$

In parallel, the maintenance program would be extended with the rewritings generated by the rewriting generators that create the maintenance rewriting for facts $(\theta_{idb}^{New}(I), \theta_{idb}^{Ins}(I)$ and $\theta_{idb}^{Del}(I))$.

Since all maintenance rules for dealing with changes in rules are removed by Algorithm 5.2, we obtain the same maintenance program as if we would have completely regenerated the maintenance program for facts from the changed source program.

6 Materializing RDF Rules

An alternative to using OWL TBox axioms to state that INDYNASTY is a symmetric property, is the usage of either one of the RDF-based rule languages (cf. Section 2), e.g. Notation 3.

Notation 3	`{ ?x :inDynasty ?y. }`
	`  log:implies`
	`{ ?y :inDynasty ?x. }.`

Datalog	$T(x,\texttt{inDynasty},y)\colon\!-T(y,\texttt{inDynasty},x).$

Table 6. Datalog Translation of RDF Rule Languages

If an RDF rule system internally uses one single predicate within the rules, however, our technique for incrementally maintaining the materialization in case of changes is useless. The evaluation of the maintenance program then corresponds to a total recomputation, since all rules defining this predicate have to be evaluated.

In order to use our approach to materialization, more optimized data structures to represent an RDF graph have to be chosen, such that the part of the knowledge base which takes part in the evaluation can be limited.

6.1 Selection-Based Optimization

We will briefly sketch a possible optimization, which we called *selection-based optimization* [33]. The optimization is based on the idea to split the extension of the RDF graph according to *split points*, which are given by constants that occur at a certain argument position of a predicate. Useful split points can be derived from the vocabulary of an ontology or an ontology language such as RDF Schema. In case of arbitrary graph data, a useful split point can be frequently occurring constants, which can be easily determined using counting. The choice of a good split point, however, clearly depends on the application of the RDF rule base.

We can transform a Datalog program into an equivalent program that incorporates split points, if all references to a predicate P (in queries, facts and rules) where a split point occurs are replaced by appropriate split predicates.

In the following, we will assume that a split point is constituted by a constant c that is used as the i-th argument in the predicate P. To generate split predicates, we then split the extension of a predicate P_{edb} into several edb predicates of the form $P^{c_i}_{edb}(Var_1, Var_2, \ldots, Var_{i-1}, c, Var_{i+1}, Var_n)$ to store tuples based on equal constant values c in their i-th component.

Hence, instead of using a single extensional predicate P_{edb} for representing direct RDF assertions, the extensional database is split into several $P^{c_i}_{edb}$. Again, we can differentiate between asserted and derived information by introducing intensional predicates (views) for each component of the extension (i.e. rules of the form $P^{c_i}\text{:-}P^{c_i}_{edb}$).The complete predicate P can still be represented by means of an intensional predicate, which is axiomatized by a collection of rules that unify the individual split predicates: $P\text{:-}P^{c_i}$.

Example 6. Returning to the triple based axiomatization (cf. Figure 2) of the N3 example, we can transform the program by introducing a split point $T^{inDynasty_2}$ for the INDYNASTY constant (when used as second argument in the ternary predicate T):

- We use two extensional predicates: $T^{Rest}_{edb}, T^{inDynasty_2}_{edb}$ to store the extension in two disjoint sets.
- We capture the intensional predicates and integrate the splits into a complete extension of T and rewrite the example such that split predicates are used instead of the full predicate:

$$
\begin{aligned}
T^{Rest}(X,Y,Z) &\text{ :- } T^{Rest}_{edb}(X,Y,Z). \\
T^{inDynasty_2}(X,Y,Z) &\text{ :- } T^{inDynasty_2}_{edb}(X,Y,Z). \\
T(X,Y,Z) &\text{ :- } T^{Rest}(X,Y,Z). \\
T(X,Y,Z) &\text{ :- } T^{inDynasty_2}(X,Y,Z). \\
T^{inDynasty_2}(X,\text{inDynasty},Y) &\text{ :- } T^{inDynasty_2}(Y,\text{inDynasty},X).
\end{aligned}
$$

Any other rule that is inserted into the RDF rule base can be transformed into a set of rules, which use the available split predicates.

However, the maintenance of a materialized predicate $T^{inDynasty_2}$ can now be carried out by ignoring all non-relevant rules for T. Hence, the whole extension of T can be updated via the insert and delete maintenance rules that were presented in the previous sections, i.e. without using the complete database.

7   Implementation

The incremental maintenance of materializations is implemented in the KAON Datalog engine[14], which handles materialization on a per predicate, i.e. per class or property, level. In case of the materialization of a predicate all changes to facts relevant for the predicate and the rule set defining a predicate are monitored.

The maintenance process is carried out as follows. When a program is designated for materialization, all maintenance rules are generated, the maintenance program itself is evaluated and the extension of all predicates P designated for materialization is stored explicitly. The maintenance program is then used for evaluation instead of the original program which is kept as auxiliary information to track changes to rules. All rules of the original program which define non-materialized predicates are added to the maintenance program.

Updates to facts are handled in a transactional manner. All individual changes are put into the appropriate p_{edb}^{Ins} and p_{edb}^{Del} predicates. Committing the transaction automatically triggers the evaluation of the maintenance rules. After this evaluation, the extensions of all materialized predicates P are updated by adding the extension of P_{idb}^{+} and removing the extension of P_{idb}^{-}. Similarly, the extension of all extensional predicates P_{edb} is updated by adding P^{Ins} and removing P^{Del}. As a last step, the extension of P^{Ins} and all other auxiliary predicates are cleared for a new evaluation.

Changes in rules are carried out in the three phase process described in Section 5: First, the new maintenance rules of rule change are generated. Then, the maintenance program is evaluated and the extensions of materialized predicates are updated as described for the change of facts. As the last step, the maintenance rules for rule change are replaced with maintenance rules for fact changes.

8   Evaluation

This section reports on the evaluation of our approach which was carried out with various synthetically generated OWL ontologies that are expressible in the DLP fragment.

8.1   Evaluation Setting

Test Assumptions. The evaluation has been carried out with changing OWL ontologies that are operationalized in logic databases using the DLP approach. It is assumed that all predicates are materialized. We assume that an inference engine builds its knowledge base by aggregating data from several web sources. Therefore bulk updates will be predominant.

---

[14] The engine is part of the open source KAON tool suite, which can be freely downloaded from http://kaon.semanticweb.org/.

Test Procedure. Each test is characterized by a certain ontology structure and a class whose extension is read. The ontology structure has been generated for different input parameters, resulting in ontologies of different sizes. The average of five such invocations has been taken as the performance measure for each test.

We obtain six measures: *(a)* the time of query processing without materialization, *(b)* the time required to set up the materialization and the maintenance program, *(c)* the time required to perform maintenance when rules are added, *(d)* rules are removed, *(e)* facts are added, and *(f)* facts are removed. Finally, *(g)* assesses the time of query processing with materialization.

Test Platform. We performed the tests on a laptop with Pentium IV Mobile processor running at 2 GHz, 512 MB of RAM using the Windows XP operating system. The implementation itself is written in Java and executed using Sun's JDK version 1.4.1_01.

8.2 Evaluation Scenarios

First we give an overview of the types of tests we conducted. In the following we use D to denote the depth of the class hierarchy, NS to denote the number of sub classes at each level in the hierarchy, NI to denote the number of instances per class and P to denote the number of properties.

To test changes in facts, we add and remove a random percentage *Change* of the facts. For rules, we add and remove a random rule. This is due to the limitation of the underlying engine, which currently does not allow to alter rules in a bulk manner. The test was performed for different depths of the taxonomy $D = 3, 4, 5$ while the number of sub classes and the number of instances was not altered ($NS = 5$; $NI = 5$). Test 2 and 3 made use of properties. Here, every class had five properties, which are instantiated for every third instance of the class ($NI = 5$). We carried out each test using varying *Change* ratios of 10% and 15% of the facts.

Test 1: Taxonomy Extended taxonomies, e.g. WordNet, currently constitute a large portion of the ontologies that are in use. Our goal with this test is to see how the very basic task of taking the taxonomy into account when retrieving the extension of a class is improved. The taxonomy is constituted by a symmetric tree of classes. We did not make use of properties, hence $P = 0$. The test query involved computing the extension of one of the concepts on the first level of the class hierarchy. This is a realistic query in systems where taxonomies are used for navigation in document collections. Here, navigation typically starts with top-level classes and the set of documents is displayed as the class extension.

Test 2: Database-like The goal of this test was to see how ontologies with larger number of properties are handled. Our goal was to answer a simple conjunctive query on top of this ontology. The DL-like query is c1 ⊓ ∃p0.c12.

Test 3: DL-like This test shows how materialization performs in DL-like ontologies, which contain simple class definitions. Each class in the class tree is defined using the following axiom: $c_i \sqcup \exists p_k.c_{i-1} \sqsubseteq c$ (where c_i denotes i-th child of concept c). The query retrieves the extension of some random class in the first-level of the taxonomy.

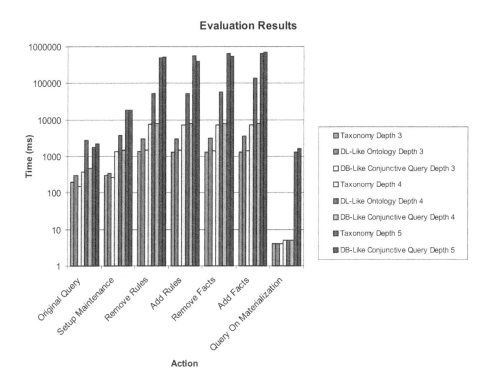

Fig. 5. Evaluation Results (Average Values for 10% change)

8.3   Results

Figure 5 depicts the average time[15] for querying an ontology without using materialization, setting up the materialization and cost of maintenance for different types of changes (adding and removing rules and facts). Finally, the time for answering the same query using the materialization is depicted. The exact results of the evaluation can be found in the appendix.

As we can see in the appendix, maintenance costs do not vary significantly with the quantity of updates, therefore Figure 5 only shows the results for 10%

---

[15] in milliseconds on a logarithmic scale

change. All costs are directly related to the size of the ontologies. The performance behavior between the taxonomy and DB-like ontologies do also not alter significantly. However, more complex rules as they are constituted by DL-like ontologies are always more expensive to evaluate, therefore setup costs and the cost of evaluating the maintenance rules is also higher.

We want to stress that we measured the performance of concrete tools. Although algorithms implemented by a system are certainly important, the overall performance of a system is influenced by many other factors as well, such the quality of the implementation or the language. It is virtually impossible to exclude these factors from the performance measurement. For example, our Datalog engine ran out of memory with the DL-like ontology where the taxonomic depth was five, viz. the set of rules was generated from 3950 class and 19750 property definitions, while the underlying knowledge base contained 19750 class instantiations and 32915 property instantiations. The other ontologies of taxonomic depth 5 were still handled by the engine, but due to inefficient memory management, most of the time was not actually used for query processing but for memory management (swapping), such that the query on the materialization in this only showed little improvement.

8.4   Discussion

The different costs of each step in the maintenance procedure are always higher than the costs of evaluating a single query. The question whether or not to materialize is therefore determined by the application and the issue whether the system can handle its typical workload, e.g. can it handle the intended number of users if answering a single query takes almost 3 seconds ?

With materialization the cost of accessing the materialized predicates can be neglected. However, the time for the evaluation of the maintenance rules can be a significant bottleneck for a system especially for large knowledge-bases. For example, in one of our test runs it took almost 16 minutes to recompute the materialization after fact changes for the DB-like test with taxonomic depth 5. Fortunately, materialization can be carried out in parallel to answering queries on top of the existing materialization.

In consequence, users will have to operate on stale copies of data. Staleness of data cannot be avoided in distributed scenarios like the Web in the first place, and existing experiences, e.g. with outdated page ranks of a web pages in Google, show that the quality of query answering is still good enough, if data is updated occasionally.

9   Related Work

We can find related work in two areas: Firstly, incremental maintenance of materialized views in deductive databases. Secondly, truth maintenance systems in the Artificial Intelligence context.

9.1   Incremental Maintenance of Materialized Views

Several algorithms have been devised for the incremental maintenance of materialized views in deductive databases. All of these approaches do not consider changes in the set of rules and differ in the techniques used to cope with changes in facts.

In order to cope with changing facts, [1, 17] effectively compute the Herbrand model of a stratified database after a database update. The proposed solution of [1] uses sets of positive and negative dependencies that are maintained for all derived facts. This leads to low space efficiency and high cost for maintaining the dependencies. [17] derives rules (so-called meta-programs) to compute the difference between consecutive database states for a stratified Datalog program. Some of the generated rules are not safe, making it impossible to implement the rules in Datalog engines. Additionally, duplicate derivations are not discarded in the algorithm.

[11] presents the Delete and Re-Derive (DRed) algorithm, which is a procedural approach to view maintenance in Datalog with stratified negation. We will follow their principal approach for the computation of changes, in fact their procedural algorithm has been altered to a declarative algorithm [30] which we will extend.

The Propagation Filtration algorithm of [12] is similar to the DRed algorithm, except that changes are propagated on a 'predicate by predicate' basis. Hence, it computes changes in one intensional predicate due to changes in one extensional predicate, and loops over all derived and extensional predicates to complete the maintenance procedure. In each step of the loop, the delete, re-derive and insert steps are executed. The algorithm ends up fragmenting computation and rederiving changed and deleted facts over and over again, i.e. it is less efficient than the DRed algorithm.

9.2   Truth Maintenance Systems (TMS)

Truth maintenance [16] is an area of AI concerned with revising sets of beliefs and maintaining the truth in a reasoning system when new information alters existing information. A representation of beliefs and their dependencies is used to achieve the retraction of beliefs and to identify contradictions. For example, justification-based TMS [9] uses a graph data structure where nodes are augmented with two fields indicating their belief status and supporting justification. When the belief status is changed, dependencies are propagated through the graph.

Making TMSs more efficient was a cottage industry in the late 1980s, with most of the attention focused on the Assumption-based TMS (ATMS) [6]. The primary advantage of the ATMS is its ability to rapidly switch among many different contexts, which allows a simpler propagation of fact withdrawals, but comes at the cost of an exponential node-label updating process when facts are added. The main disadvantage of TMS is that the set of justifications (and

---

[16] also called *belief revision* or *reason maintenance*.

nodes) grows monotonically as it is not allowed to retract a justification, but only disable information. The fact that the set of assumptions is always in flux introduces most of the complexity in the TMS algorithms. More recent work (e.g. [23]) primarily tried to reduce the cost for incremental updates.

10   Conclusion

10.1   Contribution

We presented a technique for the incremental maintenance of materialized Datalog programs. Our technique can therefore be applied for ontology languages which can be axiomatized in Datalog, i.e. RDF Schema and OWL DLP[17] as well as the Datalog-fragments of Semantic Web rule languages.

We contributed a novel solution to the challenge of updating a materialization incrementally when the rules of a Datalog program change, which has, to our best knowledge, not been addressed in the deductive database context[18].

In order to cope with changing rules, we applied a declarative, rewriting-based algorithm for the incremental maintenance of views [30] and introduced two novel techniques: Firstly, we extended the rewriting to deal with changing rules. Secondly, we introduced two algorithms for the maintenance of the rewritten rules when the underlying source rules change.

Our solution has been completely implemented and evaluated. We reported on our prototypical implementation and presented the results of our empirical analysis of the costs of incremental maintenance, which shows the feasibility of our solution.

The techniques proposed in this article are not specific to any ontology language, but can generally be used for the incremental maintenance of materialized Datalog programs. Due to this generic solution, future developments, e.g. for the rule layer of the Semantic Web, are likely to benefit from our technique as well.

Materialization is certainly not a panacea to all tractability problems. For example, one drawback is that it trades off required inferencing time against storage space and access time. In spite of this restriction, which remains to be assessed by more practical experience and cost models that are derived from those experiences, we conjecture that materialization as explained in this article will help to progress the Semantic Web and to build the large Semantic Web engines of tomorrow.

10.2   Further Uses

We can reuse our approach for incremental maintenance of a materialization in several other contexts:

---

[17] We cannot maintain function symbols other than constants, therefore our approach can not be used for $\mathcal{L}_3$.

[18] [10] address the maintenance of views after redefinition for the relational data model.

- *Integrity Constraint Checking*: Incremental maintenance can also be used as a fundamental technique in an implementation of integrity constraints on Semantic Web data, i.e. we can incrementally check the validity of a constraint by maintaining an empty view.
- *Continuous Queries*: [18] The auxiliary maintenance predicates P^+ and P^- can be used as a basis for implementing continuous queries or publish/subscribe systems, which are used to monitor a flow of data. This monitoring can use the extensions of P^+ and P^- as a basis for notification messages that are sent to the subscribers.
- *Interoperability with systems of limited inferencing capabilities*: We can use materialization to explicate data for clients that cannot entail information on their own. In particular, we can store materializations in relational databases which are agnostic about the semantics of the data but may be used for fast query answering.

References

[1] K. Apt and J.-M. Pugin. Maintenance of stratified databases viewed as belief revision system. In *Proc. of the 6th Symposium on Principles of Database Systems (PODS)*, pages 136–145, San Diego, CA, USA, March 1987.

[2] S. Bechhofer, I. Horrocks, C. Goble, and R. Stevens. OilEd: A reasonable ontology editor for the Semantic Web. In *Proceedings of KI2001, Joint German/Austrian conference on Artificial Intelligence*, volume 2174 of *LNAI*, pages 396–408. Springer, 2001.

[3] S. Bechhofer, R. Volz, and P. Lord. Cooking the Semantic Web with the OWL API. In *[10]*, pages 659–675, 2003.

[4] T. Berners-Lee. CWM - closed world machine. Internet: http://www.w3.org/2000/10/ swap/doc/cwm.html, 2000.

[5] D. Brickley and R. V. Guha. RDF vocabulary description language 1.0: RDF Schema. W3C Working Draft, 10 October 2003, October 2003. Internet: http://www.w3.org/TR/2003/WD-rdf-schema-20031010/.

[6] J. de Kleer. An assumption-based truth maintenance system. *Artificial Intelligence*, 28:127–162, 1986.

[7] S. Decker, D. Brickley, J. Saarela, and J. Angele. A query and inference service for RDF. In *QL98 - Query Languages Workshop*, December 1998.

[8] S. Decker, M. Erdmann, D. Fensel, and R. Studer. Ontobroker: Ontology based Access to Distributed and Semi-structured Information. In *Database Semantics: Semantic Issues in Multimedia Systems.*, pages 351–369. Kluwer Academic, 1999.

[9] J. Doyle. A truth maintenance system. In B. Webber and N. J. Nilsson, editors, *Readings in Artifcial Intelligence*, pages 496–516. Morgan Kaufmann, Los Altos, California, 1981.

[10] A. Gupta, I. S. Mumick, and K. A. Ross. Adapting materialized views after redefinitions. In M. J. Carey and D. A. Schneider, editors, *Proceedings of the 1995 ACM SIGMOD International Conference on Management of Data, San Jose, California, May 22-25, 1995*, pages 211–222. ACM Press, 1995.

[11] Ashish Gupta, Inderpal Singh Mumick, and V. S. Subrahmanian. Maintaining views incrementally. In *Proceedings of the 1993 ACM SIGMOD international conference on Management of data*, pages 157–166. ACM Press, 1993.

[12] J. Harrison and S. Dietrich. Maintenance of materialized views in a deductive database: An update propagation approach. In *Workshop on Deductive Databases held in conjunction with the Joint International Conference and Symposium on Logic Programming (JICSLP)*, pages 56–65, Washington, D.C., November 1992.

[13] P. Hayes. RDF Semantics. W3C Working Draft, 10 October 2003, October 2003. Internet: http://www.w3.org/TR/rdf-mt/.

[14] J. Heflin, J. Hendler, and S. Luke. SHOE: A knowledge representation language for internet applications. Technical Report CS-TR-4078, Institute for Advanced Computer Studies, University of Maryland, 1999.

[15] M. Jarke, R. Gallersdoerfer, M. A. Jeusfeld, and M. Staudt. ConceptBase - A Deductive Object Base for Meta Data Management. *JIIS*, 4(2):167–192, 1995.

[16] M. Kifer, G. Lausen, and J. Wu. Logical foundations of object-oriented and frame-based languages. *Journal of the ACM*, 42:741–843, 1995.

[17] V. Kuchenhoff. On the efficient computation of the difference betwen consecutive database states. In C. Delobel, M. Kifer, and Y. Masunaga, editors, *Proc. of 2nd Int. Conf. on Deductive and Object-Oriented Databases*, volume 566 of *Lecture Notes in Computer Science (LNCS)*, pages 478–502, Munich, Germany, December 1991. Springer.

[18] L. Liu, C. Pu, and W. Tang. Continual queries for internet scale event-driven information delivery. *IEEE TKDE*, 11(4), 1999.

[19] A. Maedche, B. Motik, L. Stojanovic, R. Studer, and R. Volz. Managing multiple ontologies and ontology evolution in ontologging. In *Proc. of IIP-2002*, Montreal, Canada, 08 2002.

[20] A. Maedche, B. Motik, L. Stojanovic, R. Studer, and R. Volz. An infrastructure for searching, reusing and evolving distributed ontologies. In *Proc. of WWW-2003*, Budapest, Hungary, 05 2003.

[21] D. L. McGuinness and F. van Harmelen. OWL Web Ontology Language Overview. Technical report, World Wide Web Consortium (W3C), August 2003. Internet: http://www.w3.org/TR/owl-features/.

[22] B. Motik, A. Maedche, and R. Volz. A conceptual modeling approach for semantics-driven enterprise applications. In *Proc. 1st Int'l Conf. on Ontologies, Databases and Application of Semantics (ODBASE-2002)*, October 2002.

[23] P. P. Nayak and B. C. Williams. Fast context switching in real-time propositional reasoning. In T. Senator and B. Buchanan, editors, *Proceedings of the Fourteenth National Conference on Artificial Intelligence and the Ninth Innovative Applications of Artificial Intelligence Conference*, pages 50–56, Menlo Park, California, 1998. AAAI Press.

[24] R. Ramakrishnan, D. Srivastava, S. Sudarshan, and P. Seshadri. The CORAL Deductive System. *VLDB Journal: Very Large Data Bases*, 3(2):161–210, 1994.

[25] J. De Roo. Euler proof mechanism. Internet: http://www.agfa.com/w3c/euler/, 2002.

[26] K. Sagonas, T. Swift, and D. S. Warren. XSB as an efficient deductive database engine. In R. T. Snodgrass and M. Winslett, editors, *Proc. of the 1994 ACM SIGMOD Int. Conf. on Management of Data (SIGMOD'94)*, pages 442–453, 1994.

[27] M. Sintek and S. Decker. TRIPLE - an RDF query, inference and transformation language. In *Deductive Databases and Knowledge Management (DDLP)*, 2001.

[28] P. Spyns, D. Oberle, R. Volz, J. Zheng, M. Jarrar, Y. Sure, R. Studer, and R. Meersman. OntoWeb - A Semantic Web community portal. In *Proc. ofProc. Fourth International Conference on Practical Aspects of Knowledge Management (PAKM)*, pages 189–200, Vienna, Austria, 2002.

[29] M. Staudt and M. Jarke. Incremental maintenance of externally materialized views. Technical Report AIB-95-13, RWTH Aachen, 1995.

[30] M. Staudt and M. Jarke. Incremental maintenance of externally materialized views. In T. M. Vijayaraman, A. P. Buchmann, C. Mohan, and N. L. Sarda, editors, *VLDB'96, Proceedings of 22th International Conference on Very Large Data Bases, September 3-6, 1996, Mumbai (Bombay), India*, pages 75–86. Morgan Kaufmann, 1996.

[31] R. Studer, Y. Sure, and R. Volz. Managing user focused access to distributed knowledge. *Journal of Universal Computer Science (J.UCS)*, 8(6):662–672, 2002.

[32] R. Volz, S. Staab, and B. Motik. Incremental maintenance of dynamic datalog programs. In *[?]*, 2003.

[33] R. Volz, S. Staab, and B. Motik. Incremental Maintenance of Materialized Ontologies. In R. Meersman, Z. Tari, D. C. Schmidt, B. Kraemer, M. van Steen, S. Vinoski, R. King, M. Orlowska, R. Studer, E. Bertino, and D. McLeod, editors, *Proc. of CoopIS/DOA/ODBASE 2003*, volume 2888 of *LNCS*, pages 707–724, Sicily, 2003.

[34] Raphael Volz. *Web Ontology Reasoning in Logic Databases*. PhD thesis, Universitaet Fridericiana zu Karlsruhe (TH), http://www.ubka.uni-karlsruhe.de/cgi-bin/psview?document=20042, February 2004.

A   Appendix

The reader may note that OoM is an acronym for "Out Of Memory", i.e. the prototypical implementation could not deal with the problem size.

Original Query	D	NS	NI	P	Change	Orig Average	Minimum	Maximum
Taxonomy	3	5	5	0	10	197	80	491
Taxonomy	4	5	5	0	10	373	290	571
Taxonomy	5	5	5	0	10	1767	1482	2463
Taxonomy	3	5	5	0	15	147	60	311
Taxonomy	4	5	5	0	15	378	280	581
Taxonomy	5	5	5	0	15	1765	1373	2464
DL-Like Ontology	3	5	5	5	10	310	170	640
DL-Like Ontology	4	5	5	5	10	2764	2523	3475
DL-Like Ontology	5	5	5	5	10	OoM	OoM	OoM
DL-Like Ontology	3	5	5	5	15	263	150	511
DL-Like Ontology	4	5	5	5	15	2774	2523	3515
DL-Like Ontology	5	5	5	5	15	OoM	OoM	OoM
DB-Like Conjunctive Query	3	5	5	5	10	152	70	341
DB-Like Conjunctive Query	4	5	5	5	10	482	310	701
DB-Like Conjunctive Query	5	5	5	5	10	2165	19963	2403
DB-Like Conjunctive Query	3	5	5	5	15	172	70	430
DB-Like Conjunctive Query	4	5	5	5	15	425	301	701
DB-Like Conjunctive Query	5	5	5	5	15	2078	1722	2374

Setup Maintenance	D	NS	NI	P	Change	Average	Minimum	Maximum
Taxonomy	3	5	5	0	10	305	200	441
Taxonomy	4	5	5	0	10	1347	1212	1622
Taxonomy	5	5	5	0	10	18391	16694	19318
Taxonomy	3	5	5	0	15	245	141	251
Taxonomy	4	5	5	0	15	1382	1232	1683
Taxonomy	5	5	5	0	15	18293	16714	19017
DL-Like Ontology	3	5	5	5	10	355	230	531
DL-Like Ontology	4	5	5	5	10	3715	2894	4747
DL-Like Ontology	5	5	5	5	10	OoM	OoM	OoM
DL-Like Ontology	3	5	5	5	15	368	241	571
DL-Like Ontology	4	5	5	5	15	3720	2894	4757
DL-Like Ontology	5	5	5	5	15	OoM	OoM	OoM
DB-Like Conjunctive Query	3	5	5	5	10	265	151	431
DB-Like Conjunctive Query	4	5	5	5	10	1464	1322	1663
DB-Like Conjunctive Query	5	5	5	5	10	18536	16935	19999
DB-Like Conjunctive Query	3	5	5	5	15	272	160	440
DB-Like Conjunctive Query	4	5	5	5	15	1467	1352	1652
DB-Like Conjunctive Query	5	5	5	5	15	18536	16905	20019

Removing Rules	D	NS	NI	P	Change	Average	Minimum	Maximum
Taxonomy	3	5	5	0	10	1386	1292	1592
Taxonomy	4	5	5	0	10	7581	7291	8352
Taxonomy	5	5	5	0	10	494726	227747	717452
Taxonomy	3	5	5	0	15	1452	1292	1772
Taxonomy	4	5	5	0	15	7615	7330	8372
Taxonomy	5	5	5	0	15	273874	189933	386005
DL-Like Ontology	3	5	5	5	10	2979	2864	3195
DL-Like Ontology	4	5	5	5	10	52613	47128	65214
DL-Like Ontology	5	5	5	5	10	OoM	OoM	OoM
DL-Like Ontology	3	5	5	5	15	33128	3055	3555
DL-Like Ontology	4	5	5	5	15	61979	50944	66395
DL-Like Ontology	5	5	5	5	15	OoM	OoM	OoM
DB-Like Conjunctive Query	3	5	5	5	10	1492	1382	1722
DB-Like Conjunctive Query	4	5	5	5	10	8011	7281	8732
DB-Like Conjunctive Query	5	5	5	5	10	517994	284389	723009
DB-Like Conjunctive Query	3	5	5	5	15	1557	1422	1783
DB-Like Conjunctive Query	4	5	5	5	15	8112	7822	8723
DB-Like Conjunctive Query	5	5	5	5	15	507760	132901	709009

Removing Facts	D	NS	NI	P	Change	Average	Minimum	Maximum
Taxonomy	3	5	5	0	10	1302	1282	1332
Taxonomy	4	5	5	0	10	7328	7281	7361
Taxonomy	5	5	5	0	10	631956	487551	759261
Taxonomy	3	5	5	0	15	1301	1291	1312
Taxonomy	4	5	5	0	15	7350	7340	7371
Taxonomy	5	5	5	0	15	542294	381628	650265
DL-Like Ontology	3	5	5	5	10	3071	2974	3184
DL-Like Ontology	4	5	5	5	10	56754	56371	57002
DL-Like Ontology	5	5	5	5	10	OoM	OoM	OoM
DL-Like Ontology	3	5	5	5	15	3242	3125	3355
DL-Like Ontology	4	5	5	5	15	58339	58104	58655
DL-Like Ontology	5	5	5	5	15	OoM	OoM	OoM
DB-Like Conjunctive Query	3	5	5	5	10	1402	1392	1412
DB-Like Conjunctive Query	4	5	5	5	10	7991	7952	8022
DB-Like Conjunctive Query	5	5	5	5	10	537931	299260	787843
DB-Like Conjunctive Query	3	5	5	5	15	1409	1382	1422
DB-Like Conjunctive Query	4	5	5	5	15	7876	7841	7901
DB-Like Conjunctive Query	5	5	5	5	15	424565	292671	482925

Adding Rules	D	NS	NI	P	Change	Average	Minimum	Maximum
Taxonomy	3	5	5	0	10	1317	1252	1463
Taxonomy	4	5	5	0	10	7265	7240	7290
Taxonomy	5	5	5	0	10	559407	393666	706696
Taxonomy	3	5	5	0	15	1286	1251	1332
Taxonomy	4	5	5	0	15	7308	7291	7331
Taxonomy	5	5	5	0	15	464588	247826	611980
DL-Like Ontology	3	5	5	5	10	3009	2834	3345
DL-Like Ontology	4	5	5	5	10	51864	47047	65444
DL-Like Ontology	5	5	5	5	10	OoM	OoM	OoM
DL-Like Ontology	3	5	5	5	15	3307	2884	3565
DL-Like Ontology	4	5	5	5	15	61283	47528	67037
DL-Like Ontology	5	5	5	5	15	OoM	OoM	OoM
DB-Like Conjunctive Query	3	5	5	5	10	1469	1392	1662
DB-Like Conjunctive Query	4	5	5	5	10	8051	7801	8523
DB-Like Conjunctive Query	5	5	5	5	10	400638	150226	541619
DB-Like Conjunctive Query	3	5	5	5	15	1462	1422	1552
DB-Like Conjunctive Query	4	5	5	5	15	7936	7902	7981
DB-Like Conjunctive Query	5	5	5	5	15	484394	141163	691164

Adding Facts	D	NS	NI	P	Change	Average	Minimum	Maximum
Taxonomy	3	5	5	0	10	1284	1262	1312
Taxonomy	4	5	5	0	10	7310	7270	7380
Taxonomy	5	5	5	0	10	649123	522761	781173
Taxonomy	3	5	5	0	15	1367	1282	1612
Taxonomy	4	5	5	0	15	7310	7271	7350
Taxonomy	5	5	5	0	15	648495	576319	756978
DL-Like Ontology	3	5	5	5	10	3620	3565	3685
DL-Like Ontology	4	5	5	5	10	136128	134463	137928
DL-Like Ontology	5	5	5	5	10	OoM	OoM	OoM
DL-Like Ontology	3	5	5	5	15	3790	3725	3895
DL-Like Ontology	4	5	5	5	15	90277	89940	90910
DL-Like Ontology	5	5	5	5	15	OoM	OoM	OoM
DB-Like Conjunctive Query	3	5	5	5	10	1399	1392	1402
DB-Like Conjunctive Query	4	5	5	5	10	7931	7761	8012
DB-Like Conjunctive Query	5	5	5	5	10	714216	460882	878814
DB-Like Conjunctive Query	3	5	5	5	15	1434	1412	1452
DB-Like Conjunctive Query	4	5	5	5	15	8011	7891	8262
DB-Like Conjunctive Query	5	5	5	5	15	763873	482964	955724

Query on Materialization	D	NS	NI	P	Change	
Taxonomy	3	5	5	0	10	0
Taxonomy	4	5	5	0	10	0
Taxonomy	5	5	5	0	10	1331
Taxonomy	3	5	5	0	15	0
Taxonomy	4	5	5	0	15	0
Taxonomy	5	5	5	0	15	1252
DL-Like Ontology	3	5	5	5	10	10
DL-Like Ontology	4	5	5	5	10	0
DL-Like Ontology	5	5	5	5	10	OoM
DL-Like Ontology	3	5	5	5	15	0
DL-Like Ontology	4	5	5	5	15	0
DL-Like Ontology	5	5	5	5	15	OoM
DB-Like Conjunctive Query	3	5	5	5	10	0
DB-Like Conjunctive Query	4	5	5	5	10	0
DB-Like Conjunctive Query	5	5	5	5	10	1633
DB-Like Conjunctive Query	3	5	5	5	15	0
DB-Like Conjunctive Query	4	5	5	5	15	0
DB-Like Conjunctive Query	5	5	5	5	15	1282

Ontology Translation on the Semantic Web*

Dejing Dou, Drew McDermott, and Peishen Qi

Yale Computer Science Department
New Haven, CT 06520, USA
{dejing.dou,drew.mcdermott,peishen.qi}@yale.edu

Abstract. Ontologies are a crucial tool for formally specifying the vocabulary and relationship of concepts used on the Semantic Web. In order to share information, agents that use different vocabularies must be able to translate data from one ontological framework to another. Ontology translation is required when translating datasets, generating ontology extensions, and querying through different ontologies. OntoMerge, an online system for ontology merging and automated reasoning, can implement ontology translation with inputs and outputs in OWL or other web languages. Ontology translation can be thought of in terms of formal inference in a merged ontology. The merge of two related ontologies is obtained by taking the union of the concepts and the axioms defining them, and then adding *bridging axioms* that relate their concepts. The resulting *merged ontology* then serves as an inferential medium within which translation can occur. Our internal representation, *Web-PDDL*, is a strong typed first-order logic language for web application. Using a uniform notation for all problems allows us to factor out syntactic and semantic translation problems, and focus on the latter. Syntactic translation is done by an automatic translator between Web-PDDL and OWL or other web languages. Semantic translation is implemented using an inference engine (*OntoEngine*) which processes assertions and queries in Web-PDDL syntax, running in either a data-driven (forward chaining) or demand-driven (backward chaining) way.

1 Introduction

One major goal of the Semantic Web is that web-based agents should process and "understand" data rather than merely display them as at present [24]. Ontologies, which are defined as the formal specification of a vocabulary of concepts and axioms relating them, are seen playing a key role in describing the "semantics" of the data. Using ontologies, web-based agents can treat web documents as sets of assertions, and, in particular, draw inferences from them.[1]

---

* This research was supported by the DARPA DAML program. This is an extended version of the paper presented in ODBASE2003 [29].

[1] We use scare quotes for "semantic" and "understand" because many people use the former term without knowing what it means, and no one knows what the latter term means. We will avoid the word "understand" wherever possible, but "semantic" in the recent sense of "seeming to reveal a grasp of the meaning of the terms occurring in," as in "semantic translation," seems unavoidable.

S. Spaccapietra et al. (Eds.): Journal on Data Semantics II, LNCS 3360, pp. 35–57, 2004.

More and more ontologies are being developed [4] as formal underpinnings for RDF-based data. An obvious desideratum of this movement is that two ontologies should not cover the same area; instead, those interested in formalizing descriptions in that area should agree on a standard set of concepts. However, this goal cannot always be met, for a variety of reasons. Some standard vocabularies arise in different parts of the world or among different linguistic communities, and attain popularity before their overlap is noticed. Even more likely is that two vocabularies will partially overlap, usually because what is central to one is peripheral to the other. For instance, a vocabulary devised by glove manufacturers will have something to say about the parts of the hand and how they mesh with the parts of gloves. A vocabulary devised by orthopedic surgeons will also talk about the parts of the hand, but in very different ways, including, obviously, going into much more detail.

These vocabulary differences make life difficult for agents on the Semantic Web. It is much simpler to program two agents to communicate if they use the same vocabulary and the terms have same meaning or interpretation. But in cases where their vocabularies differ, we must resort to *ontology translation* to allow them to communicate. This paper describes our contribution to the solution of this problem.

Our focus is on translation between languages that use the same syntax but have different vocabularies. We will have little to say about eliminating syntactic differences, and instead will generally assume that the facts or queries to be translated will be in the same logical notation after translation as before; only the vocabulary will change. Syntactic translation is not always trivial, but we will assume it is solved.

1.1   The Differences Between Ontologies on Similar Domains

The kinds of semantic differences between ontologies are innumerable, and rarely correspond to simple correspondences between symbols in one and symbols in the other, as we will discuss in section 1.2. For example, one genealogy ontology might use two properties — firstname and lastname — to represent a person's name, where another might use only one property, fullname.

Some more subtle examples arise in translation between two bibliographical ontologies developed at Yale [18] and CMU [3].[2] While they are both obviously derived from the Bibtex terminology, different decisions were made when ontology experts developed them.

EXAMPLE 1.1.1. Both ontologies have a class called Article. In the yale_bib ontology, Article is a class which is disjoint with other classes such as Inproceedings and Incollection. Therefore, in the yale_bib ontology, Article only includes those articles which were published in a journal. But in the cmu_bib ontology, Article

---

[2] These are "toy" ontologies developed as exercises to help populate the DARPA DAML ontology library [4]. They are much simpler than real-world ontologies would be. Their very simplicity helps reveal the phenomena we are after.

includes all articles which were published in a journal, proceedings or collection. There are no Inproceedings and Incollection classes in the cmu_bib ontology.

Complicated semantic differences can be caused by different understandings about similar concepts. Even if the concepts from two ontologies share the same class or property name, it is still possible that they have quite different meanings. The following example is about the booktitle property in the yale_bib ontology and cmu_bib ontology.

EXAMPLE 1.1.2. In the cmu_bib ontology, booktitle's domain is the Book class and its range is String. A booktitle relationship means that a Book has some string as its title. In the yale_bib ontology, booktitle's domain is Publication and its range is Literal, which can be taken to be the same class as String. However, yale_bib's booktitle domain is Publication. The assertion that publication P has booktitle S means that P was published in a conference proceedings or anthology, and that it is this proceedings or collection that has S as its title.

Another reason for complicated semantic differences is that they can be inherited from those between basic concepts, such as time, space etc.

EXAMPLE 1.1.3. There are several ontologies about time, such as DAML Time [6] and the time ontology in OpenCyc [11]. Those time ontologies have semantic differences among their concepts, such as events. Two genealogy ontologies, one based on DAML Time and the other on Cyc, might take identical positions on all design choices about specifically genealogical questions, but look different because of their differing assumptions about time, as expressed in the way they make assertions about genealogically relevant events such as birth and marriage.

1.2   The Relationship Between Ontology Translation and Ontology Mapping

It's important to distinguish ontology translation from *ontology mapping*, which is the process of finding correspondence (mappings) between the concepts of two ontologies. If two concepts correspond, they mean the same thing, or closely related things. Obviously, finding such mappings can be a valuable preprocessing step in solving the ontology-translation problem for the two ontologies. Automating the process of ontology mapping is an active area of research [40,42,27,46].

However, the emphasis on finding mappings has led, we believe, to a distorted view of the translation problem. Suppose one starts by assuming a particular notation for ontologies, such as OWL [12]. These notations are often represented visually as graph structures. Then it is natural to express a mapping between two ontologies as a network of "meta-links" that join nodes and links in one ontology graph with nodes and links in the other [36]. Each such link can be annotated with labels specifying whether the two constructs it joins mean exactly the same thing, or which of them covers a larger set of objects or relationships. It seems almost inevitable at that point to think of translation as a process of substitution of labels. One might identify a role R_1 in one ontology with a role R_2 in another. (In the terminology of relational databases, the columns R_1 and R_2 would be labelled as equivalent.) Translation then becomes a matter of relabelling data.

Complexities arise when the labels aren't exactly equivalent. Two classes might be connected by a subclass link instead of being exactly equivalent.

Meanwhile, there is a competing paradigm for translation, centered around the problem of answering queries in federated databases. Here the problem is that a query asked with respect to one schema (say, a central ontology) may require retrieval from a database using a different schema. This process is usually thought of as translating the *query* rather than translating the data used to answer it. The rules required to translate a query are essentially logical axioms (or logic-programming rules) of the form $A \leftarrow B$, where A is in the query vocabulary and B is in the vocabulary of the remote database [35,41].[3] The reason that this is not normally described as translating data from notation B is that the spotlight is not on arbitrary data expressed in that notation. Instead the main question is, Does the query result in finding all the bindings for its free variables that follow from the contents of the B database?

In this and our previous papers [28,29], we explore the idea of abolishing the distinction between "ontology translation" and "query translation," assimilating the former to the latter. Translation may be thought of abstractly as a two-stage process: *Inference* and *projection*. That is, to translate a set of facts S_1 expressed in ontology 1 to ontology 2, we draw all possible inferences from S_1, then *project* the results into the vocabulary of S_2. That is, we discard conclusions that are not in the *target vocabulary* used by S_2.

As stated, this proposal is highly schematic, and we will explain how it gets instantiated into a practical algorithm. In this section, however, the discussion will stay at a fairly abstract level. The first remark to make is that query translation already fits our paradigm, using backward chaining to keep the inference headed toward relevant results.

However, backward chaining is not always the best option, or even a feasible option. If an agent wants to do data mining on information supplied by another, then it won't know ahead of time what set of queries to use. Or an agent might be asked for a description of an object it is trying to find (e.g., "a recent book by Neal Stephenson"). It has in essence a small dataset that it wants to translate in its entirety to the language of the agent that asked for the description. In such cases we do *not* throw the infer-and-project framework overboard, we just use it in a forward direction.

From this point of view, translation rules are just axioms. The purpose of ontology mapping should be to find these axioms. Finding correspondences between symbols is just the first step. Unfortunately, in many papers, it often seems to be the last step. We seek to tilt in the other direction by focusing on the axioms and not worrying about automatic mapping at all. Unlike many other approaches (e.g., [27]), we do not manage axioms as links between otherwise disparate ontologies. Instead, we work in the *merge* of two related ontologies, obtained by taking the union of the concepts and the axioms defining them, and using XML

---

[3] We're oversimplifying somewhat here, by assuming that axioms define A predicates in terms of B predicates. In the competing, "local as view" paradigm, the axioms run the other way, and query translation is more difficult. See [44].

namespaces [17] to avoid name clashes. *Bridging axioms* are then added to relate the concepts in one ontology to the concepts in the other through the terms in the merge. This framework frees us from having to think in terms of just two ontologies joined by a slender "bridge." Instead, as many ontologies as are relevant can't be mixed together, and the bridging axioms can relate terms from these ontologies in whatever ways seem appropriate.

Devising and maintaining a merged ontology is a job for human experts, both domain experts and "knowledge engineers." Once the merged ontology is obtained, ontology translation can proceed without further human intervention. The inference mechanism we use is a theorem prover optimized for the ontology-translation task, called *OntoEngine*. We use it for deductive dataset translation (section 3), ontology-extension generation(section 4), and query handling through different ontologies (section 5). We will also discuss related work in section 6. In the last section, we will give some conclusions for our work so far and discuss our future plans for developing interactive tools for ontology merging based on our recent work on integrating different neuronal databases.

1.3   Three Kinds of Ontology Translation Problems

As we said above, we focus on three kinds of ontology translation problems: dataset translation, ontology-extension generation and querying through different ontologies.

Dataset translation can be defined as the translation of a "dataset" from one ontology to another. We use the term *dataset* to mean a set of facts expressed in a particular ontology [38]. The translation problem arises when web-based agents try to exchange their datasets but they use different ontologies to describe them.

EXAMPLE 1.2.1. Suppose there is a web-based agent which uses the cmu_bib ontology to collect and process the bibliography information of researchers in the area of computer science. A web-based agent at Yale can provide such information about publications by members of the Yale CS department. The CMU agent needs an ontology translation service to translate those datasets into the cmu_bib ontology before it can combine them with information it already has.

The problem of *ontology extension generation* is defined thus: given two related ontologies O_1 and O_2 and an extension (sub-ontology) O_{1s} of O_1, construct the "corresponding" extension O_{2s}.

EXAMPLE 1.2.2. DAML-S [5] is a general ("upper") ontology describing web services at the application level (i.e., focusing on business processes), and WSDL Schema [16] is another general ontology describing web services at the communication level (i.e., focusing on messages and protocols). To use DAML-S to model a particular service, one must manually develop a sub-ontology that uses the DAML-S vocabulary to describe, say, a book seller's or airline's web service. But the description of a service is not complete or usable until it extends all the way down to the communication level. In other words, given the DAML-S sub-ontology for Congo.com, we would like to derive the "analogous" sub-ontology of WSDL Schema. To oversimplify, if property P_D maps to P_W at the upper level, and if P_{DC} is a sub-property of P_D belonging to the Congo ontology, we should be able to infer the corresponding sub-property P_{WC} of Congo.com's counterpart at the communication level. This process is part of *grounding*, to use the terminology of [22].

Finally, we have the problem of *querying through ontologies*, in which a query made by one agent has the potential to be answered by another agent (perhaps a database manager) that uses a different ontology. answer a query

EXAMPLE 1.2.3. Suppose a web agent using the drc_ged [8] genealogy ontology wants to find the marriage date of King Henry_VI of England. It finds a knowledge base that it has reason to trust, which contains information about the individuals and families of European royalty, but it uses a different genealogy ontology, bbn_ged [2]. Ontology translation is required for the agent to get its query answered.

2 Our Approach: Ontology Merging and Automated Reasoning

In this section, we flesh out the inference-then-projection schema, yielding an approach we call *ontology translation by ontology merging and automated reasoning*. We have developed *Web-PDDL* as a strongly typed, first-order logic language to describe axioms, facts, and queries, which we use as our internal representation language for the formal inference. We have also designed and implemented a first-order theorem prover, *OntoEngine*, which is optimized for the ontology-translation task.

2.1 Separate Syntactic and Semantic Translation

Past work [32,25] on ontology translation has addressed both syntactic and semantic-issues, but tends to focus more on syntactic translation [25] because it is easier to automate. "Semantic" translation is more difficult because creating mapping rules often requires subtle judgments about the relationships between meanings of concepts in one ontology and their meanings in another. We assume that, at least for the foreseeable future, it can't be fully automated.[4]

We break ontology translation into three parts: syntactic translation from the source notation in a web language to an internal representation, semantic translation by inference using the internal notation, and syntactic translation from the internal representation to the target web language. All syntactic issues are dealt with in the first and third phases, using a translator, *PDDAML* [14] for translating between our internal representation and OWL. If a new web language becomes more popular for the Semantic Web, we only need extend PDDAML to

---

[4] The translation problem is certainly "AI-complete" in the sense that a program that solved it would have to be as intelligent as a person; but in fact it may be even harder than that, because agreeing on a translation in the most difficult cases might require bargaining between experts about what their notations really mean. This is not really the sort of problem a single program could solve, even in principle.

handle it (assuming it is no more expressive than first-order logic). This allows us to focus on semantic translation from one ontology to another.

Our internal representation language is *Web-PDDL* [39], a strongly typed first order logic language with Lisp-like syntax. It extends the Planning Domain Definition Language (PDDL) [37] with XML namespaces, multi-type inheritance and more flexible notations for axioms. Web-PDDL can be used to represent ontologies, datasets and queries. Here is an example, part of the yale_bib ontology written in Web-PDDL.

```
(define (domain yale_bib-ont)
    (:extends (uri "http://www.w3.org/2000/01/rdf-schema#" :prefix rdfs))
    (:types Publication - Obj
            Article Book Incollection Inproceedings - Publication
            Literal - @rdfs:Literal)
    (:predicates (author p - Publication a - Literal)
                 .....))
```

The :extends declaration expresses that this domain (i.e., ontology) is extended from one or more other ontologies identified by the URIs. To avoid symbol clashes, symbols imported from other ontologies are given prefixes, such as @rdfs:Literal. These correspond to XML namespaces, and when Web-PDDL is translated to RDF [39], that's exactly what they become. Types start with capital letters and are the same concept as classes in some other web languages, such as OWL. A type T_1 is declared to be of a subtype of a type T_0 by writing "T_1 - T_0" in the :types field of a domain definition. In other contexts, the hyphen notation is used to declare a constant or variable to be of a type T, by writing "x - T". Predicates correspond roughly to "properties" in OWL, but they can take any number of arguments. There are also functions, including Skolem functions and built-in functions such as + and − that can be evaluated when appropriate.

Assertions are written in the usual Lisp style: (author pub20 "Tom Jefferson"), for instance. We'll discuss quantifiers shortly.

Web-PDDL reflects a fundamentally different philosophy about knowledge-representation (KR) languages than that embodied in notations such as RDF and OWL. The latter reflect the strong opinions in the Description Logic community that a KR language should make it impossible to pose undecidable (or even intractable) problems. Our attitude is that languages should be as expressive as different reasoning applications will require. There are many interesting application areas where useful programs exist in spite of scary worst-case performance. As we hope to show below, ontology translation is a good example, where certain simple techniques from theorem proving solve a large portion of the problem, even though theorem proving is in principle undecidable.

2.2   Axiom-Based Ontology Merging

If all ontologies, datasets and queries can be expressed in terms of the same internal representation, such as Web-PDDL, semantic translation can be implemented as formal inference working with a *merged ontology* of the source and target ontologies. Ontology merging is the process of taking the union of the concepts of source and target ontologies together and adding the *bridging axioms* to express the relationship (mappings) of the concepts in one ontology to the concepts in the other. Such axioms can express both simple and complicated semantic mappings between concepts of the source and target ontologies. The simple semantic mappings include "subClassOf," "subPropertyOf" or "equivalent" relationships. For example, if two types (class) are equivalent (sameClassAs), such as the Book type in the yale_bib ontology is equivalent to the Book type in the cmu_bib ontology. Because types are not objects, we cannot write an axiom such as $(= T_1\ T_2)$. So we have to use a pseudo-predicate (or, perhaps, "meta-predicate") T-> and write bridging axioms about equivalent types. In the merged ontology of yale_bib and cmu_bib, the equivalent relationship about their Book types is written in Web-PDDL:

```
(:axioms
    (T-> @yale_bib:Book Book)
    (T-> @cmu_bib:Book Book)
    ...
```

Namespace prefixes distinguish yale_bib's Book and cmu_bib's Book. The symbols without a prefix are native to the merged ontology. Our axiom defines a new Book type in the merged ontology, and makes yale_bib's Book equivalent to cmu_bib's Book by making both of them be equivalent to the new defined Book in the merged ontology.

The reason we need a Book type in the merge is: the merge will be a totally new ontology which can be merged further with other ontologies. Suppose we have got the cyb ontology as the merge of the cmu_bib and yale_bib ontologies. There is another foo_bib ontology needs to be merged with the cyb ontology and the foo_bib ontology also has a Book type. Since we already have cyb's Book, we don't need to specify the relationship between foo_bib's Book and cmu_bib's Book, or the relationship between foo_bib's Book and yale_bib's Book. What we need to do is specify the relationship between foo_bib's Book and cyb's Book. Therefore, we need to define types and predicates in the merge, even through they are the same as one of two related types or predicates in the component ontologies.

The more complicated semantic mappings, such as the one about yale_bib's booktitle and cmu_bib's booktitle in Example 1.1.2, can be expressed as bridging axioms in the merged ontology. But we must be careful to distinguish the two senses of (booktitle a s), which in yale_bib means "Inproceedings or Incollection a appeared in a book with title s" and in cmu_bib means "The title of book a is s". Namespace prefixes suffice for the distinguishing two booktitles. The more interesting task is to relate the two senses, which we accomplish with the bridging axioms

```
(forall (a - Article tl - String)
        (iff (@yale_bib:booktitle a tl) (booktitle a tl)))

(forall (a - @yale_bib:Inproceedings tl - String)
        (iff (booktitle a tl)
                (exists (p - Proceedings)
```

```
    (and (contain p a)
         (@cmu_bib:inProceedings a p)
         (@cmu_bib:booktitle p tl)))))
```

Note that the bridging axioms can be used to go from either ontology to the other. The second axiom uses an existential quantifier and p is a existential quantified variable. It also can be written in the form of skolem functions after skolemization [45]:

```
(forall (a - @yale_bib:Inproceedings tl - String)
        (if (booktitle a tl)
            (and (contains (@skolem:aProc a tl) - Proceedings a)
                 (@cmu_bib:inProceedings a (@skolem:aProc a tl))
                 (@cmu_bib:booktitle (@skolem:aProc a tl) tl)))))
```

We use the prefix @skolem: as a convention for the skolem functions.

Some bridging axioms may need "callable" functions. For example, yale_bib's year predicate uses Number to represent the year when a publication was published. However, cmu_bib's year predicate uses String to represent the year. When we try to express the mapping between these two predicates, we select yale_bib's year predicate as the one in the merge. We have to use two functions, one for converting a number to a string and the other one for converting a string to a number, to express these mapping axioms:

```
(forall (p - Publication yn - @cmu_bib:Year)
        (if (@cmu_bib:year p yn)
            (year p (@built_in:NumbertoString yn))))

(forall (p - Publication y - String)
        (if (year p y)
            (@cmu_bib:year p (@built_in:StringtoNumber y))))
```

We use the prefix built_in to indicate that these two functions are built-in functions.

For the foreseeable future the construction of merged ontologies has to involve the efforts of human experts. If necessary, when the source and target ontologies are very large, automatic mapping tools can give some suggestions to human experts, but, in our view, before we know what bridging axioms look like, there's no point in spending a lot of effort on building automated tools.

2.3   OntoEngine: An Optimized Theorem Prover for Semantic Translation

Our decision to use a theorem prover for semantic translation may cause some concern, given that in general a theorem prover can run for a long time and conclude nothing useful. However, in our experience, the sorts of inferences we need to make are focused on the following areas:

- Forward chaining from facts in source ontology to facts in target ontology.
- Backward chaining from queries in one ontology to get bindings from datasets in another.
- Introduction of skolem terms from existential quantified variables or skolem functions.
- Use of equalities to substitute existing constant terms for skolem terms.

Our theorem prover, called *OntoEngine*, is specialized for these sorts of inference. OntoEngine uses generalized Modus Ponens chaining through bridging axioms with specified directions. To avoid infinite loops, we set a limit to the complexity of terms that OntoEngine generates; and, of course, OntoEngine stops when it reaches conclusions (or, in the case of backward chaining, goals) in the target ontology, which is called *target control.* Target control can avoid some redundant inference back from target ontology to source ontology. In addition, OntoEngine has a good type-checking system based on the strongly typed feature of Web-PDDL. The type-checking system can be used in both forward and backward chaining and can terminate blind alleys at the unification stage, without generating goals to prove that a term is of the correct type.

OntoEngine can use equalities to substitute existing constant terms for skolem terms or other general function terms. Equality substitutions can decrease redundant inference results, such as redundant facts and queries. In OWL ontologies, equalities occur mainly in *cardinality axioms,* which state that there is exactly one or at most one object with a given property.[5] For example, in a genealogy ontology, there are two predicates husband and wife, whose cardinality axioms say that one family has only one husband and only one wife. The cardinality axiom about husband can be expressed in Web-PDDL:

```
(forall (f - Family h1 - Male h2 - Male)
    (if (and (husband f h1)
             (husband f h2))
        (= h1 h2)))
```

It is important to compare OntoEngine with other inference systems, such as Datalog systems, description logic systems and resolution theorem provers, which may be used to do reasoning with bridging axioms to implement semantic translations. The comparisons also can explain why we designed and built OntoEngine rather than use other existing inference systems.

A Datalog system can do backward chaining with Prolog-like rules to answer queries using view relations in databases [44]. To avoid generating an infinite number of answers, Datalog rules are required to satisfy some *safety* conditions [47]. Hence, there are not any existentially quantified variable in the head (conclusion) side of a Datalog rule and Datalog systems don't have any mechanism to generate skolem terms or do equality substitution. However, relationships between concepts from different ontologies may require bridging axioms with existentially quantified variable in the conclusion side, such as the bridging axiom about booktitle in section 2.2. OntoEngine can generate skolem terms and do

---

[5] Actually, you can specify other cardinalities, but it is pretty rare to do so.

equality substitution to avoid redundant answers so that it can handle such kind of complicated axioms.

Description logics [23] are subsets of first order logic. Compared to the standard predicate calculus, the expressivity of description logic is limited, in order to guarantee the decidability of inference. There is a tradeoff between the expressivity of a representation language and the difficulty of reasoning over the representation built using that language. Although description logic (DL) reasoning systems are usually quite efficient, sometimes guaranteeably so, they cannot generate new objects — only select subsets of existing objects. For example, the DL systems cannot generate skolem terms although description logics have existential quantifier. The DL rules (axioms) do not allow (built-in) functions which is necessary in some bridging axioms, such as year example in section 2.2. OntoEngine can generate skolem terms and process the axioms with (built-in) functions.

OntoEngine is not a complete first-order theorem prover, unlike resolution-based systems, such as Otter [48]. One reason (besides our obvious desire for efficiency) is that we have empirically observed that some deductive techniques are not necessary for ontology translation. Most important, so far we have had little need for *case analysis,* in which a proposition is proved by showing that it follows from A and from B, when $A \vee B$ is the strongest conclusion that can be drawn about A and B.

3   Deductive Ontology Translation Between Datasets

In this section we describe how to apply our new approach to implement dataset translation. We set up an online ontology translation service, OntoMerge, to do deductive dataset translation on the Semantic Web. A more detailed account on the forward chaining algorithm for our generalized modus ponens reasoner appears in [28].

The problem for translating datasets can be expressed abstractly thus: given a set of facts in one vocabulary (the *source*), infer the largest possible set of consequences in another (the *target*). We break this process into two phases:

1. *Inference:* working in a *merged ontology* that combines all the symbols and axioms from both the source and target, draw inferences from source facts.
2. *Projection:* Retain conclusions that are expressed purely in the target vocabulary.

In *Example* 1.2.1, suppose the source ontology is yale_bib and the target ontology is cmu_bib. Considering the semantic difference mentioned in Example 1.1.2, the fact "The publication BretonZucker96 appeared in the Proceedings of IEEE Conf. on Computer Vision and Pattern Recognition" is expressed in the yale_bib ontology thus:

```
(:objects ... BretonZucker96 - InProceedings)
(:facts ... (booktitle BretonZucker96 "Proceedings of  CVPR'96"))
```

In the cmu_bib ontology, the same fact should be expressed thus:

```
(:objects ... BretonZucker96 - Article proc38 - Proceedings)
(facts ... (inProceedings BretonZucker96 proc38)
           (booktitle proc38 "Proceedings of  CVPR'96") ...)
```

Recall the bridging axioms related to this booktitle example:

```
(forall (a - Article tl - String)
        (iff (@yale_bib:booktitle a tl) (booktitle a tl)))

(forall (a - @yale_bib:Inproceedings tl - String)
        (iff (booktitle a tl)
             (exists (p - Proceedings)
                (and (contain p a)
                     (@cmu_bib:inProceedings a p)
                     (@cmu_bib:booktitle p tl)))))
```

When used from left to right, the bridging axioms causes the inference engine to introduce a new constant (proc38) to designate the proceedings that the article (BretonZucker96) appears in. Such *skolem terms* are necessary whenever the translation requires talking about an object that can't be identified with any existing object.

On the Semantic Web model, the knowledge is mostly represented in XML-based web languages. We have set up an online ontology-translation system called OntoMerge. OntoMerge serves as a semi-automated nexus for agents and humans to find ways of coping with notational differences, both syntactic and semantic, between ontologies. OntoMerge wraps OntoEngine with PDDAML, which implement the syntactic translation for the input and output DAML or OWL files. The architecture of OntoMerge for translating datasets is shown in Figure 1.

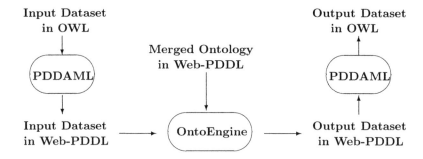

Fig. 1. The OntoMerge Architecture for Translating Datasets

When receiving an input dataset to translate, OntoEngine needs a merged ontology that covers the source and target ontologies. If no such merged ontology is available, all OntoEngine can do is to record the need for a new merger. (If enough such requests come in, the ontology experts may wake up and get to work.) Assuming that a merged ontology exists, located typically at some URL, OntoEngine tries to load it in. Then it loads the dataset (facts) in and does forward chaining with the bridging axioms, until no new facts in the target ontology are generated.

OntoMerge has worked well so far, although our experience is inevitably limited by the demand for our services. In addition to the small example from the dataset[6] using the yale_bib ontology to the equivalent dataset using the cmu_bib ontology, we have also run it on some big ones.

Experiment 1: OntoMerge translates a dataset[7] with 7564 facts about the geography of Afghanistan using more than 10 ontologies into a dataset in the map ontology [10]. 4611 facts are related to the geographic features of Afghanistan described by the geonames ontology [9] and its airports described by the airport ontology [1]. Some facts about an airport of Afghanistan are:

```
(@rdfs:label @af:OAJL "JALALABAD")
(@airport:icaoCode @af:OAJL "OAJL")
(@airport:location @af:OAJL "Jalalabad, Afghanistan")
(@airport:latitude @af:OAJL 34.399166666666666)
(@airport:longitude @af:OAJL 70.49944444444445)
```

Actually either of these two ontologies just partly overlaps with the map ontology. The main semantic difference between their overlapping with the map ontology is: in the map ontology, any location in a map is a point whether it is an airport or other kind of geographic feature such as a bridge. But in the airport and geonames ontologies, an airport is a special location which is different from a bridge, and it's not a point. We have merged the geonames ontology and the airport ontology with the map ontology. One of bridging axioms in the merge of the airport ontology and the map ontology is below:

```
(forall (x - Airport y z  - Object)
   (if (and (@airport:latitude x y) (@airport:longitude x z))
       (and (location (@skolem:aPoint x y z) - Point
                      (@skolem:aLocation x y z) - Location)
            (latitude (@skolem:aLocation x y z) y)
            (longitude (@skolem:aLocation x y z) z))))
```

After OntoEngine loads the two merged ontologies and all 7564 facts in, those 4611 facts in the airport and geonames ontologies are translated to 4014 facts in the map ontology by inference. The translated dataset for the above airport like:

```
(@map:label Point31 "JALALABAD")
(@map:label Point31 "OAJL")
(@map:label Point31 "Jalalabad, Afghanistan")
(@map:location Point31 Location32)
(@map:latitude Location32 34.399166666666666)
(@map:longitude Location32 70.49944444444445)
```

---

[6] http://cs-www.cs.yale.edu/homes/dvm/daml/datasets/yale_bib_dataset.daml

[7] http://www.daml.org/2001/06/map/af-full.daml

As part of DAML Experiment 2002, the result can be used by a map agent (BBN's OpenMap) to generate a map image about the airports and geographic features of Afghanistan. The semantic translation (inference) process by Onto-Engine, which contains 21232 reasoning steps, only takes 18 seconds (including the time for loading the input dataset and merged ontologies) on our PC in PIII 800MHZ with 256M RAM.

Experiment 2: OntoEngine translates a bigger dataset[8] with 21164 facts (on 3010 individuals and 1422 families of European royalty) in the bbn_ged genealogy ontology [2] to 26956 facts in the drc_ged genealogy ontology [8]. Here are some facts in the bbn_ged ontology about a King of France :

```
(@bbn_ged:name @royal92:@I1248@ "Francis_II")
(@bbn_ged:sex @royal92:@I1248@ "M")
(@bbn_ged:spouseIn @royal92:@I1248@ @royal92:@F456@)
(@bbn_ged:marriage @royal92:@F456 @royal92:event3138)
(@bbn_ged:date @royal92:event3138 "24 APR 1558")
(@bbn_ged:place @royal92:event3138 "Paris,France")
```

Although these two genealogy ontology are very similar and overlap a lot, there are still some differences. For example, in the drc_ged ontology, there are two properties wife and husband, but the most related concept in the bbn_ged ontology is the spouseIn property. As our general understanding, if a person is a male (his sex is "M") and he is spouseIn some family which is related to some marriage event, he will be the husband of that family. We have written the bridging axioms for the bbn_ged and drc_ged ontologies to express such semantic differences. The one for the above example is given below.

```
(forall (f - Family h - Individual m - Marriage)
    (if (and (@bbn_ged:sex h "M") (@bbn_ged:spouseIn h f)
            (@bbn_ged:marriage f m))
        (husband f h)))
```

This merged genealogy ontology works well for semantic translation. After loading the input dataset and merged ontology, OntoEngine runs 85555 reasoning steps to generate all the 26956 facts. The whole process takes 59 seconds. The translated dataset for King Francis_II in the drc_ged ontology is:

```
(@drc_ged:name @royal92:@I1248@ "Francis_II")
(@drc_ged:sex @royal92:@I1248@ "M")
(@drc_ged:husband @royal92:@F456 @royal92:@I1248@)
(@drc_ged:marriage @royal92:@F456 @royal92:event3138)
(@drc_ged:date @royal92:event3138 "24 APR 1558")
(@drc_ged:location @royal92:event3138 "Paris,France")
```

Prospective users should check out the OntoMerge website[9]. We have put all URLs of existing merged ontologies there. OntoMerge is designed to solicit descriptions of ontology-translation problems, even when OntoMerge can't solve them. However, according to our experience, we believe that in most cases we

---

[8] http://www.daml.org/2001/01/gedcom/royal92.daml
[9] http://cs-www.cs.yale.edu/homes/dvm/daml/ontology-translation.html

can develop and debug a merged ontology within days that will translate any dataset from one of the ontologies in the merged set to another. It's not difficult for a researcher who knows first-order logic to write bridging axioms in Web-PDDL. We encourage other people to develop their own merged ontology to solve ontology translation problems they encounter.

4 Ontology Extension Generation

As we have said, manually developing sub-ontologies extended from existing ontology(s) is tedious at the Web scale. Tools are needed to make it easier because the number of sub-ontologies is usually much larger. In this section, we will introduce our approach to generate ontology extensions automatically by ontology translation.

One scenario is that ontology experts have some sub-ontologies of the existing ontology(s), and they want to generate the corresponding sub-ontologies of other related existing ontology(s). If they know the relationships between those existing ontologies, ontology-translation tools can automate this process. Another scenario is that ontology experts often need to update some existing ontologies when new knowledge or new requirement comes up. This work has to be done manually, but how about updating their sub-ontologies? Since they know the relationships between the old and updated ontologies, new sub-ontologies can be generated automatically.

In *Example* 1.2.2, if ontology experts can merge DAML-S and WSDL Schema first, they can translate Congo.com into its "grounding." The advantage is they only need to get one merged ontology for DAML-S and WSDL Schema. Further translation from the sub web service ontologies of DAML-S to their groundings on WSDL Schema can be implemented automatically.

The structure for OntoMerge to generate ontology extensions is similar to that shown in Figure 1. The difference is the input and output are not datasets but sub-ontologies. Instead of a set of facts, we input a set of sub-property definitions. In *Example* 1.2.2, the following sub-property occurs in the Congo.com ontology:

```
(deliveryAddress sp1 - SpecifyDeliveryDetails st2 - @xsd:string)
```

where SpecifyDeliveryDetails is a subtype of @DAML-S:Process. To find the corresponding sub-property of a WSDL property, we create an instance of deliveryAddress, with new skolem constants for the variables:

```
(deliveryAddress SDD-1 str-2)
;;SDD-1 and str-2 are skolem constants of types SpecifyDeliveryDetails
;;and @xsd:string respectively
```

Hypothetically assume that this is a true fact, and draw conclusions using forward chaining. This inference process uses the axioms in the Congo ontology, and the bridging axioms in the merged ontology for DAML-S and WSDL Schema such as:

```
(forall (ob1 ob2)
   (if (deliveryAddress ob1 ob2) (@process:input ob1 ob2)))
;;the above axiom is from the Congo ontology to express that
;;deliveryAddress is a sub property of @process:input in DAML-S.

(forall (x - @DAML-S:Process)
        (exists (sg - ServiceGrounding) (ground sg x)))

(forall (p - Process sg - ServiceGrounding ob1 - String)
    (if (and (ground sg p) (@process:input p ob1))
        (exists (ms - Message pa - Part pm - Param)
          (and (@wsdl:input p pm) (paramMessage pm ms)
                (part ms pa) (partElement pa ob1)))))
;;these two axioms are from merged ontology for DAML-S and WSDL Schema.
```

OntoEngine can generate the translated facts in Web-PDDL:

```
(@wsdl:input SDD-1 Param374)
(@wsdl:operation PortType367 SDD-1)
(@wsdl:partElement Part376 str-2)
(@wsdl:part Message375 Part376)
(@wsdl:paramMessage Param374 Message375)
```

where Param374 and such are further skolem terms produced by instantiating existential quantifiers during inference.

All of the conclusions are expressed in the WSDL Schema ontology. The first three mention the two skolem constants in the original assumption. These are plausible candidates for capturing the entire meaning of the deliveryAddress predicate as far as WSDL Schema is concerned. So to generate the new extension WSDL_congo, simply create new predicates for each of these conclusions and make them sub-properties of the predicates in the conclusions:

```
(define (domain WSDL_congo)
   (:extends (uri "http://schemas.xmlsoap.org/wsdl/"))
   (:types SpecifyDeliveryDetails - Operation ....)
   (:predicates
      (deliveryAddress_input arg1 - SpecifyDeliveryDetails arg2 - Param)
      (deliveryAddress_operation arg1 - PortType
                                 arg2 - SpecifyDeliveryDetails)
      (deliveryAddress_partElement arg1 - Part arg2 - @xsd:string)
   ...
```

The corresponding axioms for sub-property relationships are:

```
(forall (ob1 ob2) (if (deliveryAddress_input ob1 ob2)
                      (@wsdl:input ob1 ob2)))
(forall (ob1 ob2) (if (deliveryAddress_operation ob1 ob2)
                      (@wsdl:operation ob1 ob2)))
(forall (ob1 ob2) (if (deliveryAddress_partElement ob1 ob2)
                      (@wsdl:partElement ob1 ob2)))
```

The output sub-ontology is a grounding of Congo in WSDL Schema and it can be represented in WSDL after feeding it into a translator between Web-PDDL and WSDL. That translator has been embedded in PDDAML and the output for the grounding of Congo in WSDL looks like:

```
<wsdl:message name="SpecifyDeliveryDetailsInputMsg">
   <wsdl:part name="deliveryAddressPart"
              element="xsd:string"/>
   ...
</wsdl:message>

<wsdl:portType name="SpecifyDeliveryDetails_PortType">
   <wsdl:operation name="SpecifyDeliveryDetails">
     <wsdl:input name="SpecifyDeliveryDetailsInput"
                 message="SpecifyDeliveryDetailsInputMsg"
     </wsdl:input>
   </wsdl:operation>
</wsdl:portType>
```

Our automatically generated WSDL_congo is very similar to the manually produced grounding by the DAML-S group[10].

This result is encouraging, but obviously much remains to be done. The technique of treating skolemized definitions as pseudo-axioms can translate only axioms expressing sub-property relationships in the source sub-ontology. Although this technique works fine for grounding Congo to WSDL, other ontology extension generation problems may need translating more general axioms from the source sub-ontology to the target sub-ontology. We have developed an algorithm called *automatic axiom derivation* to deal with it[11].

5   Querying Through Different Ontologies

Forward-chaining deduction is a data-driven inference technique that works well for translating datasets and ontology-extension generation. We have also embedded a more traditional backward-chaining reasoner into OntoEngine. This module becomes the central component of an end-to-end workflow (similar to that in figure 1) to translate queries expressed in the standard query language DQL [7] to Web-PDDL, answer the queries using backward chaining, and translate the results back as a DQL response. As usual, we will focus on the semantic internals of this process, not the syntactic translations between Web-PDDL and DQL.

To extend OntoMerge to handle querying problem through different ontologies, we embedded some tools for query selection and query reformulation. One input query can be the conjunction of some sub-queries and each of them may

---

[10] http://www.daml.org/services/daml-s/0.7/CongoGrounding.wsdl

[11] The full solution about general axioms translation can be found in Dejing Dou's Ph.D. Dissertation *Ontology Translation by Ontology Merging and Automated Reasoning* (Technical Report 1300, Yale Computer Science, August, 2004).

be answered by different knowledge bases. We might not be able to "translate" the whole input query in one ontology to the query in another. For example, suppose we add to the query of *Example* 1.2.3 a conjunct asking for the name of the woman Henry VI married (the @xsd prefix is for "XML Schema Datatype"):

```
(:query (freevars (?k ?q - Individual ?f - Family ?m - Marriage
                ?n - @xsd:string ?d - @xsd:date)
      (and (@drc_ged:name ?k "Henry_VI") (@drc_ged:husband ?f ?k)
           (@drc_ged:wife ?f ?q) (@drc_ged:name ?q ?n)
           (@drc_ged:marriage ?f ?m) (@drc_ged:date ?m ?d))))
```

The required answer must give the bindings for variables ?d and ?n.

This query is expressed using the drc_ged ontology. Suppose an agent asks OntoMerge for help in answering it, and OntoMerge's library of merged ontologies includes some with drc_ged ontology as a component. This means that OntoMerge might be able to help answer the query with those web resources described by the other component ontologies of the merged one. In particular, suppose OntoMerge has a merged ontology for the drc_ged and bbn_ged ontologies. It can would ask some broker agent to find some web knowledge bases using the bbn_ged ontology. In this experiment, we just assume one such web knowledge base exists (and is trustworthy!).

The whole process is described as follows. OntoMerge calls the query selection tool to select one sub-query. Here, the tool will first select (@drc_ged:name ?k "Henry_VI") because it has only one variable. OntoEngine then does backward chaining for this sub-query and translates it into a query in the bbn_ged ontology, (@bbn_ged:name ?k "Henry_VI"). The new one is sent to the web knowledge base described by the bbn_ged ontology, which returns the binding {?k/@royal92:@I1217@}. (@royal92:@I1217@ is an Individual in the web knowledge base.) With this binding, OntoMerge call the query-reformulation tool to reform the rest of the sub-queries and get another selection: (@drc_ged:husband ?f @royal92:@I1217@). After backward chaining and querying, the next binding we get is {?f/ @royal92:@F448@}, which leads to a new sub-query

```
(and (@drc_ged:wife @royal92:@F448@ ?q)
     (@drc_ged:marriage @royal92:@F448@ ?m))
```

and its corresponding one in the bbn_ged ontology:

```
(and (@bbn_ged:sex ?q "F") (@bbn_ged:spouseIn ?q @royal92:@F448@)
     (@bbn_ged:marriage @royal92:@F448@ ?m))
```

The bindings this time are {?q/@royal92:@I1218@}, and {?m/@royal92:event3732}. Repeat the similar process and the final query in the bbn_ged ontology is

```
(and (@bbn_ged:name @royal92:@I1218@ ?n)
     (@bbn_ged:date @royal92:event3732 ?d))
```

The ultimate result is {?n/"Margaret of_Anjou"} and {?d/"22 APR 1445"}.

In addition, answering query by backward chaining may be necessary in the middle of forward chaining. For example, when OntoEngine is unifying the fact (P c1) with (P ?x) in the axiom:

$$(P\ ?x) \wedge (member\ ?x\ [c1, c2, c3]) \Rightarrow (Q\ ?x)$$

it can't conclude (Q c1) unless it can verify that c1 is a member of the list [c1,c2,c3], and the only way to implement this deduction is by answering that query by backward chaining.

6   Related Work

As we said at the beginning of this paper, one can consider our work to be the application of insights from query translation to the general ontology-translation problem. We have been able to draw on a long tradition of work in query translation for databases [42,44,20], and for web searching [21,41]. Much of this work (e.g., [30,20]) has tackled the *query optimization* problem, which we have not focused much on yet, although there are some query selection and reformulation tools in OntoMerge.

There has been some previous work on developing deductive-rule systems for the semantic web [33]. The emerging standard is OWL Rules [13], which can be characterized as an XML serialization of logic-programming rules. While we use heuristics similar to those embodied in logic programming, we believe that ontology translation requires equality substitution and a more systematic treatment of existential quantifiers than logic programming can provide. The dominant paradigm for the Semantic Web is description logics (DLs), and there has been work on reconciling the rule-based approach with DLs [31]. We would rather "layer" logic on top of RDF in a way that leaves it completely independent of the constraints of description logics [39].

Our ontology merging is rather different from what some other people have emphasized in talking about ontology combination, because traditionally merging two ontologies has meant finding mappings between them and using those to weed out redundancies. The PROMPT [43] and Chimaera [40] are two prominent examples. As we said in section 1, our interest is not in mapping, but in the content of the rules that mapping might help discover. The large literature on ontology mapping(e.g., [27]) is therefore only tangentially relevant to our work.

One approach to ontology translation is to create a global, centralized ontology that all other notations can be translated into [32,34]. The problem with this strategy is that it is difficult to keep the central ontology updated and in harmony with all sub-ontologies, especially since new sub-ontologies will appear every day. If someone creates a simple, lightweight ontology for a particular domain, he may be interested in translating it to neighboring domains, but can't be bothered to think about how it fits into a grand unified theory of knowledge representation.

The idea of building up merged ontologies incrementally, starting with local mergers, has been explored in a recent paper [19], in which bridging rules are assumed to map database relations by permuting and projecting columns. These rules are simpler than ours, but in return the authors get some very interesting algorithms for combining local ontology mappings into more global views.

People working in specific domains have tried to use ontology techniques to help their own data integration tasks. For example, some eCommerce and Tourism researchers have proposed a way to do data translation between real-world (e.g. travel and tourism) ontologies [26].

7   Conclusions and Future Work

The distributed nature of the Web makes ontology translation one of the most difficult problems web-based must cope with. We described our new approach to implement ontology translation on the Semantic Web. Here are the main points we tried to make:

1. *Ontology translation* is required when translating datasets, generating ontology extensions, or querying through different ontologies. It must be distinguished from ontology mapping, which is the process of finding likely correspondences between symbols in two different ontologies. This sort of mapping can be a prelude to translation, but it is likely to be necessary for the foreseeable future for a human expert to produce useful translation rules from proposed correspondences.
2. Ontology translation can be thought of in terms of formal inference in a merged ontology. The merge of two related ontologies is obtained by taking the union of the terms and the axioms defining them, then adding bridging axioms that relate the terms in one ontology to those in the other through the terms in the merge.
3. If all ontologies, datasets and queries can be expressed in terms of the same internal representation, semantic translation can be implemented by automatic reasoning. We believe the reasoning required can be thought of as typed, first-order inference with equality substitution, easily implemented using a language such as Web-PDDL for expressing type relationships and axioms. The syntactic translation can be done by an automatic syntax translator between Web-PDDL and other Web agent languages.

We set up an online ontology translation server, OntoMerge, to apply and validate our method. We have evaluated our approach by the experiments for large web knowledge resources and its performance is good so far. We also discuss the efficiency and completeness of our inference system. We hope the existence of OntoMerge will get more people interested in the hard problem of generating useful translation rules.

Our results so far open up all sorts of avenues of further research, especially in the area of automating the production of bridging axioms. Although these can be quite complicated, many of them fall into standard classes. We are working on tools that allow domain experts to build most such axioms themselves, through a set of dialogues about the form of the relation between concepts in one ontology and concepts in the other. We also will develop tools to check the consistency of the generated bridging axioms. The long-range goal is to allow domain experts to generate their own merged ontologies without being familiar with the technicalities of Web-PDDL.

Recently, we began cooperating with the medical informatics researchers of Yale to apply our approach to integrate different Web-based neuronal databases: Yale's SenseLab database and Cornell's CNDB database. Although both of their data and database schemas have been marked up by using some XML specifications, there are still some major differences between what the data of each database concerns. The differences exist because the database designers had different views and purposes: SenseLab's data is about model and structure information of a particular class of neurons but CNDB's is about experimental data for individual neurons measured at a particular day. These kind of differences make data integration very difficult. Based on OntoMerge structure, we are designing some initial tools to support construction and testing of axioms for merging two different database schemas. Our future work will focus on designing human computer interactive tools to help domain experts, such as neuroscientists, to find and build bridging axioms between the concepts from different ontologies or database schemas. The biggest obstacle is that domain experts may not be familiar with any formal logic languages but only know the knowledge of their domains. Therefore, this future work will involve automatic ontology mapping, bridging axiom production from machine learning and natural language processing, pattern reuse and consistency testing for merged ontologies.

Acknowledgements

We would like to thank Mike Dean and Troy Self from BBN Technologies for providing the data used for our experiments. We are grateful for helpful comments from the anonymous referees.

References

1. http://www.daml.org/2001/10/html/airport-ont.daml.
2. http://www.daml.org/2001/01/gedcom/gedcom.daml.
3. http://www.daml.ri.cmu.edu/ont/homework/atlas-publications.daml.
4. http://www.daml.org/ontologies/
5. http://www.daml.org/services/.
6. http://www.ai.sri.com/daml/ontologies/time/Time.daml.
7. http://www.daml.org/2003/04/dql/.
8. http://orlando.drc.com/daml/Ontology/Genealogy/3.1/Gentology-ont.daml.
9. http://www.daml.org/2002/04/geonames/geonames-ont.daml.
10. http://www.daml.org/2001/06/map/map-ont.daml.
11. http://opencyc.sourceforge.net/daml/cyc.daml.
12. http://www.w3.org/TR/webont-req/.
13. http://www.daml.org/2003/11/swrl/.

14. http://www.cs.yale.edu/homes/dvm/daml/pddl_daml_translator.html.
15. http://www.w3c.org/TR/wsdl.
16. http://schemas.xmlsoap.org/wsdl/.
17. http://www.w3.org/TR/REC-xml-names/
18. http://www.cs.yale.edu/homes/dvm/daml/ontologies/daml/yale_bib.daml.
19. K. Aberer, P. Cudré-Mauroux, and M. Hauswirth. The chatty web: emergent semantics through gossiping. In *Proc. International World Wide Web Conference*, 2003.
20. S.Adali, K.Candan, Y.Papakonstantinou, and V. Subrahmanian. Query Caching and Optimization in Distributed Mediator Systems. In *Proc. ACM SIGMOD Conf. on Management of Data*, pages 137–148, 1996.
21. Yigal Arens, Craig A. Knoblock and Wei-Min Shen. Query reformulation for dynamic information integration. *J. Intelligent Information Systems — Special Issue on Intelligent Information Integration* **6**(2/3), pp. 99–130
22. D.-S. C. A. Ankolekar, M. Burstein, J. R. Hobbs, O. Lassila, D. Martin, D. McDermott, S. A. McIlraith, S. Narayanan, M. Paolucci, T. Payne, and K. Sycara. Daml-s: Web service description for the semantic web. In *Proceedings of International Semantic Web Conference 2002*, pages 348–363, 2002.
23. F. Baader, D. McGuinness, D. Nardi, and P. P. Schneider. *The Description Logic Handbook*. Cambridge University Press, 2002.
24. T.Berners-Lee, J.Hendler, and O.Lassila. The Semantic Web. *Scientific American*, 284(5):34–43, 2001.
25. H. Chalupsky. OntoMorph: A translation system for symbolic logic. In *Proc. Int'l. Con. on Principles of Knowledge Representation and Reasoning*, pages 471–482, San Francisco, 2000. Morgan Kaufmann.
26. M. Dell'Erba, O. Fodor, F. Ricci, and H. Werthner. Harmonise: A Solution for Data Interoperability. In *I3E 2002*, 2002.
27. A. Doan, J. Madhavan, P. Domingos, and A. Halevy. Learning to map between ontologies on the semantic web. In *Proceedings of the World-Wide Web Conference (WWW-2002)*, 2002.
28. D. Dou, D. McDermott, and P. Qi. Ontology Transaltion by Ontology Merging and Automated Reasoning. In *Proceedings of EKAW02 Workshop on Ontologies for Multi-Agent Systems*, 2002. Available at http://cs-www.cs.yale.edu/homes/dvm/papers/DouMcDermottQi02.ps
29. Dejing Dou, Drew McDermott, and Peishen Qi. Ontology Translation on the Semantic Web. In *Proceedings of International Conference on Ontologies, Databases and Application of SEmantics (ODBASE) 2003*, pages 952–969.
30. M. R. Genesereth, A. Keller, and O. Duschka. Infomaster: An information integration system. In *Proc 97 ACM SIGMOD International Conference on Management of Data*, pages 539–542, 1997.
31. B. N. Grosof, I. Horrocks, R. Volz, and S. Decker. Description logic programs: Combining logic programs with description logic. In *Proc. International World Wide Web Conference*, 2003.
32. T. Gruber. Ontolingua: A Translation Approach to Providing Portable Ontology Specifications. *Knowledge Acquisition*, 5(2):199–200, 1993.
33. Jeff Heflin and James Hendler Searching the web with SHOE. In *Artificial Intelligence for Web Search. Papers from the AAAI Workshop. WS-00-01*, pp. 35–40. Menlo Park, CA: AAAI Press. 2000
34. Douglas B. Lenat and R.V. Guha *Building Large Knowledge-Based Systems*. Reading: Addison-Wesley 1990

35. J. Madhavan, P. A. Bernstein, P. Domingos, and A. Halevy. Representing and Reasoning about Mappings between Domain Models. In *Proc. AAAI 2002*, 2002.
36. A. Maedche, B. Motik, N. Silva, and R. Volz. MAFRA - A Mapping Framework for Distributed Ontologies. In *Proceedings of the 13th International Conference, EKAW 2002.*
37. D. McDermott. The Planning Domain Definition Language Manual. Technical Report 1165, Yale Computer Science, 1998. (CVC Report 98-003).
38. D. McDermott, M. Burstein, and D. Smith. Overcoming ontology mismatches in transactions with self-describing agents. In *Proc. Semantic Web Working Symposium*, pages 285–302, 2001.
39. D. McDermott and D. Dou. Representing Disjunction and Quantifiers in Rdf. In *Proceedings of International Semantic Web Conference 2002*, pages 250–263, 2002.
40. D. L. McGuinness, R. Fikes, J. Rice, and S. Wilder. An Environment for Merging and Testing Large Ontologies. In *Proceedings of the Seventh International Conference on Principles of Knowledge Representation and Reasoning (KR2000)*, 2000.
41. E. Mena, A. Illarramandi, V. Kashyap, and A. Sheth OBSERVER: An approach for query processing in global information systems based on interoperation across pre-existing ontologies. In *Int. J. Distributed and Parallel Database (DAPD)* **8**(2), pp. 223–271
42. P. Mitra, G. Wiederhold, and M. Kersten. A graph-oriented model for articulation of ontology interdependencies. In *Proceedings of Conference on Extending Database Technology (EDBT 2000)*, 2000.
43. N. F. Noy and M. A. Musen. Prompt: Algorithm and tool for automated ontology merging and alignment. In *Proceedings of the Seventeenth National Conference on Artificial Intelligence (AAAI-2000)*, 2000.
44. Rachel Pottinger and Alon Levy. A scalable algorithm for answering queries using views. In *Proceedings of the 26th VLDB Conference*, 2000.
45. S. Russell and P. Norvig. *Artificial Intelligence: A Modern Approach*. Prentice-Hall, Inc, 1995.
46. L. Serafini, P. Bouquet, B. Magnini, and S. Zanobini. An algorithm for matching contextualized schemas via sat. In *Proceedings of CONTEXT'03.*
47. Abraham Silberschatz, Henry F. Korth, and S. Sudarshan. *Database System Concepts, 4th Edition.* McGraw-Hill Companies, 2001.
48. Larry Wos. *The Automation of Reasoning: An Experimenter's Notebook with Otter Tutorial.* Academic Press, 1996.

Compound Term Composition Algebra: The Semantics

Yannis Tzitzikas[1][*], Anastasia Analyti[2], and Nicolas Spyratos[3]

[1] Institut d'Informatique, F.U.N.D.P. (University of Namur), Belgium
ytz@info.fundp.ac.be
[2] Institute of Computer Science, FORTH, Heraklion, Greece
analyti@ics.forth.gr
[3] Laboratoire de Recherche en Informatique, Universite de Paris-Sud, France
spyratos@lri.fr

Abstract. The *Compound Term Composition Algebra* (CTCA) is an algebra with four algebraic operators, whose composition can be used to specify the meaningful (valid) compound terms (conjunctions of terms) in a given faceted taxonomy in an efficient and flexible manner. The "positive" operations allow the derivation of valid compound terms through the declaration of a small set of valid compound terms. The "negative" operations allow the derivation of valid compound terms through the declaration of a small set of invalid compound terms. In this paper, we formally define the model-theoretic semantics of the operations and the closed-world assumptions adopted in each operation. We prove that CTCA is monotonic with respect to both valid and invalid compound terms, meaning that the valid and invalid compound terms of a subexpression are not invalidated by a larger expression. We show that CTCA cannot be directly represented in Description Logics. However, we show how we could design a metasystem on top of Description Logics in order to implement this algebra.

Keywords: Faceted Taxonomies, Semantics, Description Logics.

1 Introduction

A *faceted taxonomy* is a set of taxonomies, each describing a given domain from a different aspect, or *facet* (for more about faceted classification and analysis see [12, 6, 18, 7, 9, 10, 8]). Having a faceted taxonomy, the indexing of domain objects is done through conjunctive combinations of terms from the facets, called *compound terms*. Faceted taxonomies are used in Web Catalogs [11], Libraries [8], Software Repositories [9, 10], and several others application domains. Current interest in faceted taxonomies is also indicated by several recent or ongoing projects (like FATKS[4], FACET[5], FLAMENGO[6]) and the emergence of XFML

---

[*] Part of this work was done while the author was an ERCIM fellow at the VTT Technical Research Centre of Finland.

[4] http://www.ucl.ac.uk/fatks/database.htm

[5] http://www.glam.ac.uk/soc/research/hypermedia/facet_proj/index.php

[6] http://bailando.sims.berkeley.edu/flamenco.html

S. Spaccapietra et al. (Eds.): Journal on Data Semantics II, LNCS 3360, pp. 58–84, 2004.
© Springer-Verlag Berlin Heidelberg 2004

[1] (Core-eXchangeable Faceted Metadata Language) a markup language for applying the faceted classification paradigm on the Web.

For example, assume that the domain of interest is a set of hotel Web pages in Greece, and suppose that we want to provide access to these pages according to the *Location* of the hotels and the *Sports* facilities they offer. Figure 1 shows these two facets. Each object is described using a *compound term*. For example, a hotel in Crete providing sea ski and wind-surfing facilities would be described by the compound term $\{Crete, SeaSki, Windsurfing\}$.

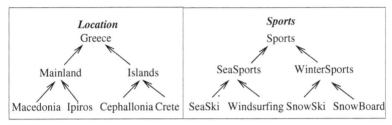

Fig. 1. Two facets for indexing hotel Web pages

Faceted taxonomies carry a number of well known advantages over single hierarchies in terms of building and maintaining them, as well as using them in multicriteria indexing. For instance, assume that the Web consists of 1 billion pages and suppose we want to create terms that allow partitioning the pages of the Web in blocks of 10 pages as it is illustrated in Figure 2. For doing so we need at least 100 millions (10^8) different terms, assuming each page is indexed by one term. If we want these terms to be the leaves of a complete balanced decimal tree, then this tree would have: 111,111,111 terms in total. By adopting a faceted taxonomy we can obtain the same discrimination capability with much fewer terms. For example, consider 4 facets, each one having 100 leaf terms. The number of all combinations of these leaf terms, with one term from each facet, equals 100 millions. If each facet is a complete balanced decimal tree, then the entire faceted taxonomy would have: (100 + 10 + 1) x 4 = 444 terms in total. We can obtain the same discrimination capability with even fewer terms! For example, we can have 10^8 different combinations by adopting 8 facets, each one having 10 leaf terms. In this case, the entire faceted taxonomy has only 88 terms! Notice the tremendous difference between 111,111,111 and 88. It is therefore evident that a faceted taxonomy has several advantages by comparison to a single taxonomy (of the kind of Yahoo! or ODP), such as conceptual clarity, compactness and scalability (e.g. see [10]). A drawback, however, is the cost of avoiding *invalid* combinations, i.e. compound terms that do not apply to any object in the domain. For example, the compound term $\{Crete, SnowBoard\}$ is an invalid compound term, as there are no hotels in Crete offering snow-board facilities (because Crete never has enough snow). These meaningless or invalid compound terms may give rise to problems and errors during object indexing.

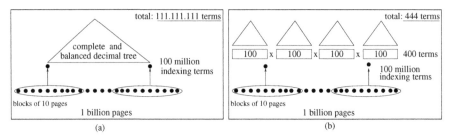

Fig. 2. The benefits of using faceted instead of non-faceted taxonomies

In [13], we proposed the *Compound Term Composition Algebra* (CTCA), an algebra that allows the efficient and flexible specification of the valid compound terms over a faceted taxonomy. Having defined the set of valid compound terms, a navigation tree can be derived dynamically, whose nodes correspond to valid compound terms, only. Such a navigation tree can aid object indexing and browsing, and can prevent some of the indexing errors that may occur in an open and collaborative environment like the Web. Following this approach, given a faceted taxonomy, one can use an *algebraic expression* to define the desired set of compound terms. In each algebraic operation, the designer has to declare either a small set of valid compound terms from which other valid compound terms are inferred, or a small set of invalid compound terms from which other invalid compound terms are inferred. Then, a *closed-world assumption* is adopted for the rest of the compound terms in the range of the operation. For example, if a user declares in a positive operation that the compound term {$Crete, SeaSki$} is valid then it is inferred that the compound term {$Crete, SeaSports$} is also valid. If a user declares in a negative operation that the compound term {$Crete, WinterSports$} is invalid then it is inferred that the compound term {$Crete, SnowBoard$} is also invalid. In our example, this means that the designer can specify all valid compound terms of the faceted taxonomy by providing a relatively small number of (valid or invalid) compound terms. This is an important feature as it minimizes the effort needed by the designer.

From an application point of view, an important remark is that there is no need to store the set of valid compound terms that are defined by an expression, as an inference mechanism (given in [13]) can check whether a compound term belongs to the set of compound terms defined by an expression in polynomial time. So, only the faceted taxonomy and the expression have to be stored. Another final remark, is that the recently emerged markup language XFML+CAMEL (*C*ompound term composition *A*lgebraically-*M*otivated *E*xpression *L*anguage) [2], allows publishing and exchanging faceted taxonomies *and* expressions of CTCA in an XML format. An authoring system based on CTCA has just been developed by VTT and Helsinki University of Technology (HUT), under the name FASTAXON [14].

In this paper, we emphasize on the *semantics* of the algebra. Specifically, we formally define the model-theoretic semantics of the operations and the closed-world assumptions adopted in each operation. First, intermediate semantics are defined for the particular operations, and then intermediate semantics are synthesized to define the semantics of the complete algebraic operation. Based on these, we define the models of an algebraic expression, and we prove that every *well-formed* algebraic expression is satisfiable. We also prove that CTCA is *monotonic* with respect to both valid and invalid compound terms, meaning that the valid and invalid compound terms of a subexpression are not invalidated by a larger expression. The importance of this property is demonstrated through an example.

We also show that CTCA cannot be directly represented in Description Logics. However we show how a meta-system (on top of a Description Logics-based system) could be designed in order to implement CTCA.

The remaining of this paper is organized as follows: Section 2 describes the algebra, and justifies the definition of a well-formed algebraic expression based on the monotonicity property. Section 3 defines the model-theoretic semantics of the algebra and proves monotonicity. Section 4 compares the approach with Description Logics. Finally, Section 5 concludes the paper and discusses applications. Proofs of all propositions are given in Appendix A. Appendix B illustrates the application of the algebra and the benefits of its monotonic nature by an example. A table of symbols is given in Appendix C.

2   The Compound Term Composition Algebra

In this section, we present in brief the *Compound Term Composition Algebra*, defined in [13]. For more explanations, and examples the reader should refer to that article.

A *terminology* is a finite set of names, called *terms*. A *taxonomy* is a pair $(T, \leq)$, where T is a *terminology* and $\leq$ is a reflexive and transitive relation over T, called *subsumption*.

A *compound term* over T is any subset of T. For example, the following sets of terms are compound terms over the terminology *Sports* of Figure 1: $s_1 = \{SeaSki, Windsurfing\}$, $s_2 = \{SeaSports\}$, and $s_3 = \emptyset$.

A *compound terminology* S over T is any set of compound terms that contains the compound term $\emptyset$.

The set of all compound terms over T can be ordered using the *compound ordering* over T, defined as: $s \preceq s'$ iff $\forall t' \in s' \; \exists t \in s$ such that $t \leq t'$.

That is, $s \preceq s'$ iff s contains a narrower term for every term of s'. In addition, s may contain terms not present in s'. Roughly, $s \preceq s'$ means that s carries more specific information than s'. For example, $\{SeaSki, Windsurfing\} \preceq \{SeaSports\} \preceq \emptyset$.

We say that two compound terms s, s' are *equivalent* iff $s \preceq s'$ and $s' \preceq s$. For example, $\{SeaSki, SeaSports\}$ and $\{SeaSki\}$ are equivalent. Intuitively, equivalent compound terms carry the same information.

Definition 1. A *compound taxonomy* over T is a pair $C = (S, \preceq)$, where S is a compound terminology over T, and $\preceq$ is the compound ordering over T restricted to S.

Let $P(T)$ be the set of all compound terms over T (i.e. the powerset of T). Clearly, $(P(T), \preceq)$ is a compound taxonomy over T.

Let s be a compound term. The broader and the narrower compound terms of s are defined as follows:

$$\mathrm{Br}(s) = \{s' \in P(T) \mid s \preceq s'\}$$
$$\mathrm{Nr}(s) = \{s' \in P(T) \mid s' \preceq s\}$$

Let S be a compound terminology over T. The broader and the narrower compound terms of S are defined as follows:

$$Br(S) = \cup\{\mathrm{Br}(s) \mid s \in S\}$$
$$Nr(S) = \cup\{\mathrm{Nr}(s) \mid s \in S\}$$

One way of designing a taxonomy is by identifying a number of different aspects of the domain of interest and then designing one taxonomy per aspect. As a result we obtain a set of taxonomies called *facets*. Given a set of facets we can define a *faceted taxonomy*.

Definition 2. Let $\{F_1, ..., F_k\}$ be a finite set of taxonomies, where $F_i = (T_i, \leq_i)$, and assume that the terminologies $T_1, ... ,T_k$ are pairwise disjoint. Then the pair $\mathcal{F} = (T, \leq)$, where

$$T = \bigcup_{i=1}^{k} T_i \quad \text{and} \quad \leq \; = \bigcup_{i=1}^{k} \leq_i,$$

is a taxonomy which we shall call the *faceted taxonomy generated* by $\{F_1, ..., F_k\}$. We shall call the taxonomies $F_1, ..., F_k$ the *facets* of $\mathcal{F}$.

Clearly, all definitions introduced so far apply also to $(T, \leq)$. For example, the set $S = \{\{Greece\}, \{Sports\}, \{SeaSports\}, \{Greece, Sports\}, \{Greece,$ $SeaSports\}, \emptyset\}$ is a compound terminology over the terminology T of the faceted taxonomy shown in Figure 1. Additionally, the pair $(S, \preceq)$ is a compound taxonomy over T.

Let $\mathcal{F} = (T, \leq)$ be the faceted taxonomy generated by a given set of facets $\{F_1, ..., F_k\}$. The problem is that $\mathcal{F}$ does not itself specify which compound terms, i.e. which elements of $P(T)$, are valid (i.e. meaningful) and which are not (i.e. meaningless). To tackle this problem, we introduce an algebra for defining a compound terminology over T (i.e. a subset of $P(T)$) which consists of the valid compound terms.

2.1   Algebraic Operations

For defining the desired compound taxonomy the designer has to formulate an algebraic expression e, using four operations, namely:

- *plus-product,*
- *minus-product,*
- *plus-self-product,* and
- *minus-self-product.*

Let us now see which are the initial operands of these operations. To each facet terminology $\mathcal{T}_i$ we associate a compound terminology, denoted by T_i, that we call the *basic compound terminology* of $\mathcal{T}_i$, given by:

$$T_i = \cup\{ \text{ Br}(\{t\}) \mid t \in \mathcal{T}_i\} \tag{1}$$

So the initial operands (or "building blocks") of the algebraic operations are the basic compound terminologies $\{T_1, .., T_k\}$. Let us now explain the role of "Br" in the formula (1). We by default assume that every individual term of a taxonomy is valid (meaningful), i.e. there are real-world objects (at least one) to which this term applies. It follows easily that all compound terms in $\text{Br}(\{t\})$ are valid too. We used $\text{Br}(\{t\})$ instead of just $\{t\}$ in order to capture the case where $\mathcal{T}_i$ is not a tree. For example, suppose three terms a, b and c such that $a \leq b$ and $a \leq c$. It follows that the compound term $\{b, c\}$ is certainly valid as it subsumes $\{a\}$. Formula (1) captures this case, as $\{b, c\} \in \text{Br}(\{a\})$. Of course, if $\mathcal{T}_i$ had a tree structure then we could omit "Br" and rewrite formula (1) as: $T_i = \cup\{ \{t\} \mid t \in \mathcal{T}_i\} \cup \{\emptyset\}$.

Let $\mathcal{S}$ be the set of all compound terminologies over $\mathcal{T}$. Before defining the four algebraic operations, we shall first define an auxiliary n-ary operation $\oplus$ over $\mathcal{S}$, called *product*. This operation results in an "unqualified" compound terminology whose compound terms are *all* possible combinations of compound terms from its operands. Specifically, if $S_1, ..., S_n$ are compound terminologies, then:

$$S_1 \oplus ... \oplus S_n = \{s_1 \cup ... \cup s_n \mid s_i \in S_i\}$$

Now *plus-product* and *minus-product* are two "variations" of the $\oplus$ operation. Each of these two operations has an extra parameter denoted by P or N, respectively. The set P is a set of compound terms that the designer considers as <u>valid</u>. On the other hand, the set N is a set of compound terms that the designer considers as <u>invalid</u>. These parameters are declared by the designer (domain expert).

To proceed and explain the role of these parameters we need to distinguish what we shall call *genuine compound terms*. Intuitively, a genuine compound term combines non-empty compound terms from more than one compound terminology.

Definition 3. The set of *genuine* compound terms over a set of compound terminologies $S_1, ..., S_n$, denoted by $G_{S_1,...,S_n}$, is defined as follows:

$$G_{S_1,...,S_n} = S_1 \oplus ... \oplus S_n - \bigcup_{i=1}^{n} S_i$$

For example if
$S_1 = \{\{Greece\}, \{Islands\}, \emptyset\}$,
$S_2 = \{\{Sports\}, \{WinterSports\}, \emptyset\}$, and
$S_3 = \{\{Pensions\}, \{Hotels\}, \emptyset\}$, then

$$\{Greece, WinterSports, Hotels\} \in G_{S_1,S_2,S_3},$$
$$\{WinterSports, Hotels\} \in G_{S_1,S_2,S_3} \text{ , but}$$
$$\{Hotels\} \notin G_{S_1,S_2,S_3}$$

One can easily see, that as we are interested in characterizing the validity of *compound terms*, the parameters P and N must contain *genuine* compound terms only.

We can now define precisely the *plus-product* operation, $\oplus_P$.

Definition 4. Let $S_1, ..., S_n$ be compound terminologies and $P \subseteq G_{S_1,...,S_n}$. The *plus-product* of $S_1, ..., S_n$ with respect to P, denoted by $\oplus_P(S_1, ..., S_n)$, is defined as follows:

$$\oplus_P(S_1, ...S_n) = S_1 \cup ... \cup S_n \cup Br(P)$$

This operation results in a compound terminology consisting of the compound terms of the initial compound terminologies, *plus* the compound terms which are broader than an element of P. This is because, if a compound term p is valid then all compound terms in $Br(p)$ are also valid.
For any parameter P, it holds: $\bigcup_{i=1}^{n} S_i \subseteq \oplus_P(S_1, ..., S_n) \subseteq S_1 \oplus ... \oplus S_n$.

Let us now define precisely the *minus-product* operation, $\ominus_N$.

Definition 5. Let $S_1, ..., S_n$ be compound taxonomies and $N \subseteq G_{S_1,...,S_n}$. The *minus-product* of $S_1, ..., S_n$ with respect to N, denoted by $\ominus_N(S_1, ..., S_n)$, is defined as follows:

$$\ominus_N(S_1, ...S_n) = S_1 \oplus ... \oplus S_n - Nr(N)$$

This operation results in a compound terminology consisting of all compound terms in the product of the initial compound terminologies, *minus* all compound terms which are narrower than an element of N. This is because, if a compound term n is invalid then every compound term in $Nr(n)$ is invalid.
For any parameter N, it holds: $\bigcup_{i=1}^{n} S_i \subseteq \ominus_N(S_1, ..., S_n) \subseteq S_1 \oplus ... \oplus S_n$.

For example, consider the compound terminologies S and S' shown in the left part of Figure 3, and suppose that we want to define a compound terminology that does not contain the compound terms $\{Islands, WinterSports\}$ and

$\{Islands, SnowSki\}$, because they are invalid. For this purpose, we can use either a *plus-product* or a *minus-product* operation.

Specifically, we can use a plus-product operation, $\oplus_P(S, S')$, where $P = \{\{Islands, Seasports\}, \{Greece, SnowSki\}\}$. The compound taxonomy defined by this operation is shown in the right part of Figure 3. In this figure we enclose in squares the elements of P. We see that the compound terminology $\oplus_P(S, S')$ contains the compound term $s = \{Greece, Sports\}$, as $s \in Br(\{Islands, SeaSports\})$. However, it does not contain the compound terms $\{Islands, WinterSports\}$ and $\{Islands, SnowSki\}$, as they do not belong to $S \cup S' \cup Br(P)$.

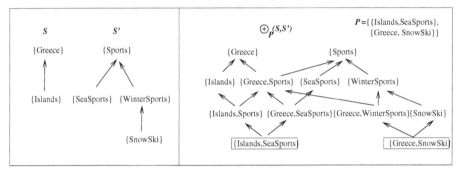

Fig. 3. An example of a *plus-product*, $\oplus_P$, operation

Alternatively, we can obtain the compound taxonomy shown at the right part of Figure 3 by using a *minus-product* operation, i.e. $\ominus_N(S, S')$, with $N = \{\{Islands, WinterSports\}\}$. The result does not contain the compound terms $\{Islands, WinterSports\}$ and $\{Islands, SnowSki\}$, as they are elements of $Nr(N)$.

The two operations introduced so far allow defining a compound terminology which consists of compound terms that contain at most one compound term from each basic compound terminology. However, in general there may exist valid compound terms that contain more than one term from the same facet (multiple classification within one facet). To capture such cases, and specify which of these compound terms are valid and which are not, the algebra supports another two operations, namely, *plus-self-product* and *minus-self-product*.

Again, we shall start from an auxiliary operation called *self-product*. *Self-product*, $\overset{*}{\oplus}$, is a unary operation which gives all possible compound terms of one facet. The *self-product* of T_i is defined as: $\overset{*}{\oplus}(T_i) = P(\mathcal{T}_i)$.

Now *plus-self-product* and *minus-self-product* are two "variations" of the $\overset{*}{\oplus}$ self-product operation. Each of these two operations has an extra parameter denoted by P or N, respectively. Again, the notion of genuine compound terms is also necessary here. The set of *genuine* compound terms over a basic compound terminology T_i is defined as:

$$G_{T_i} = \overset{*}{\oplus} (T_i) - T_i$$

Now we define precisely the *plus-self-product* operation, $\overset{*}{\oplus}_P$.

Definition 6. Let T_i be a basic compound terminology and $P \subseteq G_{T_i}$. The *plus-self-product* of T_i with respect to P, denoted by $\overset{*}{\oplus}_P (T_i)$, is defined as follows:

$$\overset{*}{\oplus}_P (T_i) = T_i \cup Br(P)$$

This operation results in a compound terminology consisting of the compound terms of the initial basic compound terminology, *plus* all compound terms which are broader than an element of P.

For any parameter P, it holds: $T_i \subseteq \overset{*}{\oplus}_P (T_i) \subseteq \overset{*}{\oplus} (T_i)$

Now *minus-self-product* operation, $\overset{*}{\ominus}_N$, is defined as:

Definition 7. Let T_i be a basic compound terminology and $N \subseteq G_{T_i}$. The *minus-self-product* of T_i with respect to N, denoted by $\overset{*}{\ominus}_N (T_i)$, is defined as follows:

$$\overset{*}{\ominus}_N (T_i) = \overset{*}{\oplus} (T_i) - Nr(N)$$

This operation results in a compound terminology consisting of all compound terms in the self-product of T_i, *minus* the compound terms which are narrower than an element in N.

For any parameter N it holds: $T_i \subseteq \overset{*}{\ominus}_N (T_i) \subseteq \overset{*}{\oplus} T_i$

Table 1 gives the definition of each operation of the algebra.

Operation	e	S_e	arity
product	$S_1 \oplus ... \oplus S_n$	$\{ s_1 \cup ... \cup s_n \mid s_i \in S_i \}$	n-ary
plus-product	$\oplus_P(S_1, ...S_n)$	$S_1 \cup ... \cup S_n \cup Br(P)$	n-ary
minus-product	$\ominus_N(S_1, ...S_n)$	$S_1 \oplus ... \oplus S_n - Nr(N)$	n-ary
self-product	$\overset{*}{\oplus} (T_i)$	$P(T_i)$	unary
plus-self-product	$\overset{*}{\oplus}_P (T_i)$	$T_i \cup Br(P)$	unary
minus-self-product	$\overset{*}{\ominus}_N (T_i)$	$\overset{*}{\oplus} (T_i) - Nr(N)$	unary

Table 1. The operations of the Compound Term Composition Algebra

2.2   Algebraic Expressions

For defining the desired compound taxonomy, the designer has to formulate an expression e, where an expression is defined as follows:

Definition 8. An expression over a set of facets $\{F_1, ..., F_k\}$ is defined according to the following grammar:

$$e ::= \ \oplus_P(e, ..., e) \mid \ominus_N(e, ..., e) \mid \overset{*}{\oplus}_P T_i \mid \overset{*}{\ominus}_N T_i \mid T_i$$

The outcome of the evaluation of an expression e is denoted by S_e and is called the *compound terminology* of e. In addition, $(S_e, \preceq)$ is called the *compound taxonomy* of e.

Let $\mathcal{T}_e$ be the union of the terminologies of the facets appearing in an expression e. The expression e actually partitions the set $P(\mathcal{T}_e)$ into two sets:

(a) the set of valid compound terms, S_e, and
(b) the set of invalid compound terms $P(\mathcal{T}_e) - S_e$

Now *well-formed* expressions are defined as follows:

Definition 9. An expression e is *well-formed* iff:

(i) each basic compound terminology T_i appears at most once in e,
(ii) each parameter P that appears in e, is a subset of the associated set of genuine compound terms, e.g. if $e = \oplus_P(e_1, e_2)$ then it should be $P \subseteq G_{S_{e_1}, S_{e_2}}$, and
(iii) each parameter N that appears in e, is also a subset of the associated set of genuine compound terms, e.g. if $e = \overset{*}{\ominus}_N(T_i)$ then it should be $N \subseteq G_{T_i}$.

For example, the expression $(T_1 \oplus_P T_2) \ominus_N T_1$ is not well-formed, as T_1 appears twice in the expression.

Constraints (i), (ii), and (iii) ensure that the evaluation of an expression is *monotonic*, meaning that the valid and invalid compound terms of an expression e increase as the length of e increases[7] (in other words, there are no conflicts). For example, if we omit constraint (i) then an invalid compound term according to an expression $T_1 \oplus_P T_2$ could be valid according to a larger expression $(T_1 \oplus_P T_2) \oplus_{P'} T_1$. If we omit constraint (ii) then an invalid compound term according to an expression $T_1 \oplus_{P_1} T_2$ could be valid according to a larger expression $(T_1 \oplus_{P_1} T_2) \oplus_{P_2} T_3$. Additionally, if we omit constraint (iii) then a valid compound term according to an expression $T_1 \oplus_P T_2$ could be invalid according to a larger expression $(T_1 \oplus_P T_2) \ominus_N T_3$.

This monotonic behaviour in the evaluation of a well-formed expression results in a number of useful properties. Specifically, due to their monotonicity,

---

[7] Proof of this property is given in Section 3.

well-formed expressions can be formulated in a systematic, gradual manner (intermediate results of subexpressions are not invalidated by larger expressions). Appendix B offers examples of the algebra. The benefits of monotonicity are also demonstrated there.

In the rest of the paper, we assume that expressions are *well-formed*. In [13], we presented the algorithm $IsValid(e, s)$ that checks the validity of a compound term s according to a well-formed expression e in $O(|T|^2 * |s| * |\mathcal{P} \cup \mathcal{N}|)$ time, where $\mathcal{P}$ denotes the union of all P parameters and $\mathcal{N}$ denotes the union of all N parameters appearing in e. Polynomial is also the time needed for checking if an expression e is well-formed.

Let us define the *size* of an expression e as follows: $size(e) = |\mathcal{P} \cup \mathcal{N}|$. Obviously, reducing the size of e is desirable, as both the storage space requirements of e and the time for checking compound term validity are reduced. It is easy to see that if we replace each parameter P of e with $minimal_{\preceq}(P)$ and each parameter N of e with $maximal_{\preceq}(N)$, we derive an expression e' such that $S_e = S_{e'}$ and $size(e') \leq size(e)$. Yet, e' may not be the shortest expression with these properties. The problem of finding the shortest expression e' such that $S_e = S_{e'}$ is treated in [16].

3   Semantic Interpretation

At first we shall give a model-theoretic interpretation to faceted taxonomies and to compound taxonomies. Using this framework, we shall formally define the validity of a compound term. In the sequent, we will define the models of the compound taxonomies that *satisfy* a well-formed algebraic expression. At that point, it will become evident that the algebraic operations and their parameters actually pose constraints to the models of the compound taxonomy $(P(T), \preceq)$. Moreover, we will show that the operations as defined in Section 2, are also justified by the semantic interpretation of this section.

We conceptualize the world as a set of objects, that is, we assume an arbitrary domain of discourse and a corresponding set of objects Obj. A typical example of such a domain is a set of Web pages. The only constraint that we impose on the set Obj is that it must be a denumerable set.

The set of objects described by a term is the *interpretation* of that term.

Definition 10. Given a terminology T, we call *interpretation* of T over Obj any function $I : T \rightarrow 2^{Obj}$.

Intuitively, the interpretation $I(t)$ of a term t is the set of objects to which the term t is correctly applied. In our discussion the set Obj will be usually understood from the context. So, we shall often say simply "an interpretation" instead of "an interpretation over Obj". Interpretation, as defined above, assigns to a term denotational or extensional meaning [19].

Definition 11. An interpretation I of T is a *model* of a taxonomy $(T, \leq)$, if for each $t, t' \in T$:   if $t \leq t'$ then $I(t) \subseteq I(t')$.

Now, any interpretation I of $\mathcal{T}$ can be extended to an interpretation $\hat{I}$ of $P(\mathcal{T})$ as follows:

$$\hat{I}(\{t_1, ..., t_n\}) = I(t_1) \cap I(t_2) \cap ... \cap I(t_n)$$

Definition 12. Let $(\mathcal{T}, \leq)$ be a taxonomy. An interpretation $\hat{I}$ of $P(\mathcal{T})$ is a *model* of $(P(\mathcal{T}), \preceq)$, if for each $s, s' \in P(\mathcal{T})$:   if $s \preceq s'$ then $\hat{I}(s) \subseteq \hat{I}(s')$.

Proposition 1. Let S be a compound taxonomy over a taxonomy $\mathcal{T}$, and let s and s' be two elements of S. It holds:

$$s \preceq s' \text{ iff } \hat{I}(s) \subseteq \hat{I}(s') \text{ in every model } I \text{ of } (\mathcal{T}, \leq)$$

We can see that the compound ordering $\preceq$ is also justified semantically (it coincides with extensional subsumption).

From the above, it easily follows that an interpretation I is a model of $(\mathcal{T}, \leq)$ iff $\hat{I}$ is a model of $(P(\mathcal{T}), \preceq)$.

For brevity hereafter we shall denote by I both I and $\hat{I}$. Additionally, in the following, by model I we refer to a model I of $(\mathcal{T}, \leq)$.

For describing the semantics of compound terminologies that are defined by algebraic expressions, we shall equate validity with non-empty interpretation and invalidity with empty interpretation. For simplicity, we consider only expressions of the form $e \oplus_P e'$ and $e \ominus_N e'$, with no plus-self-product and minus-self-product operations. We will define the *valid* and *invalid compound terms* of an expression e, denoted by $VC(e)$ and $IC(e)$, recursively starting by $VC(T_i) = T_i$.

At first, we define the *valid genuine compound terms* of e *op* e' (denoted by $VG(e \ op \ e')$) and the *invalid genuine compound terms* of e *op* e' (denoted by $IG(e \ op \ e')$), based on $VC(e)$ and $VC(e')$. Intuitively, we first define the validity of the genuine compound terms over $VC(e)$ and $VC(e')$.

The valid genuine compound terms of $e \oplus_P e'$ are defined as follows:

$$VG(e \oplus_P e') = \{ \ s \in G_{VC(e), VC(e')} \ | $$
$$I(s) \neq \emptyset \text{ in every model } I \text{ such that: } I(s') \neq \emptyset, \forall s' \in P\}$$

Now by adopting a closed-world assumption for the invalid genuine compound terms, we assume that all elements of $G_{S_e, S_{e'}} - VG(e \oplus_P e')$ are invalid. Thus we write:

$$IG(e \oplus_P e') = G_{VC(e), VC(e')} - VG(e \oplus_P e')$$

The following proposition holds:

Proposition 2. $VG(e \oplus_P e') = Br(P) \cap G_{VC(e), VC(e')}$

Below we define the invalid genuine compound terms of $e \ominus_N e'$:

$$IG(e \ominus_N e') = \{\ s \in G_{VC(e),VC(e')}\ |$$
$$I(s) = \emptyset \text{ in every model } I \text{ such that: } \quad I(s') = \emptyset, \forall s' \in N\}$$

Now we again adopt a closed-world assumption for the valid genuine compound terms, specifically we assume that all elements of $G_{VC(e),VC(e')} - IG(e \ominus_N e')$ are valid. Thus we write:

$$VG(e \ominus_N e') = G_{VC(e),VC(e')} - IG(e \ominus_N e')$$

The following proposition holds:

Proposition 3. $IG(e \ominus_N e') = Nr(N) \cap G_{VC(e),VC(e')}$

Until now, for every operation e op e' we partitioned the set $G_{VC(e),VC(e')}$ to the sets $VG(e$ op $e')$ and $IG(e$ op $e')$. Let $\mathcal{T}_e$ denote the union of the terminologies of the facets that appear in e. Now for any well-formed expression e, we will partition the elements of the entire $P(\mathcal{T}_e)$ into the set of *valid compound terms*, $VC(e)$, and the set of *invalid compound terms*, $IC(e)$. We define[8]:

$$VC(T_i) = T_i, \text{ for } i = 1, ...k$$
$$VC(e \text{ } op \text{ } e') = VG(e \text{ } op \text{ } e') \cup VC(e) \cup VC(e')$$
$$IC(e) = P(\mathcal{T}_e) - VC(e)$$

Clearly, the sets $VC(e)$ and $IC(e)$ constitute a partition of $P(\mathcal{T}_e)$.

Definition 13. Let e be a well-formed expression, and let I be a model of $(\mathcal{T}, \leq)$. We say that I *satisfies* e if:
  (1) $\forall\ s \in VC(e),\ I(s) \neq \emptyset$, and
  (2) $\forall\ s \in IC(e),\ I(s) = \emptyset$.

The following proposition expresses that every expression e is satisfiable.

Proposition 4. Let e be a well-formed expression. There always exists a model I of $(\mathcal{T}, \leq)$ that satisfies e.

The following proposition expresses that the compound taxonomy S_e of an algebraic expression e (as computed from our operations) consists of exactly those compound terms which are valid according to the semantic interpretation that we described in this section.

Proposition 5. Let e be a well-formed expression. It holds:

$$VC(e) = S_e \text{ and } IC(e) = P(\mathcal{T}_e) - S_e$$

---

[8] Note that in the definition, there is double recursion.

The following proposition gives a very important property of our theory, that is, intermediate results of subexpressions are not invalidated by larger expressions. Thus, expressions can be formed in a constructive, gradual manner, allowing use of intermediate results.

Proposition 6. Let e be a well-formed expression and e' be a subexpression of e. Then, it holds

$$VC(e') \subseteq VC(e) \text{ and } IC(e') \subseteq IC(e)$$

To see the significance of this proposition, let $\{F_1, ..., F_k\}$ be the facets of a faceted taxonomy and let e' be an expression that defines the current desired compound taxonomy. Assume that now the designer adds some new facets of interest. Then, he has only to extend (and not to rewrite) e' with a subexpression e'' such that the new expression, $e = e' \text{ op } e''$, defines the new desired compound taxonomy (see the examples of Appendix B).

The following proposition expresses that the valid and invalid genuine compound terms of a subexpression of an expression e are indeed valid and invalid compound terms, respectively.

Proposition 7. Let e be a well-formed expression and $e_1 \text{ op } e_2$ be a subexpression of e. Then, it holds

$$VG(e_1 \text{ op } e_2) \subseteq VC(e) \text{ and } IG(e_1 \text{ op } e_2) \subseteq IC(e)$$

From the above proposition and propositions 2 and 3, it easily follows that for any parameter P and N of e, it holds: $P \subseteq VC(e)$ and $N \subseteq IC(e)$.

In Section 2, we informally indicated that if a compound term s is valid then every compound term in $\text{Br}(s)$ is also valid. Additionally, if a compound term s is invalid then every compound term in $\text{Nr}(s)$ is also invalid. This property is formally proved in the following proposition.

Proposition 8. Let e be a well-formed expression. It holds:

$$Br(VC(e)) = VC(e) \text{ and } Nr(IC(e)) = IC(e)$$

The semantic interpretation that we described can be extended in a straightforward manner, so as to also capture the plus-self-product operation and the minus-self-product operation.

4   Comparison with Description Logics

In this section we will investigate whether we can represent the compound taxonomies that are defined by CTCA expressions, in Description Logics (DL) [5]. This involves finding a method for representing in DL, taxonomies and the constraints that are imposed by the CTCA expressions, in a way that allows reducing compound term validity checking to the semantics (and inference rules) of DL.

Recall that any Description Logic (DL) is a fragment of First Order Logic (FOL). In particular, any (basic) DL is a subset of the function-free FOL using at most *three* variable names. In DL, a knowledge base, also referred as a DL theory, denoted by Σ, is formed by two components: the *intensional* one, called TBox, (denoted by TB), and the *extensional* one, called ABox (denoted by AB), i.e. $\Sigma = (TB, AB)$. The first is a general schema concerning the classes of individuals to be represented, their general properties and mutual relationships. The latter is a (partial) instantiation of this schema, containing assertions relating either individuals to classes, or individuals to each other. Specifically, the language used is composed by symbols denoting *concept names* and *individual names*[9]. Besides the above symbols, the alphabet includes a number of *constructors* that permit the formation of *concept expressions*. In our case, we only need to use the bottom concept $\bot$ and the conjunctive constructor $\sqcap$. Now a DL knowledge base comprises expressions belonging to one of the following two categories where C, C_1, C_2 stand for concepts, and a for individual constants:

- $C(a)$, called *concept assertions*, asserting that a is an instance of C;
- $C_1 \sqsubseteq C_2$, asserting that C_1 is more specific than C_2.

The set of concept assertions constitute the ABox of Σ, while the latter, which are called *concept axioms*, constitute the TBox of Σ.

The semantics is specified through the notion of interpretation. An *interpretation* $\mathcal{I}$ is a pair $\mathcal{I} = (\Delta^{\mathcal{I}}, \cdot^{\mathcal{I}})$ consisting of a non-empty set $\Delta^{\mathcal{I}}$ (called the *domain*) and of an *interpretation function* $\cdot^{\mathcal{I}}$. The latter maps different individual constants into different elements of $\Delta^{\mathcal{I}}$ and primitive concepts into subsets of $\Delta^{\mathcal{I}}$. The interpretation of complex concepts is defined by structural induction, in our case by the rules: $\top^{\mathcal{I}} = \Delta^{\mathcal{I}}$, $\bot^{\mathcal{I}} = \emptyset$ and $(C_1 \sqcap C_2)^{\mathcal{I}} = C_1^{\mathcal{I}} \cap C_2^{\mathcal{I}}$. Semantically, the assertion $C(a)$ is *satisfied* by an interpretation $\mathcal{I}$ iff $a^{\mathcal{I}} \in C^{\mathcal{I}}$. An axiom $C_1 \sqsubseteq C_2$ is *satisfied* by an interpretation $\mathcal{I}$ iff $C_1^{\mathcal{I}} \subseteq C_2^{\mathcal{I}}$. An interpretation $\mathcal{I}$ *satisfies* (*is a model of*) a KB Σ iff $\mathcal{I}$ satisfies each axiom in TB and each assertion in AB. A KB Σ *entails* an assertion α (written $\Sigma \models \alpha$) iff every model of Σ satisfies α.

One can easily see that a faceted taxonomy $F = (\mathcal{T}, \leq)$ can be expressed as a TBox containing one primitive concept $\mathbf{t}$ for each term $t \in \mathcal{T}$, and one concept axiom $\mathbf{t} \sqsubseteq \mathbf{t}'$ for each relationship $t \leq t'$ of the taxonomy.

Recall that we have equated compound term validity with non-empty interpretation and compound term invalidity with empty interpretation. One can easily see that invalidity reduces quite straightforwardly to unsatisfiability of DL. On the other hand, in order to express that each term t of a taxonomy is valid, we will create an ABox that contains one concept assertion $\mathbf{t}(a_t)$, where a_t is a new individual constant (different terms are associated with different constants, i.e. if $t \neq t'$ then $a_t \neq a_{t'}$). If $(T, \leq)$ is a taxonomy we shall use Σ_T to denote

---

[9] We skip *roles* as they are not needed for the problem at hand.

the DL theory that is derived according to the above. For example, if $(T, \leq) = (\{t_1, t_2, t_3\}, \{t_2 \leq t_1, t_3 \leq t_1\})$, then $\Sigma_T = \{t_2 \sqsubseteq t_1, t_3 \sqsubseteq t_1, t_1(1), t_2(2), t_3(3)\}$

We will now generalize, and describe how we can construct a DL theory Σ_e for every well-formed expression e of the CTCA[10]. The method is described in Table 2. At first note that a compound term $s = \{t_1, ..., t_n\}$ in the DL framework corresponds to the conjunctively defined concept $d_s = t_1 \sqcap ... \sqcap t_n$.

In the case of a plus-product operation, for each $p = \{t_1, ..., t_n\} \in P$ we derive the concept assertion $(t_1 \sqcap ... \sqcap t_n)(a_p)$, where a_p is a fresh new constant.

Now in the case of a minus-product operation, for each $\{t_1, ..., t_n\} \in N$ we derive the concept axiom $t_1 \sqcap ... \sqcap t_n \sqsubseteq \bot$.

e	Σ_e
T_i	$\{\, t(a_t) \mid$ for each $t \in \mathcal{T}_i\} \cup$ $\{\, t \sqsubseteq t' \mid$ for each $t, t' \in \mathcal{T}_i$ s.t. $t \leq t'\}$
$\oplus_P^* (T_i)$	$\Sigma_{T_i} \cup \{\, (t_1 \sqcap ... \sqcap t_n)(a_p) \mid p = \{t_1, ..., t_n\} \in P\}$
$\ominus_N^* (T_i)$	$\Sigma_{T_i} \cup \{\, t_1 \sqcap ... \sqcap t_n \leq \bot \mid \{t_1, ..., t_n\} \in N\}$
$e_1 \oplus_P e_2$	$\Sigma_{e_1} \cup \Sigma_{e_2} \cup \{\, (t_1 \sqcap ... \sqcap t_n)(a_p) \mid p = \{t_1, ..., t_n\} \in P\}$
$e_1 \ominus_N e_2$	$\Sigma_{e_1} \cup \Sigma_{e_2} \cup \{\, t_1 \sqcap ... \sqcap t_n \leq \bot \mid \{t_1, ..., t_n\} \in N\}$

Table 2. Using DL for representing the compound terminology of a CTCA expression

Having defined Σ_e in this way, Table 3 sketches how we can check whether a compound term $s = \{t_1, ..., t_n\}$ belongs to the compound terminology S_e of an expression e by using Σ_e and the inference mechanisms of DL. In this table we consider that $s_1 = \{t \in s \mid F(t) \in F(e_1)\}$ and $s_2 = \{t \in s \mid F(t) \in F(e_2)\}$, where $F(t)$ is the facet of term t, and $F(e)$ are the facets appearing in e.

Notice the difference between the algorithm for the plus-products with that of the minus-products: if the current operation is a plus-product then validity checking reduces to query answering, while if the current operation is a minus-product then validity checking reduces to satisfiability checking. It follows that if we would like to use a DL-based system for checking the validity of a compound term then we should design a *metasystem* (on top of DL inference engine) that parses the expression e and recursively calls the inference mechanisms of DL (i.e. query answering and concept satisfiability) as described in Table 3. We omit the proof that this metasystem would function correctly, because the recursive calls of Table 3 are based exactly on the algorithm $IsValid(e, s)$ as it has been given in [13].

Alternatively, if we want to use the classical reasoning services of DL, then we cannot create the Σ_e by the method described in Table 2. Instead, we have to either:

---

[10] It is important that the expression e be well-formed. Otherwise, the TBOX may be inconsistent.

$CTCA$ approach	A DL-based approach
$IsValid(T_i, s) = \text{TRUE}$	$\{\, a \mid \Sigma_{T_i} \models d_s(a) \,\} \neq \emptyset$
$IsValid(\overset{*}{\oplus}_P (T_i), s) = \text{TRUE}$	$\{\, a \mid \Sigma_{\overset{*}{\oplus}_P(T_i)} \models d_s(a) \,\} \neq \emptyset$
$IsValid(\overset{*}{\ominus}_N (T_i), s) = \text{TRUE}$	$\Sigma_{\overset{*}{\ominus}_N(T_i)} \not\models d_s \equiv \bot$
$IsValid(e_1 \oplus_P e_2, s) = \text{TRUE}$	$(\{\, a \mid \Sigma_{e_1 \oplus_P e_2} \models d_s(a) \,\} \neq \emptyset)\ \vee$ $IsValid(e_1, s)\ \vee$ $IsValid(e_2, s)$
$IsValid(e_1 \ominus_N e_2, s) = \text{TRUE}$	$(\Sigma_{e_1 \ominus_N e_2} \not\models d_s \equiv \bot)\ \wedge$ $IsValid(e_1, s_1)\ \wedge$ $IsValid(e_2, s_2),$ where $s_1 = \{t \in s \mid F(t) \in F(e_1)\}$ and $s_2 = \{t \in s \mid F(t) \in F(e_2)\}$

Table 3. Using DL for checking the validity of a compound term

(a) convert all minus-products to plus-products (and then translate the resulting plus-products to DL), or
(b) convert all plus-products to minus-products (and then translate the resulting minus-products to DL).

We can convert a minus-product operation $e_1 \ominus_N e_2$ to a plus-product operation (and vice-versa) as follows:

$$e_1 \ominus_N e_2 = e_1 \oplus_P e_2 \text{ where } P = G_{S_{e_1}, S_{e_2}} - Nr(N)$$
$$e_1 \oplus_P e_2 = e_1 \ominus_N e_2 \text{ where } N = G_{S_{e_1}, S_{e_2}} - Br(P)$$

So according to approach (a), we translate each plus-product operation as described in Table 2, and each minus-product operation $e_1 \ominus_N e_2$ as:

$$\Sigma_{e_1} \cup \Sigma_{e_2} \cup \{\, d_s(a_s) \mid \ s \in G_{S_{e_1}, S_{e_2}} - Nr(N) \}$$

It is evident that if we derive Σ_e in this way, it holds:

$$s \in S_e \text{ iff } \{\, a \mid \Sigma_e \models d_s(a) \} \neq \emptyset$$

Now according to approach (b) we translate each minus-product operation as described in Table 2, and each plus-product operation $e_1 \oplus_P e_2$ as follows:

$$\Sigma_{e_1} \cup \Sigma_{e_2} \cup \{\, d_s \sqsubseteq \bot \mid \ s \in G_{S_{e_1}, S_{e_2}} - Br(P) \}$$

It is again evident that if we derive Σ_e in this way, it holds:

$$s \in S_e \text{ iff } \Sigma_e \not\models d_s \equiv \bot$$

However note, that in both (a) and (b) approaches, the conversion of plus-products to minus-products (or the reverse) requires computing $G_{S_{e_1}, S_{e_2}}$ which in turn requires computing S_{e_1} and S_{e_2}. This might turn out computationally heavy. Recall that the reason that CTCA supports both positive and negative statements (i.e. plus-products and minus-products) is to allow the designer to select at each step the most economical operation i.e. the one that requires providing the less number of parameters. Under this assumption, it follows that the above conversion is expected to result in an expression with much more parameters, i.e. to a much bigger in size DL theory.

From the above discussion it is evident that we cannot represent CTCA expressions in DL in a straightforward manner (due to the closed-world assumptions inherent to the operations of CTCA). In addition, in the DL framework there is no clear method for deciding whether an expression is well-formed.

5   Conclusion

In this paper, we defined the semantics of the Compound Term Composition Algebra (CTCA). Specifically, we justified the definition of the algebraic operations, based on the model-theoretic definition of the valid and invalid genuine compound terms. Having defined the valid (resp. invalid) genuine compound terms of a positive (resp. negative) operation, the invalid (resp. valid) genuine compound terms are computed based on a closed-world assumption. The valid compound terms according to an expression e is the union of the valid genuine compound terms of all operations of e.

Additionally, we defined the models of an algebraic expression. Intuitively, a model of an algebraic expression, is an interpretation which is non-empty for each valid compound term, and empty for each invalid compound term. We proved that every well-formed algebraic expression is satisfiable. Moreover, we proved that well-formed algebraic expressions are monotonic, which ensures that results of subexpressions are not invalidated by larger expressions. We also showed that we cannot directly represent the compound taxonomies defined by CTCA directly in Description Logics, and a metasystem was designed on top of Description Logics to implement the algebra.

CTCA can be used in any application that indexes objects using a faceted taxonomy. For example, it can be used for designing compound taxonomies for products, for fields of knowledge (e.g. indexing the books of a library), etc.

As we can infer the valid compound terms of a faceted taxonomy, we are able to generate a single hierarchical navigation tree *on the fly*, having only valid compound terms as nodes. The algorithm for deriving navigation trees on the fly is given in [13]. Such a navigational tree can be used for object indexing, preventing indexing errors, as well as for object retrieval, guiding the user to only meaningful selections.

Moreover, CTCA can be used for providing compact representations. This is because, there is no need to store the complete set of valid compound terms of a faceted taxonomy. Only the faceted taxonomy and the expression have to be stored. A novel application of CTCA for compressing Symbolic Data Tables is described in [15]. For more about Symbolic Data Analysis, see [3, 4].

The algebra can also be used for query answering optimization. For example, consider Figure 1, and assume that the user wants to retrieve all hotels located in Greece and offer winter sports. As $\{Islands, WinterSports\}$ is an invalid compound term, the system (optimizing execution) does not have to look for hotels located in islands at all.

Another application of the algebra is consistency control. In certain applications, objects may be indexed to non-meaningful compound terms (due to lack of information or other factors). In such case, the algebra can help to point-out the incorrectly indexed objects. Genomic experiments belong to this category, as several aspects of the genomic domain are still unknown, and experimental methods may be inaccurate or based on erroneous assumptions. The *Gene Ontology* (GO)[11] is a faceted taxonomy with 3 facets, namely *Molecular Function, Biological Process*, and *Cellular Component*. Genes may be indexed to one or more terms of each facet. The annotation guide of GO indicates that indexing of genes to contradictory compound terms is allowed, as long as indexing of a gene by a term is associated with the type of evidence and a cited source. Specifying the valid compound terms of GO using the algebra, genes indexed by an invalid compound term, can be immediately designated by an inconsistency flag. Certainly, knowing the genes indexed by an invalid compound term is of interest to biologists who need to perform more elaborate experiments to correct inconsistencies.

The algebra can also be used for configuration management. Consider a product whose configuration is determined by a number of parameters, each associated with a finite number of values. However, some configurations may be unsupported, unviable, or unsafe. For this purpose, the product designer can employ an expression which specifies all valid configurations, thus ensuring that the user selects only among these.

As future work, we plan to study how updates on the faceted taxonomy, or changes to the desired compound terminology should update the expression that defines the compound terminology. This process can be automated. This is very important in practice, as it adds flexibility to the design process: the designer during the formulation of the expression e can update the faceted taxonomy, without having to bother that e will become obsolete. Additionally, the designer can add or delete compound terms from the desired compound terminology without having to worry that e will no longer reflect his/her desire.

References

[1] "XFML: eXchangeable Faceted Metadata Language". http://www.xfml.org.
[2] "XFML+CAMEL:Compound term composition Algebraically-Motivated Expression Language". http://www.csi.forth.gr/markup/xfml+camel.
[3] H. H. Bock and E. Diday. *Analysis of Symbolic Data*. Springer-Verlag, 2000. ISBN: 3-540-66619-2.

---

[11] http://www.geneontology.org/

[4] Edwin Diday. "An Introduction to Symbolic Data Analysis and the Sodas Software". *Journal of Symbolic Data Analysis*, 0(0), 2002. ISSN 1723-5081.

[5] F.M. Donini, M. Lenzerini, D. Nardi, and A. Schaerf. "Reasoning in Description Logics". In Gerhard Brewka, editor, *Principles of Knowledge Representation*, chapter 1, pages 191–236. CSLI Publications, 1996.

[6] Elizabeth B. Duncan. "A Faceted Approach to Hypertext". In Ray McAleese, editor, *HYPERTEXT: theory into practice, BSP*, pages 157–163, 1989.

[7] P. H. Lindsay and D. A. Norman. *Human Information Processing*. Academic press, New York, 1977.

[8] Amanda Maple. "Faceted Access: A Review of the Literature", 1995. http://theme.music.indiana.edu/tech_s/mla/facacc.rev.

[9] Ruben Prieto-Diaz. "Classification of Reusable Modules". In *Software Reusability. Volume I*, chapter 4, pages 99–123. acm press, 1989.

[10] Ruben Prieto-Diaz. "Implementing Faceted Classification for Software Reuse". *Communications of the ACM*, 34(5):88–97, 1991.

[11] U. Priss and E. Jacob. "Utilizing Faceted Structures for Information Systems Design". In *Proceedings of the ASIS Annual Conf. on Knowledge: Creation, Organization, and Use (ASIS'99)*, October 1999.

[12] S. R. Ranganathan. "The Colon Classification". In Susan Artandi, editor, *Vol IV of the Rutgers Series on Systems for the Intellectual Organization of Information*. New Brunswick, NJ: Graduate School of Library Science, Rutgers University, 1965.

[13] Y. Tzitzikas, A. Analyti, N. Spyratos, and P. Constantopoulos. "An Algebraic Approach for Specifying Compound Terms in Faceted Taxonomies". In *Information Modelling and Knowledge Bases XV, 13th European-Japanese Conference on Information Modelling and Knowledge Bases, EJC'03*, pages 67–87. IOS Press, 2004.

[14] Y. Tzitzikas, R. Launonen, M. Hakkarainen, P. Kohonen, T. Leppanen, E. Simpanen, H. Tornroos, P. Uusitalo, and P. Vanska. "FASTAXON: A system for FAST (and Faceted) TAXONomy design". In *Procs. of 23th Int. Conf. on Conceptual Modeling, ER'2004*, Shanghai, China, November 2004. (an on-line demo is available at http://fastaxon.erve.vtt.fi/).

[15] Yannis Tzitzikas. "An Algebraic Method for Compressing Very Large Symbolic Data Tables". In *Procs. of the Workshop on Symbolic and Spatial Data Analysis of ECML/PKDD 2004*, Pisa, Italy, September 2004.

[16] Yannis Tzitzikas and Anastasia Analyti. "Mining the Meaningful Compound Terms from Materialized Faceted Taxonomies ". In *Procs. of the 3rd Intern. Conference on Ontologies, Databases and Applications of Semantics, ODBASE'2004*, pages 873–890, Larnaca, Cyprus, October 2004.

[17] Yannis T. Tzitzikas. *"Collaborative Ontology-based Information Indexing and Retrieval"*. PhD thesis, Department of Computer Science - University of Crete, September 2002.

[18] B. C. Vickery. "Knowledge Representation: A Brief Review". *Journal of Documentation*, 42(3):145–159, 1986.

[19] W. A. Woods. "Understanding Subsumption and Taxonomy". In *Principles of Semantic Networks*, chapter 1. Morgan Kaufmann Publishers, 1991.

Appendix A: Proofs

In this Appendix, we give the proofs of the propositions appearing in the paper.

We first prove an auxiliary lemma.

Lemma 1 Let S be the compound terminology of an algebraic expression. It holds $Br(S) = S$.

Proof:
We will prove Lemma 1, recursively. Obviously, it holds $S \subseteq Br(S)$.
Let $S = T_i$ then from the definition of a basic compound taxonomy, it follows $Br(T_i) = T_i$.

Let $S = \overset{*}{\oplus}_P T_i$, then $Br(S) = Br(T_i \cup Br(P)) = Br(T_i) \cup Br(Br(P)) = T_i \cup Br(P) = S$.

Let $S = \overset{*}{\ominus}_N T_i$, then $Br(S) = Br(\overset{*}{\oplus} T_i - Nr(N))$. We will show $Br(\overset{*}{\oplus} T_i - Nr(N)) \subseteq \overset{*}{\oplus} T_i - Nr(N)$. Let $s \in Br(\overset{*}{\oplus} T_i - Nr(N))$. Then, there is $s' \in \overset{*}{\oplus} T_i - Nr(N)$ such that $s' \preceq s$. If $s \in Nr(N)$ then $s' \in Nr(N)$, which is impossible. Thus, $s \in \overset{*}{\oplus} T_i - Nr(N)$. Therefore, $Br(S) = S$.

Let $S = \oplus_P(S_1, ..., S_n)$, such that $Br(S_i) = S_i$, for $i = 1, ..., n$. It holds $Br(S) = Br(S_1) \cup ... \cup Br(S_n) \cup Br(Br(P)) = S_1 \cup ... \cup S_n \cup Br(P) = S$.

Let $S = S_1 \oplus ... \oplus S_n$ such that $Br(S_i) = S_i$, for $i = 1, ..., n$. We will show $Br(S) = S$. Let $s \in Br(S_1 \oplus ... \oplus S_n)$. Then, $\exists s' \in S_1 \oplus ... \oplus S_n$ such that $s' \leq s$. Let $s' = s'_1 \cup ... \cup s'_n$, where $s'_i \in S_i$, for $i = 1, ..., n$. Thus, $s = s_1 \cup ... \cup s_n$, where $s_i \in S_i$ and $s'_i \leq s_i$, for $i = 1, ..., n$. Thus, $s_i \in Br(S_i)$, for $i = 1, ..., n$. Therefore, $s \in Br(S_1) \oplus ... \oplus Br(S_n) = S_1 \oplus ... \oplus S_n$.

Let $S = \ominus_N(S_1, ..., S_n)$ such that $Br(S_i) = S_i$, for $i = 1, ..., n$. It holds $Br(S) = Br(S_1 \oplus ... \oplus S_n - Nr(N))$. We will show $Br(S_1 \oplus ... \oplus S_n - Nr(N)) \subseteq S_1 \oplus ... \oplus S_n - Nr(N)$. Let $s \in Br(S_1 \oplus ... \oplus S_n - Nr(N))$. Then, there is $s' \in S_1 \oplus ... \oplus S_n - Nr(N)$ such that $s' \preceq s$. If $s \in Nr(N)$ then $s' \in Nr(N)$, which is impossible. Thus, $s \in Br(S_1 \oplus ... \oplus S_n) - Nr(N) = S_1 \oplus ... \oplus S_n - Nr(N)$. Therefore, $Br(S) = S$. ◇

Proposition 1 Let S be a compound taxonomy over a taxonomy T, and let s and s' be two elements of S. It holds:

$$s \preceq s' \text{ iff } I(s) \subseteq I(s') \text{ in every model } I \text{ of } (T, \leq)$$

Proof:
($\Rightarrow$)

Let $s = \{a_1, ..., a_m\}$ and $s' = \{b_1, ..., b_n\}$. If $s \preceq s'$, then for each b_i exists a_j such that $a_j \leq b_i$. This means that in every model I of $(T, \leq)$, it holds $I(a_j) \subseteq I(b_i)$. Now, as $I(s) = I(a_1) \cap ... \cap I(a_k)$ and $I(s') = I(b_1) \cap ... \cap I(b_m)$, it is evident that it holds $I(s) \subseteq I(s')$ in every model I of $(T, \leq)$.

($\Leftarrow$)

Let $s = \{a_1, ..., a_m\}$ and $s' = \{b_1, ..., b_n\}$. As it has been shown in [17], $I(s) \subseteq I(s')$ in every model of $(T, \leq)$ iff $r(s \cup s') = r(s)$, where $r(\{t_1, ..., t_n\}) = minimal_\leq(\{c(t_1), ..., c(t_k)\})$ where $c(t)$ denotes the equivalence class of a term t. However, $r(s \cup s') = r(s)$ can hold only if for each $t' \in s'$ exists $t \in s$ such that $t \leq t'$. Thus it must hold $s \preceq s'$. ⋄

Proposition 2 $VG(e \oplus_P e') = Br(P) \cap G_{VC(e),VC(e')}$
Proof:
First, we will show that $VG(e \oplus_P e') \subseteq Br(P) \cap G_{VC(e),VC(e')}$. Let $s \in VG(e \oplus_P e')$. It holds $I(s) \neq \emptyset$, in every model I such that $I(p) \neq \emptyset$, $\forall p \in P$. Therefore, it holds that exists $p \in P$ such that $I(p) \subseteq I(s)$, for every model I. From Prop. 1, it follows that $p \preceq s$. Therefore, $s \in Br(P)$. As $VG(e \oplus_P e') \subseteq G_{VC(e),VC(e')}$, it follows that $s \in Br(P) \cap G_{VC(e),VC(e')}$.

We will now show that $Br(P) \cap G_{VC(e),VC(e')} \subseteq VG(e \oplus_P e')$. Let $s \in Br(P) \cap G_{VC(e),VC(e')}$. Thus, there is $p \in P$ such that $p \preceq s$. From Prop. 1, it follows that $I(p) \subseteq I(s)$, for every model I. Thus, $s \in VG(e \oplus_P e')$. ⋄

Proposition 3 $IG(e \ominus_N e') = Nr(N) \cap G_{VC(e),VC(e')}$
Proof:
First, we will show that $IG(e \ominus_N e') \subseteq Nr(N) \cap G_{VC(e),VC(e')}$. Let $s \in IG(e \ominus_N e')$. It holds $I(s) = \emptyset$, in every model I such that $I(n) = \emptyset$, $\forall n \in N$. Therefore, it holds that exists $n \in N$ such that $I(s) \subseteq I(n)$, for every model I. From Prop. 1, it follows that $s \preceq n$. Therefore, $s \in Nr(N)$. As $IG(e \ominus_N e') \subseteq G_{VC(e),VC(e')}$, it follows that $s \in Nr(N) \cap G_{VC(e),VC(e')}$.

We will now show that $Nr(N) \cap G_{VC(e),VC(e')} \subseteq IG(e \ominus_N e')$. Let $s \in Nr(N) \cap G_{VC(e),VC(e')}$. Thus, there is $n \in N$ such that $s \preceq n$. From Prop. 1, it follows that $I(s) \subseteq I(n)$, for every model I of $(\mathcal{T}, \leq)$. Thus, $s \in IG(e \ominus_N e')$. ⋄

Proposition 4 Let e be a well-formed expression. There always exists a model I of $(\mathcal{T}, \leq)$ that satisfies e.
Proof:
We create a model I of $(\mathcal{T}, \leq)$ as follows:
Initially, $I(t) = \emptyset$, for every $t \in \mathcal{T}$. Let $VC(e) = \{s_1, ..., s_n\}$. For each $s_i = \{t_{i,1}, ..., t_{i,n_i}\} \in VC(e)$, we insert an object o_i to each $I(t_{i,j})$, for $i = 1, ...n$ and $j = 1, ..., n_i$.
For each $t \leq t'$, we extend $I(t')$ such that $I(t) \subseteq I(t')$. For each $t \in \mathcal{T}$, $I(t)$ contains nothing else.

From the construction, I is a model of $(\mathcal{T}, \leq)$. Additionally, $\forall s \in VC(e)$, obviously, it holds that $I(s) \neq \emptyset$. We will show that $\forall s \in IC(e)$, it holds that $I(s) = \emptyset$. Assume that $\exists s \in IC(e)$ such that $I(s) \neq \emptyset$. Then, there should be an $s' \in VC(e)$ such that $s' \preceq s$. From Prop. 5 and Lemma 1. it follows that $Br(VC(e)) = VC(e)$. Thus, $s \in VC(e)$, which is impossible as $VC(e) \cap IC(e) = \emptyset$. Therefore, $\forall s \in IC(e)$, it holds that $I(s) = \emptyset$. ⋄

Proposition 5 Let e be a well-formed expression. It holds:

$$VC(e) = S_e \text{ and } IC(e) = P(\mathcal{T}_e) - S_e$$

Proof:
We will prove the proposition recursively.
The proposition obviously holds for $e = T_i$.

Let $e = e_1 \oplus_P e_2$, and assume that the proposition holds for e_1 and e_2. Using Proposition 2 and assumption, we have: $VC(e_1 \oplus_P e_2) = VG(e_1 \oplus_P e_2) \cup VC(e_1) \cup VC(e_2) = (Br(P) \cap G_{S_{e_1}, S_{e_2}}) \cup S_{e_1} \cup S_{e_2} = (Br(P) \cap (S_{e_1} \oplus S_{e_2})) \cup S_{e_1} \cup S_{e_2}$. As e is well-formed, it holds $Br(P) \subseteq S_{e_1} \oplus S_{e_2}$. Therefore, $VC(e_1 \oplus_P e_2) = Br(P) \cup S_{e_1} \cup S_{e_2} = S_e$.

Now, let $e = e_1 \ominus_N e_2$, and assume that the proposition holds for e_1 and e_2. Using Proposition 3 and assumption, we have: $VC(e_1 \ominus_N e_2) = VG(e_1 \ominus_N e_2) \cup VC(e_1) \cup VC(e_2) = (G_{S_{e_1}, S_{e_2}} - Nr(N)) \cup S_{e_1} \cup S_{e_2}$. As e is well-formed, it holds $Nr(N) \cap S_{e_1} = \emptyset$ and $Nr(N) \cap S_{e_2} = \emptyset$. Therefore, $VC(e_1 \ominus_N e_2) = S_{e_1} \oplus S_{e_2} - Nr(N) = S_e$.

Therefore, for any expression e, $VC(e) = S_e$. Now, it follows immediately that $IC(e) = P(\mathcal{T}_e) - S_e$. ◊

Proposition 6 Let e be a well-formed expression and e' be a subexpression of e. Then, it holds

$$VC(e') \subseteq VC(e) \text{ and } IC(e') \subseteq IC(e)$$

Proof:
The fact that $VC(e') \subseteq VC(e)$ follows recursively from the definition of $VC(e)$. We will now show that $IC(e') \subseteq IC(e)$.

Let $e = e_1 \ op \ e_2$. Then, $IC(e) = P(\mathcal{T}_e) - VC(e) = P(\mathcal{T}_e) - VC(e_1 \ op \ e_2) = P(\mathcal{T}_e) - VG(e_1 \ op \ e_2) - VC(e_1) - VC(e_2) \supseteq P(\mathcal{T}_{e_1}) - VG(e_1 \ op \ e_2) - VC(e_1) - VC(e_2)$. As $VG(e_1 \ op \ e_2) \cap P(\mathcal{T}_{e_1}) = \emptyset$, and $VC(e_2) \cap P(\mathcal{T}_{e_1}) = \emptyset$, it holds that $IC(e) \supseteq P(\mathcal{T}_{e_1}) - VC(e_1) = IC(e_1)$. Similarly, $IC(e_2) \subseteq IC(e)$.

Recursively, it holds that for any subexpression e' of e, it holds that $IC(e') \subseteq IC(e)$.
◊

Proposition 7 Let e be a well-formed expression and $e_1 \ op \ e_2$ be a subexpression of e. Then, it holds

$$VG(e_1 \ op \ e_2) \subseteq VC(e) \text{ and } IG(e_1 \ op \ e_2) \subseteq IC(e)$$

Proof:
The fact that $VG(e_1 \ op \ e_2) \subseteq VC(e)$ follows recursively from the definition of $VC(e)$. We will now show that $IG(e_1 \ op \ e_2) \subseteq IC(e)$.

From Prop. 6, it holds that $IC(e_1 \ op \ e_2) \subseteq IC(e)$. Now, $IC(e_1 \ op \ e_2) = P(\mathcal{T}_{e_1 \ op \ e_2}) - VG(e_1 \ op \ e_2) - VC(e_1) - VC(e_2) \supseteq IG(e_1 \ op \ e_2)$. Therefore, $IG(e_1 \ op \ e_2) \subseteq IC(e)$. ◊

Proposition 8 Let e be a well-formed expression. It holds:

$$Br(VC(e)) = VC(e) \text{ and } Nr(IC(e)) = IC(e)$$

Proof:
For Lemma 1 and Proposition 5, it follows immediately that $Br(VC(e)) = VC(e)$.

Obviously, $IC(e) \subseteq Nr(IC(e))$. We will prove that $Nr(IC(e)) \subseteq IC(e)$. Let $s \in Nr(IC(e))$. Then, there is $s' \in IC(e)$ such that $s \preceq s'$. For the definition of $IC(e)$, it follows that $s' \in P(\mathcal{T}_e) - VC(e)$. Assume that $s \notin IC(e)$. Then, $s \in VC(e)$, which implies that $s' \in VC(e)$. However, this is impossible. Thus, $s \in IC(e)$. ◊

Appendix B: Example

Suppose that the domain of interest is a set of hotel Web pages and that we want to index these pages using a faceted taxonomy. First, we must define the taxonomy. Suppose it is decided to do the indexing according to three facets, namely the *location* of the hotels, the kind of *accommodation*, and the *facilities* they offer. Specifically, assume that the designer employs (or designs from scratch) the facets shown in Figure 4.

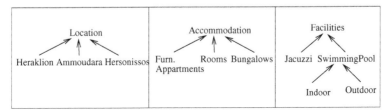

Fig. 4. Three-facets

The faceted taxonomy has 13 terms ($|\mathcal{T}|$=13) and $P(\mathcal{T})$ has 890 compound terms[12]. However, available domain knowledge suggests that only 96 compound terms are valid. Omitting the compound terms which are singletons or contain top terms of the facets, the following 23 valid compound terms remain:

$\{Heraklion, Furn.Appartments,\}, \{Heraklion, Rooms\},$
$\{Ammoudara, Furn.Appartments\}, \{Ammoudara, Rooms\},$
$\{Ammoudara, Bungalows\}, \{Hersonissos, Furn.Appartments\},$
$\{Hersonissos, Rooms\}, \{Hersonissos, Bungalows\},$
$\{Hersonissos, SwimmingPool\}, \{Hersonissos, Indoor\},$
$\{Hersonissos, Outdoor\}, \{Ammoudara, Jacuzzi\},$
$\{Rooms, SwimmingPool\}, \{Rooms, Indoor\},$
$\{Bungalows, SwimmingPool\}, \{Bungalows, Outdoor\},$
$\{Bungalows, Jacuzzi\}, \{Hersonissos, Rooms, SwimmingPool\},$
$\{Hersonissos, Rooms, Indoor\}, \{Hersonissos, Bungalows, SwimmingPool\},$
$\{Hersonissos, Bungalows, Outdoor\}, \{Ammoudara, Bungalows, Jacuzzi\}.$

Rather than being explicitly enumerated, the 96 valid compound terms can be algebraically specified. In this way, the specification of the desired compound terms can be done in a systematic, gradual, and easy manner. For example, the following plus-product operation can be used:

$$\oplus_P(Location, Accommodation, Facilities), \text{ where}$$

---

[12] Equivalent compound terms are considered the same. Thus, $|P(\mathcal{T})|$ is not 2^{13} but 890. This is computed as follows: It holds that $| \overset{*}{\oplus} (Location) |$=8, $| \overset{*}{\oplus} (Accomodation) | = 8$, and $| \overset{*}{\oplus} (Facilities) | = 10$. Thus, $|P(\mathcal{T})| = |(\overset{*}{\oplus} (Location)) \oplus (\overset{*}{\oplus} (Accomodation)) \oplus (\overset{*}{\oplus} (Facilities)| | = (8 + 8 * 8 + 8 * 10 + 8 * 8 * 10) + (8 + 8 * 10) + 10 = 890$.

$$P = \{\{Heraklion, Furn.Appartments\},$$
$$\{Heraklion, Rooms\},$$
$$\{Ammoudara, Furn.Appartments\},$$
$$\{Ammoudara, Rooms\},$$
$$\{Hersonissos, Furn.Appartments\},$$
$$\{Ammoudara, Bungalows, Jacuzzi\},$$
$$\{Hersonissos, Rooms, Indoor\},$$
$$\{Hersonissos, Bungalows, Outdoor\}\}$$

Note that the compound terms in P are only 8. Alternatively, the same result can be obtained more efficiently through the expression:

$$(Location \ominus_N Accommodation) \oplus_P Facilities,$$

where

$$N = \{\{Heraklion, Bungalows\}\}, \text{ and}$$
$$P = \{\{Hersonissos, Rooms, Indoor\},$$
$$\{Hersonissos, Bungalows, Outdoor\},$$
$$\{Ammoudara, Bungalows, Jacuzzi\}\}$$

Note that now the total number of compound terms in P and N is just 4. In summary, the faceted taxonomy of our example, includes 13 terms, 890 compound terms, and 96 valid compound terms which can be specified by providing only 4 (carefully selected) compound terms and an appropriate algebraic expression.

Consider now the additional facet *Season* shown in Figure 5, and suppose that $\{Bungalows, Winter\}$ is an invalid combination of compound terms between the previous compound taxonomy $(Location \ominus_N Accommodation) \oplus_P Facilities$ and the basic compound taxonomy *Season*.

Fig. 5. The facet *Season*

Then, the designer can declare the expression

$$((Location \ominus_N Accommodation) \oplus_P Facilities) \ominus_{N'} Season$$

where $N' = \{\{Bungalows, Winter\}\}$

Note that the total number of compound terms in N, P, and N' is 5. The number of valid compound terms is 530. Note that the new expression is well-formed. Thus, previous results are not invalidated.

The same result could be obtained through the less efficient operation

$$\oplus_{P'}(Location, Accommodation, Facilities, Season), \text{ where}$$

$P' = \{\{Heraklion, Furn.Appartments, Allyear\}, \{Heraklion, Rooms, Allyear\},$
$\quad \{Ammoudara, Furn.Appartments, Allyear\}, \{Ammoudara, Rooms, Allyear\},$
$\quad \{Hersonissos, Furn.Appartments, Allyear\}, \{Ammoudara, Bungalows, Jacuzzi, Summer\},$
$\quad \{Hersonissos, Rooms, Indoor, Allyear\}, \{Hersonissos, Bungalows, Outdoor, Summer\}\}$

In this case the number of compound terms in P' is 8.

We will now give an example of an expression which includes a *minus-self-product* operation. Consider the faceted taxonomy of Figure 6.

Fig. 6. Another faceted taxonomy

The user can declare the expression:

$$Location \oplus_P (\overset{*}{\ominus}_N (Sports)), \text{ where}$$

$N = \{\{SeaSports, WinterSports\}\}, \text{ and}$
$P = \{\{Heraklion, SeaSki, Windsurfing\}, \{Olymbus, SnowSki\}\}$

Appendix C: Table of Symbols

Symbol	Definition
$P(.)$	$Powerset$
$s \preceq s'$	$\forall t' \in s' \; \exists t \in s$ such that $t \leq t'$
$\mathcal{T}_i$	$\cup \{ Br(\{t\}) \mid t \in \mathcal{T}_i \}$
$S_1 \oplus ... \oplus S_n$	$\{ s_1 \cup ... \cup s_n \mid s_i \in S_i \}$
$\oplus_P(S_1, ...S_n)$	$S_1 \cup ... \cup S_n \cup Br(P)$
$\ominus_N(S_1, ...S_n)$	$S_1 \oplus ... \oplus S_n - Nr(N)$
$\overset{*}{\oplus}(\mathcal{T}_i)$	$P(\mathcal{T}_i)$
$\overset{*}{\oplus}_P(\mathcal{T}_i)$	$\mathcal{T}_i \cup Br(P)$
$\overset{*}{\ominus}_N(\mathcal{T}_i)$	$\overset{*}{\oplus}(\mathcal{T}_i) - Nr(N)$
$G_{S_1,...,S_n}$	$S_1 \oplus ... \oplus S_n - \cup_{i=1}^n S_i$
G_{T_i}	$\overset{*}{\oplus}(\mathcal{T}_i) - \mathcal{T}_i$
S_e	the evaluation of an expression e
$\hat{I}(\{t_1, ..., t_n\})$	$I(t_1) \cap ... \cap I(t_n)$
$d_{\{t_1,...,t_n\}}$	$\mathbf{t}_1 \sqcap ... \sqcap \mathbf{t}_n$
$F(t)$	the facet of term t
$F(e)$	the facets that appear in expression e

Table 4. Table of Symbols

Dynamic Pattern Mining:
An Incremental Data Clustering Approach

Seokkyung Chung and Dennis McLeod

Department of Computer Science
and Integrated Media System Center
University of Southern California
Los Angeles, California 90089–0781, USA
[seokkyuc, mcleod]@usc.edu

Abstract. We propose a mining framework that supports the identification of useful patterns based on incremental data clustering. Given the popularity of Web news services, we focus our attention on news streams mining. News articles are retrieved from Web news services, and processed by data mining tools to produce useful higher-level knowledge, which is stored in a content description database. Instead of interacting with a Web news service directly, by exploiting the knowledge in the database, an information delivery agent can present an answer in response to a user request. A key challenging issue within news repository management is the high rate of document insertion. To address this problem, we present a sophisticated incremental hierarchical document clustering algorithm using a neighborhood search. The novelty of the proposed algorithm is the ability to identify meaningful patterns (e.g., news events, and news topics) while reducing the amount of computations by maintaining cluster structure incrementally. In addition, to overcome the lack of topical relations in conceptual ontologies, we propose a topic ontology learning framework that utilizes the obtained document hierarchy. Experimental results demonstrate that the proposed clustering algorithm produces high-quality clusters, and a topic ontology provides interpretations of news topics at different levels of abstraction.

1 Introduction

With the rapid growth of the World Wide Web, Internet users are now experiencing overwhelming quantities of online information. Since manually analyzing the data becomes nearly impossible, the analysis would be performed by automatic data mining techniques to fulfill users' information needs quickly.

On most Web pages, vast amounts of useful knowledge are embedded into text. Given such large sizes of text datasets, mining tools, which organize the text datasets into structured knowledge, would enhance efficient document access. This facilitates information search and at the same time, provides an efficient framework for document repository management as the number of documents becomes extremely huge.

S. Spaccapietra et al. (Eds.): Journal on Data Semantics II, LNCS 3360, pp. 85–112, 2004.
© Springer-Verlag Berlin Heidelberg 2004

Given that the Web has become a vehicle for the distribution of information, many news organizations are providing newswire services through the Internet. Given this popularity of the Web news services, we have focused our attention on mining patterns from news streams.[1]

The simplest document access method within Web news services is keyword-based retrieval. Although this method seems effective, there exist at least three drawbacks. First, if a user chooses irrelevant keywords (due to broad and vague information needs or unfamiliarity with the domain of interest), retrieval accuracy will be degraded. Second, since keyword-based retrieval relies on the syntactic properties of information (e.g., keyword counting),[2] *semantic gap* cannot be overcome. Third, only expected information can be retrieved since the specified keywords are generated from users' knowledge space. Thus, if users are unaware of the airplane crash that occurred yesterday, then they cannot issue a query about that accident even though they might be interested.

The first two drawbacks stated above have been addressed by query expansion based on domain-independent ontologies [47]. However, it is well known that this approach leads to a degradation of precision. That is, given that the terms introduced by term expansion may have more than one meaning, using additional terms can improve recall, but decrease precision. Exploiting a manually developed ontology with a controlled vocabulary is helpful in this situation [27, 28, 29]. However, although ontology-authoring tools have been developed in the past decades, manually constructing ontologies whenever new domains are encountered is an error-prone and time-consuming process. Therefore, integration of knowledge acquisition with data mining, which is referred to as *ontology learning*, becomes a must [32].

In this paper, we propose a mining framework that supports the identification of meaningful patterns (e.g., topical relations, topics, and events that are instances of topics) from news stream data. To build a novel framework for an intelligent news database management and navigation scheme, we utilize techniques in information retrieval, data mining, machine learning, and natural language processing.

To facilitate information navigation and search on a news database, we first identify three key problems.

1. *Vague information needs.* Sometimes, defining keywords for a search is not an easy task, especially when a user has vague information needs. Thus, a reasonable starting point would be provided to assist the user.
2. *Lack of topical relations in concept-based ontologies.* In order to achieve rich semantic information retrieval, an ontology-based approach would be provided. However, as discussed in Agirre *et al.* [2], one of the main prob-

---

[1] In this paper, we are concerned with (news) articles, which are also referred to as documents.

[2] Like Latent Semantic Indexing (LSI) [8], the vector space model based on keyword counting can be augmented with semantics by combining other methods (e.g., Singular Value Decomposition). However, keyword-based retrieval in this paper is referred to as the method relying on only simple keyword counting.

lems with concept-based ontologies is that topically related concepts and terms are not explicitly linked.[3] That is, there is no relation between *court-attorney*, *kidnap-police*, etc. Thus, concept-based ontologies have a limitation in supporting a topical search. For example, consider the Sports domain ontology that we have developed in our previous work [27, 28, 29]. In this ontology, "Kobe Bryant", who is an NBA basketball player, is related with terms/concepts in Sports domain. However, for the purpose of query expansion, "Kobe Bryant" needs to be connected with a "court trial" concept if a user keeps "Kobe Bryant court trial" in mind. Therefore, it is essential to provide explicit links between topically related concepts/terms.

3. *High rate of document insertion.* As several hundred news articles are published everyday at a single Web news site, triggering the whole mining process whenever a document is inserted to the database is computationally impractical. To cope with such a dynamic environment, efficient incremental data mining tools need to be developed.

The first of the three problems can be approached using clustering. A collection of documents is easy to skim if similar articles are grouped together. If the news articles are hierarchically classified according to their topics, then a query can be formulated while a user navigates a cluster hierarchy. Moreover, clustering can be used to identify and deal with near-duplicate articles. That is, when news feeds repeat stories with minor changes from hour to hour, presenting only the most recent articles is probably sufficient.

To remedy the second problem, we present a *topic ontology*, which is defined as a collection of concepts and relations. In a topic ontology, concept is defined as a set of terms that characterize a topic. We define two generic kinds of relations, *generalization* and *specialization*. The former can be used when a query is generalized to increase recall or broaden the search. On the other hand, the latter is useful when refining the query. For example, when a user is interested in someone's court trial but cannot remember the name of a person, then specialization can be used to narrow down the search.

To address the third problem, we propose a sophisticated incremental hierarchical document clustering algorithm using a neighborhood search. The novelty of the proposed algorithm is the ability to identify news event clusters as well as news topic clusters while reduce the amount of computation by maintaining cluster structure incrementally. Learning topic ontologies can be performed on the obtained document hierarchy.

Figure 1 illustrates the main parts of the proposed framework. In the information gathering stage, a Web crawler retrieves a set of news documents from a news Web site (e.g., CNN). Developing an intelligent Web crawler is another research area, and it is not our main focus. Hence, we implement a simple Web spider, which downloads news articles from a news Web site on a daily basis.

---

[3] Although there exist different types of term association relationships in WordNet [36] such as "Bush versus President of US" as synonym, or "G.W. Bush versus R. Reagan" as coordinate terms, these types of relationships are limited to addressing topical relationships.

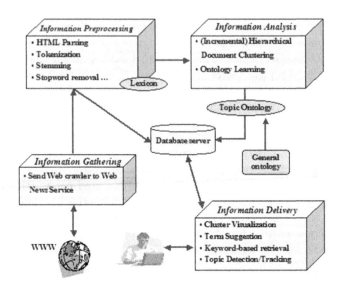

Fig. 1. Overview of a proposed framework

The retrieved documents are processed by data mining tools to produce useful higher-level knowledge (e.g., a document hierarchy, a topic ontology, etc), which is stored in a content description database. Instead of interacting with a Web news service directly, by exploiting knowledge in the database, an information delivery agent can present an answer in response to a user request.

Main contributions of our work are twofold. First, despite the huge body of research efforts on document clustering [33, 30, 22, 31, 52], little work has been conducted in the context of incremental hierarchical news document clustering. To address the problem of frequent document insertions into a database, we have developed an incremental hierarchical clustering algorithm using a neighborhood search. Since the algorithm produces a document cluster hierarchy, it can identify event level clusters as well as topic level clusters. Second, to address the lack of topical relations in concept-based ontologies, we propose a topic ontology learning framework, which can interpret news topics at multiple levels of abstraction.

The remainder of this paper is organized as follows. Section 2 presents related work. Section 3 discusses the information preprocessing step. In Section 4, we explain the information analysis component, which is a key focus of this paper. Section 5 presents experimental results. Finally, we conclude the paper and provide our future plans in Section 6.

2   Related Work

The most relevant research areas to our work are Topic Detection and Tracking (TDT) and document clustering. Section 2.1 presents a brief overview on TDT work. In Section 2.2, a survey on previous document clustering work is provided. Finally, Section 2.3 introduces previous work on intelligent news services, which utilize document clustering and TDT.

2.1   Topic Detection and Tracking

Over the past six years, the information retrieval community has developed a new research area, called Topic Detection and Tracking (TDT) [4, 5, 10, 48, 49]. The main goal of TDT is to detect the occurrence of a novel event in a stream of news stories, and to track the known event. In particular, there are three major components in TDT.

1. *Story segmentation.* It segments a news stream (e.g., including transcribed speech) into topically cohesive stories. Since online Web news (in HTML format) is supplied in segmented form, this task only applies to audio or TV news.
2. *First Story Detection (FSD).* It identifies whether a new document belongs to an existing topic or a new topic.
3. *Topic tracking.* It tracks events of interest based on sample news stories. It associates incoming news stories with the related stories, which were already discussed before. It can be also asked to monitor the news stream for further stories on the same topic.

In Allan *et al.* [4], the notion of *event* is first defined. *Event* is defined as "some unique thing that happens at some point in time". Hence, an event is different from a topic. For example, "airplane crash" is a topic while "Chinese airplane crash in Korea in April 2002" is an event. Thus, there exists M-1 mapping between event and topic (i.e., multiple events can be on a same topic). Note that it is important to identify events as well as topics. Although the user may not be interested in a flood topic, in general, she may be interested in documents about a flood event in her home town. Thus, a news recommendation system must be able to distinguish different events within a same topic.

Yang *et al.* introduced an important property of news events, referred to as *temporal locality* [48]. That is, news articles discussing the same event tend to be temporally proximate. In addition, most of the events (e.g., flood, earthquake, wildfire, kidnapping) have short duration (e.g., 1 week - 1 month). They exploited these heuristics when computing similarity between two news articles.

The most popular method in TDT is to use a simple incremental clustering algorithm, which is shown in Figure 2. Our work starts by addressing the limitations of this algorithm.

2.2   Document Clustering

In this section, we classify the widely used document clustering algorithms into two categories (partition-based clustering and hierarchical clustering), and provide a concise overview for each of them.

1. Initially, only one news article is available, and it forms a singleton cluster.

2. For an incoming document (d_*), we compute the similarity between d_* and pre-generated clusters. The similarity is computed by the distance between d_* and the representative of the cluster.

3. Selects the cluster (C_i) that has the maximum proximity with d_*.

4. If the similarity between d_* and C_i exceeds the pre-defined threshold, then all documents in C_i are considered as related stories to d_* (topic tracking), and d_* is assigned to C_i.
   Otherwise, d_* is considered as a novel story (first story detection), and a new cluster for d_* is created.

5. Repeat 2-4 whenever a new document appears in a stream.

Fig. 2. The incremental document clustering algorithm in TDT

Partition-Based Clustering Partition-based clustering decomposes a collection of documents, which is optimal with respect to some pre-defined function. Typical methods in this category include center-based clustering, Gaussian Mixture Model, etc.

Center-based algorithms identify the clusters by partitioning the entire dataset into a pre-determined number of clusters (e.g., K-means clustering), or an automatically derived number of clusters (e.g., X-means clustering) [9, 23, 13, 16, 30, 37, 39].

The most popular and the best understood clustering algorithm is K-means clustering [13]. The K-means algorithm is a simple but powerful iterative clustering method to partition a dataset into K disjoint clusters, where K must be determined beforehand. The idea of the algorithm is to assign points to the cluster such that the sum of the mean square distance of points to the center of the assigned cluster is minimized.

While the K-means clustering approach works in a metric space, medoid-based method works with a similarity space [23, 37]. It uses the medoids (representative sample objects) instead of the means (e.g., the centers of clusters) such that the sum of the distances of points to their closest medoid is minimized.

Although the center-based clustering algorithms have been widely used in document clustering, there exist at least five serious drawbacks. First, in many center-based clustering algorithms, the number of clusters (K) needs to be determined beforehand. Second, the algorithm is sensitive to an initial seed selection. Depending on the initial points, it is susceptible to a local optimum. Third, it can model only a spherical (K-means) or ellipsoidal (K-medoid) shape of clusters. Thus, the non-convex shape of clusters cannot be modeled in center-based clustering. Forth, it is sensitive to outliers since a small amount of outliers can substantially influence the mean value. Finally, due to the nature of iterative scheme in producing clustering results, it is not relevant for incremental datasets.

Hierarchical Agglomerative Clustering Hierarchical (agglomerative) clustering (HAC) finds the clusters by initially assigning each document to its own cluster and then repeatedly merging pairs of clusters until a certain stopping condition is met [13, 18, 26, 19, 52]. Consequently, its result is in the form of a tree, which is referred to as a *dendrogram*. A dendrogram is represented as a tree with numeric levels associated to its branches.

The main advantage of HAC lies in its ability to provide a view of data at multiple levels of abstraction. However, since HAC builds a dendrogram, a user must determine where to cut the dendrogram to produce actual clusters. This step is usually done by human visual inspection, which is a time-consuming and subjective process. Moreover, the computational complexity of HAC is more expensive than that of partition-based clustering. In partition-based clustering, the computational complexity is $O(nKI)$ where n is the number of documents, K is the number of clusters, and I is the number of iterations, respectively. In contrast, HAC takes $O(n^3)$ if pairwise similarities between clusters are changed when two clusters are merged. However, the complexity can be reduced to $O(n^2 log n)$ if we utilize a priority queue [52].

2.3   Intelligent News Services Systems

The one of the most successful intelligent news services is NewsBlaster [34]. The basic idea of NewsBlaster is to group the articles on the same story using clustering, and present one story using multi-document summarization. Thus, the main goal of NewsBlaster is similar to ours in that both aim to propose intelligent news analysis/delivery tools. However, the underlying methodology is different. For example, with respect to clustering, NewsBlaster is based on the clustering algorithm in Hatzivassiloglou *et al.* [22]. Main contributions of their work is to augment document representation using linguistic features. However, rather than developing their own clustering algorithm, they used conventional HAC, which has the drawbacks as discussed in Section 2.2.

Recent attempts present other intelligent news services like NewsInEssence [41, 42], or QCS (Query, Cluster, Summarize) [14]. Both services utilize a similar approach to NewsBlaster in that they separate the retrieved documents into topic clusters, and create a single summary for each topic cluster. However, their main focus does not lie in developing a novel clustering algorithm. For example, QCS utilizes generalized spherical K-means clustering whose limitations have been addressed in Section 2.2.

Therefore, it is worthwhile to develop a sophisticated document clustering algorithm that can overcome the drawbacks of previous document clustering work.

In particular, the developed algorithm must address the special requirements in news clustering such as high rate of document insertion, or ability to identify event level clusters as well as topic level clusters.

3   Information Preprocessing

The information preprocessing step extracts meaningful information from unstructured text data and transforms it into structured knowledge. As shown in Figure 1, this step is composed of the following standard IR tools.

- *HTML preprocessing.* Since downloaded news articles are in HTML format, we remove irrelevant HTML tags for each article and extract meaningful information.
- *Tokenization.* Its main task is to identify the boundaries of the terms.
- *Stemming.* There can be different forms for the same terms (e.g., *students* and *student,   go* and *went*). These different forms of the same term need to be converted to their roots. Toward this end, instead of solely relying on Porter stemmer [40], in order to deal with irregular plural/tense, we combine Porter stemmer with the lexical database [35].
- *Stopwords removal.* Stopwords are the terms that occur frequently in the text but do not carry useful information. For example, *have*, *did*, and *get* are not meaningful. Removing such stopwords provide us with a dimensionality reduction effect. We employ the stopword list that was used in Smart project [44].

After preprocessing, a document is represented as a vector in an n-dimensional vector space [44]. The simple way to do this is to employ the Bag-Of-Word (BOW) approach. That is, all content-bearing terms in the document are kept and any structure of text or the term sequence is ignored. Thus, each term is treated as a feature and each document is represented as a vector of certain weighted term frequencies in this feature space.

There are several ways to determine the weight of a term in a document. However, most methods are based on the following two heuristics.

- Important terms occur more frequently within a document than unimportant terms do.
- The more times a term occurs throughout all documents, the weaker its discriminating power becomes.

The term frequency (TF) is based on the first heuristic. In addition, TF can be normalized to reflect different document lengths. Let $freq_{ij}$ be the number of t_i's occurrence in a document j, and l_j be the length of the document j. Then, term frequency (tf_{ij}) of t_i in the document j is defined as follows:

$$tf_{ij} = \frac{freq_{ij}}{l_j} \tag{1}$$

	kidnap	abduct	child	boy	police	search	missing	investigate	suspect	return	home
d_1	1	0	1	0	1	1	0	1	0	0	0
d_2	1	1	1	1	1	0	1	1	1	0	0
d_3	0	1	0	1	0	0	1	0	0	1	1

Table 1. A sample illustrative example for document×term matrix. For simplicity, each document vector is represented as boolean values instead of TF-IDF values

The document frequency (DF) of the term (the percentage of the documents that contain this term) is based on the second heuristic. A combination of TF and DF introduces TF-IDF ranking scheme, which is defined as follows:

$$w_{ij} = tf_{ij} \times log \frac{n}{n_i} \qquad (2)$$

where w_{ij} is the weight of t_i in a document j, n is the total number of documents in the collection, and n_i is the number of documents where t_i occurs at least once.

The above ranking scheme is referred to as static TF-IDF since it is based on static document collection. However, since documents are inserted incrementally, IDF values are initialized using a sufficient amount of documents (i.e., the document frequency is generated from training corpus). After then, IDF is incrementally updated as subsequent documents are processed. In particular, we employ an incremental update of IDF value proposed by Yang et al. [48].

Finally, to measure closeness between two documents, we use the Cosine metric, which measures the similarity of two vectors according to the angle between them [44]. Thus, vectors pointing to similar directions are considered as representing similar concepts. The cosine of the angles between two m-dimensional vectors (x and y) is defined by

$$Similarity(x, y) = Cosine(x, y) = \frac{\sum_{i=1}^{m} x_i \cdot y_i}{||x||_2 \cdot ||y||_2} \qquad (3)$$

4   Information Analysis

This section presents the information analysis component of Figure 1. Section 4.1 illustrates a motivating example for the proposed incremental clustering algorithm. In Section 4.2, a non-hierarchical incremental document clustering algorithm using a neighborhood search is presented. Section 4.3 explains how to extend the algorithm into a hierarchical version. Finally, Section 4.4 shows how to build a topic ontology based on the obtained document hierarchy.

4.1   A Motivating Example

To illustrate a simple example, consider the following three documents (whose document×term matrix is shown in Table 1).

Notation	Meaning
n	The total number of documents in a database
d_*	A new document
d_i	An i-th document
ϵ	Threshold for determining the neighborhood
$N_\epsilon(d_i)$	ϵ-neighborhood for d_i
D_{d_i}	The set of documents that contain any term of d_i
C_{d_i}	The set of clusters that contain any neighbor of d_i
$|A|$	The size of a set A where A can be a neighborhood or cluster
df_{ij}	Document frequency of a term t_i within a set A_j
w_{ij}	TF-IDF value for a term t_i for a document d_j
S_j	Signature vector for a set A_j
s_i^j	i-th component of S_j

Table 2. Notations for incremental non-hierarchical document clustering

1. d_1: A child is kidnapped so police starts searching.
2. d_2: Police found the suspect of child kidnapping.
3. d_3: An abducted boy safely returned home.

In the above three documents, although d_1 and d_2 are similar, and d_2 and d_3 are similar, d_1 and d_3 are completely dissimilar since they share no terms. Consequently, transitivity relation does not hold. Why does this happen? We provide explanations to this question in terms of three different perspectives.

1. *Fuzzy similarity relation.* As discussed in the fuzzy theory [50], the similarity relation does not satisfy transitivity. To make it satisfy transitivity, a fuzzy transitivity closure approach was introduced. However, this approach is not scalable with the number of data points.
2. *Inherent characteristic of news.* As discussed in Allan *et al.* [4], event is considered as an evolving object through some time interval (i.e., content of news articles on the same story are changed throughout time). Hence, although the documents belong to a same event, the terms the documents use would be different if they discuss different aspects of the event.
3. *Language semantics.* The diverse term usage for a same meaning (e.g., kidnap and abduct) needs to be considered. Using only a syntactic property (e.g., keyword counting) aggravates the problem.

The transitivity is related with document insertion order in incremental clustering. Consider the TDT incremental clustering algorithm in Figure 2. If the order of document insertion is "$d_1 d_2 d_3$", then one cluster ($\{\{d_1, d_2, d_3\}\}$) is obtained. However, if the order is "$d_1 d_3 d_2$", then two clusters ($\{\{d_1, d_2\}, \{d_3\}\}$) are obtained. Although the order of document insertion is fixed (because the document is inserted whenever it is published), it is undesirable if the clustering result significantly depends on the insertion order. Regardless of the input order, the successful algorithm should produce a single cluster, $\{\{d_1, d_2, d_3\}\}$.

4.2   A Proposed Incremental Non-hierarchical Document Clustering Algorithm Using a Neighborhood Search

Before we present detailed discussions on the proposed clustering algorithm, definitions for basic terminology are provided first. In addition, Table 2 shows the notations, which will be used throughout this paper.

Definition 1 (similar). *If $Similarity(d_i, d_j) \geq \epsilon$, then a document d_i is referred to as similar to a document d_j.*

Definition 2 ($N_\epsilon(d_i)$). *ϵ-neighborhood for d_i is $\{x : Similarity(x, d_i) \geq \epsilon\}$.*

That is, ϵ-neighborhood for a document d_i is defined as a set of documents, which are similar to d_i. In this paper, ϵ-neighborhood and neighborhood are used interchangeably.

Definition 3 (neighbor). *A document d_j is defined as a neighbor of d_i if and only if $d_j \in N_\epsilon(d_i)$.*

The proposed clustering algorithm is based on the observation that a property of an object would be influenced by the attributes of its neighbors. Examples of such attributes are the properties of the neighbors, or the percentage of neighbors that fulfill a certain constraint. The above idea can be translated into clustering perspective as follows: a cluster label of an object depends on the cluster labels of its neighbors.

Recent data mining research has proposed density-based clustering such as Shared Nearest Neighbors (SNN) clustering [15, 24]. In SNN, the similarity between two objects is defined as the number of k-nearest neighbors they share. Thus, the basic motivation of SNN clustering is similar to ours, however, as we will explain in Section 4.3, the detailed approach is completely different.

Figure 3 shows the proposed incremental clustering algorithm. Initially, we assume that only one document is available. Thus, this document itself forms a singleton cluster. Adding a new document to existing cluster structure proceeds in three phases: neighborhood search, identification of an appropriate cluster for a new document, and re-clustering based on local information. In what follows, these three steps are explained in detail.

Neighborhood Search Achieving an efficient neighborhood search is important in the proposed clustering algorithm. Since we deal with documents in this research, we can rely on an inverted index for the purpose of the neighborhood search.[4] In an inverted index [44], the index associates a set of documents with

---

[4] Note that the neighborhood search can be supported with Multi-Dimensional Index (MDI) structure [6, 20, 7] coupling with dimensionality reduction (e.g., wavelet transforms [11] or Fourier transforms [3]) if the proposed algorithm is extended into other data types such as time-series.

> *Step 1. Initialization:*
>   Document d_0 forms a singleton cluster C_0.
>
> *Step 2. Neighborhood search:*
>   Given a new incoming document d_*, obtain $N_\epsilon(d_*)$ by performing
>   a neighborhood search.
>
> *Step 3. Identification of a cluster that can host a new document:*
>   Compute the similarity between d_* and a cluster $C_i \in C_{d_*}$.
>
>   Based on the value obtained from above,
>   if there exists a cluster (C_j) that can host d_*, then
>   add d_* to the cluster and update the DCF_j.
>   Otherwise,
>   create a new cluster for d_* and
>   create a corresponding DCF vector for this new cluster.
>
> *Step 4. Re-clustering:*
>   Let C_j be the cluster that hosts d_*.
>   If C_j is not a singleton cluster, then trigger merge operation.
>
> *Step 5.*
>   Repeat Step 2-4 whenever a new document appears in a stream.

Fig. 3. The incremental non-hierarchical document clustering algorithm

terms. That is, for each term t_i, we build a document list that contains all documents containing t_i. Given that a document d_i is composed of t_1, ... ,t_k, to identify similar documents to d_i, instead of checking whole document dataset, it is sufficient to examine the documents that contain any t_i. Thus, given a document d_i, identifying the neighborhood can be accomplished in $O(|D_{d_i}|)$.

Identification of an Appropriate Cluster To assign an incoming document (d_*) to the existing cluster, the cluster, which can host d_*, needs to be identified using the neighborhood of d_*. If there exists such a cluster, then d_* is assigned to the cluster. Otherwise, d_* is identified as an outlier and forms a singleton cluster.

Toward this end, the set of candidate clusters (C_{d_*}) is identified by selecting the cluster that contains any document belonging to $N_\epsilon(d_*)$. Subsequently, the cluster, which can host a new document, is identified by using one of the following three methods.

1. *Considering the size of an overlapped region.* Select the cluster that has the largest number of its members in $N_\epsilon(d_*)$. This approach only considers the

number of documents in the overlapped region, and ignores the proximity between neighbors and d_*.

2. *Exploiting weighted voting.* The similarities between each neighbor of d_* and the candidate clusters are measured. Then, the similarity values are aggregated using weighted voting. That is, the weight is determined by the similarity between the proximity of a neighbor to the new document. Thus, each neighbor can vote for its class with a weight proportional to its proximity to the new document.

Let W_j be a weight for representing the proximity of n_j to the new document (e.g., Cosine similarity between n_j and the new document). Then, the most relevant cluster (C_*) is selected based on the following formula:

$$C_* = argmax_{C_k \in C_{d_*}} \sum_{n_j \in N_\epsilon(d_*)} W_j \cdot Similarity(n_j, S_k) \qquad (4)$$

Equation (4) mitigates the problem of the previous method by considering the weight W_j. Moreover, it still favors the cluster with a large size of overlapped region to $N_\epsilon(d_*)$ by summing up the weighted similarity.

3. *Exploiting a signature vector.* While the weighted voting approach is effective, it is computationally inefficient since the similarities between all neighbors and all candidate clusters need to be computed. Instead, we employ a simple but effective approach, which measures the similarity between the signature vector of the neighborhood and that of the candidate clusters.

The signature vector should be composed of terms that reflect the main characteristics of the documents within a set. For example, the center of a cluster would be a signature vector for the cluster. For each term t_i in the set A_j (e.g., cluster/neighborhood), we compute the weight for the signature vector using the following formula:

$$s_i^j = \frac{df_{ij}}{|A_j|} \cdot \frac{\sum_{d_k \in A_j} w_{ik}}{|A_j|} \qquad (5)$$

In Equation (5), the first factor measures the normalized document frequency within a set, and the second factor measures the sum of the weight for the term over the whole documents within a set.

Next, the notion of Document Cluster Feature (DCF) vector[5] is presented as follows:

Definition 4 (DCF). *Document Cluster Feature (DCF) vector for a cluster C_i is defined as a triple $DCF_i = (N_i, DF_i, W_i)$ where N_i is the number of documents in C_i, DF_i is a document frequency vector for C_i, and W_i is a weight sum vector for C_i, respectively.*

---

[5] The basic notion of DCF is motivated by Cluster Feature (CF) in BIRCH clustering [51].

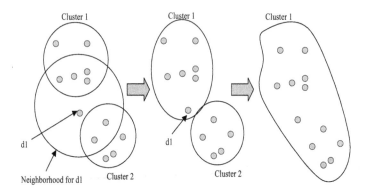

Step 1: Check whether d1 can be added to cluster 1

Step 2: Add d1 to cluster 1

Step 3: Merge cluster 1 and cluster 2 if they satisfy the merge constraint

Fig. 4. Illustration of a re-clustering phase

Theorem 1 (Additivity of DCF). *Let $DCF_i = (N_i, DF_i, W_i)$ and $DCF_j = (N_j, DF_j, W_j)$ be the document cluster feature vectors for C_i and C_j, respectively. Then, DCF for a new cluster (by merging C_i and C_j) is defined by $(N_i + N_j, DF_i + DF_j, W_i + W_j)$.*

Proof. It is straightforward by simple linear algebra.

To compute the similarity between a document and a cluster, we only need signature vectors of the cluster and the document. However, the signature vector does not need to be recomputed as a new document is inserted to the cluster. This property is based on the additivity of DCF. Since S_i (a signature vector for C_i) can be directly reconstructed from DCF_i, instead of recomputing S_i whenever a new document is inserted into C_i, the DCF_i only needs to be updated using the additivity of DCF.

In sum, if there exists a cluster (C_i) that can host a new document, then the new document is assigned to C_i and the DCF_i is updated. Otherwise, a new cluster for d_* and a DCF vector for this cluster are created.

Re-clustering If d_* is assigned to C_i, then a merge operation needs to be triggered. This is based on a locality assumption [43]. Instead of re-clustering the whole dataset, we only need to focus on the clusters that are affected by the new document. That is, a new document is placed in the cluster, and a sequence of cluster re-structuring processes is performed only in regions that have been affected by the new document. Figure 4 illustrates this idea. As shown, clusters that contain any document belonging to the neighborhood of a new document need to be considered.

Notation	Meaning
ST_{C_i}	A collection of specific terms for C_i
T	Virtual time
$df^i(T)$	Document frequency of a term t_i in whole documents at time T
$df_{IN}^{ij}(T)$	Document frequency of a term t_i within C_j at time T
K	Number of clusters at level 1 at time T
$df_{OUT}^{ij}(T)$	A quantitative value representing how much t_i occurs outside the cluster C_j at time T
$Sel_j^i(T)$	Selectivity of a term t_i for the cluster C_j at time T
C_i^j	A i-th cluster at level j

Table 3. Notations for incremental hierarchical document clustering

4.3 How to Extend the Non-hierarchical Clustering Algorithm into a Hierarchical Version?

When the algorithm in Figure 3 is applied to a news article dataset, different event clusters[6] can be obtained. Since our goal is to generate a cluster hierarchy, all event clusters on the same topic need to be combined together. For example, to reflect a court trial topic, all court trial event clusters at level 1 should be merged in a single cluster at level 2. However, in many cases, this becomes a difficult task due to the extremely high term-frequency of named entities within a document. Named entities are people/organization, time/date and location, which play a key role in defining "who", "when", and "where" of a news event. Thus, although two different event clusters belong to the same topic, similarity between the clusters becomes extremely low, consequently, the task of merging different event clusters (on a same topic) is not simple.

To address the above problem, we illustrate how to extend the algorithm (in Figure 3) into a hierarchical version. Table 3 summarizes the notations that will be used in this section. Before presenting a detailed discussion, necessary terminology is first defined.

Definition 5. Specific term (ST). *A specific term for a cluster C_i is a term, which frequently occurs within a cluster C_i, but rarely occurs outside of C_i. The collection of specific terms for C_i is denoted by ST_{C_i}.*

Definition 6. Virtual time (T). *Virtual time T is initialized by 0. At any time T, only one operation (e.g., document insertion and cluster merge) can be performed. In addition, T is increased by one only when an operation is performed.*

---

[6] These event clusters are defined at level 1. Note that level 0 corresponds to the lowest level in a cluster tree (i.e., each document itself forms a singleton cluster at level 0). Thus, clusters at level 1 are expected to contain similar documents on a certain event (i.e., event clusters) while clusters at level 2 are expected to contain similar documents on a certain topic (i.e., topic clusters).

Let $df^i(T)$ be the document frequency of a term t_i in whole document dataset at time T. Then, the document frequency of t_i at time $T+1$ is defined as follows:

$$df^i(T+1) = \begin{cases} df^i(T) + 1, & \text{if } d_* \text{ is inserted at } T \text{ and } d_* \text{ contains } t_i, \\ df^i(T), & \text{Otherwise} \end{cases} \quad (6)$$

Let $df_{IN}^{ij}(T)$ be the document frequency of a term t_i within a C_j at time T. Then $df_{IN}^{ij}(T+1)$ is recursively defined as follows:

$$df_{IN}^{ij}(T+1) = \begin{cases} df_{IN}^{ij}(T)+1, & \text{if } d_* \text{ is inserted to } C_j \text{ at } T \text{ and } d_* \text{ contains } t_i, \\ df_{IN}^{ij}(T), & \text{Otherwise} \end{cases} \quad (7)$$

We denote $K(T)$ as a number of clusters at level 1 at time T. Then, $K(T+1)$ is defined as follows:

$$K(T+1) = \begin{cases} K(T), & \text{if } d_* \text{ is inserted to an existing cluster at } T \\ K(T) + 1, & \text{if } d_* \text{ itself forms a new cluster at } T \\ K(T) - 1, & \text{if two clusters are merged at } T \end{cases} \quad (8)$$

Although $df^i(T+1) - df_{IN}^{ij}$ could be considered for representing how much t_i occurs outside C_j at $T+1$, it is not sufficient if our goal is to quantify how much t_i is informative for C_j. This is because the number of clusters can also affect on how much t_i discriminates C_j from other clusters. Thus, $df_{OUT}^{ij}(T+1)$, which represents how much t_i occurs outside C_j at time $T+1$, can be defined as follows:

$$df_{OUT}^{ij}(T+1) = \frac{df^i(T+1) - df_{IN}^{ij}(T+1)}{K(T+1) - 1} \quad (9)$$

Finally, the selectivity of a term t_i for the cluster C_j at time $T+1$ is defined as follows:

$$Sel_j^i(T+1) = log \frac{df_{IN}^{ij}(T+1)}{df_{OUT}^{ij}(T+1)} \quad (10)$$

In sum, Equation (10) assigns more weight to the terms occurring frequently within C_j, and occurring rarely outside of C_j. Therefore, a term with high selectivity for C_i can be a candidate for ST_{C_i}.

Based on the definition of ST, the proposed hierarchical clustering algorithm is described. While clusters at level 1 are generated using the algorithm in Figure 3, if no more documents are inserted to a certain cluster at level 1 during the pre-defined time interval, then we assume that the event for the cluster ends,[7] and associate ST with this cluster at level 1. We then perform a neighborhood search for this cluster at level 2. Since ST reflects the most specific characteristics for the cluster, it is not helpful if two topically similar clusters (but different

---

[7] This assumption is based on the temporal proximity of an event [48].

events) need to be merged. Hence, when we build a vector for C_i^j, terms in ST (for C_i^j) are not included for building a cluster vector.

At this moment, it is worthwhile to compare our algorithm with the SNN approach [24, 15]. The basic strategy of SNN clustering is as follows: It first constructs the nearest neighbor graph from the sparsified similarity matrix, which is obtained by keeping only k-nearest neighbor of each entry. Next, it identifies representative points by choosing the points that have high density, and removes noise points that have low density. Finally, it takes connected components of points to form clusters.

Event	Specific features
Court trial 1	winona, ryder, *actress, shoplift*, beverly
Court trial 2	andrea, yates, *drown, insanity*
Court trial 3	blake, bakley, *actor*
Court trial 4	moxley, martha, kennedy, michael
Kidnapping 1	elizabeth, smart, utah, salt, lake
Kidnapping 2	jessica, holly, soham, cambridgeshire, england
Kidnapping 3	weaver, ashlei, *miranda*, gaddis
Kidnapping 4	avila, samantha, runnion
Earthquake 1	san, giuliano, puglia, italy, sicily, etna
Earthquake 2	china, bachu, beijing, xinjiang
Earthquake 3	algeria, algerian
Earthquake 4	iran, qazvin

Table 4. A sample specific terms for the clusters at level 1. The term with regular font denotes NE. Thus, this supports the argument that NE plays a key role in defining specific details of events

The key difference between SNN and our approach is that SNN is defined on static datasets while ours can deal with incremental datasets. The re-clustering phase, and special data structures (e.g., DCF or signature vector) make our algorithm more suitable for incremental clustering than SNN. The second distinction is how a neighborhood is defined. In SNN, a neighborhood is defined as a set of k-nearest neighbors while we use ϵ-neighborhood. Thus, as discussed in Han *et al.* [21], the neighborhood constructed from k-nearest neighbors is local in that the neighborhood is defined narrowly in dense regions while it is defined more widely in sparse regions. However, for document clustering, a global neighborhood approach produces more meaningful clusters. The third distinction is that we intend to build a cluster hierarchy incrementally. In contrast, SNN does not focus on hierarchical clustering. Finally, our algorithm can easily identify singleton clusters. This is especially important in our application since an outlier document on a in a news stream may imply a valuable fact (e.g., a new event or technology that has not been mentioned in previous articles). In contrast, SNN overlooks the importance of singleton clusters.

Topic	Specific features
Court trial	attorney court defense evidence jury kill law legal murder prosecutor testify trial
Kidnapping	abduct disappear enforce family girl kidnap miss parent police
Earthquake	body collapse damage earthquake fault hit injury magnitude quake victim
Airplane crash	accident air aircraft airline aviate boeing collision crash dead flight passenger pilot safety traffic warn

Table 5. A sample specific terms for the clusters at level 2

4.4   Building a Topic Ontology

A topic ontology is a collection of concepts and relations. One view of a concept is as a set of terms that characterize a topic. We define two generic kinds of relations, specialization and generalization. The former is useful when refining a query while the latter can be used when generalizing a query to increase recall or broaden the search.

Event	General features
Court trial 1	arm arrest camera count delay drug hill injury order store stand target victim

Table 6. General terms for the court trial cluster 1 in Table 4

Table 4 and Table 5 illustrate the sample specific terms for the selected events/topics. As shown, with respect to the news event, we observed that the specific details are captured by the lower levels (e.g., level 1), while higher levels (e.g., level 2) are abstract. We can also generate general terms for the node, which is defined as follows:

Definition 7. General term (GT). *A general term for a cluster C_i is a term, which frequently occurs within a cluster C_i, and also frequently occurs outside of C_i. A collection of general terms for C_i is denoted by GT_{C_i}.*

Thus, in comparison with ST, the selectivity of GT is less than that of ST. Those ST and GT constitute the concepts of a topic ontology.[8]

Table 6 shows GT for the "court trial 1" cluster in Table 4. When the "Winona Ryder court trial" cluster (C_1) is considered, ST_{C_1} represents the most specific information for "Winona Ryder court trial event", GT_{C_1} carries the next

---

[8] There are two thresholds (for selectivity) that for ST (λ_1) and GT (λ_2), which are determined by experiments.

most specific information for the event, and specific terms for the court trial cluster describe the general information for the event. Therefore, we can conclude that a topic ontology can characterize a news topic at multiple levels of abstraction.

Human-understandable information needs to be associated with cluster structure such that clustering results are easily comprehensible to users. Since a topic ontology provides an interpretation of a news topic at multiple levels of detail, an important use of a topic ontology is automatic cluster labeling. In addition, a topic ontology can be effectively used for suggesting alternative queries in information retrieval.

There exists research work on extraction of hierarchical relations between terms from a set of documents [17, 45] or term associations [46]. However, our work is unique in that the topical relations are dynamically generated based on incremental hierarchical clustering rather than based on human defined topics such as Yahoo directory (http://www.yahoo.com).

Sample topic	Sample events
Earthquake	Algeria earthquake, Alaska earthquake, Iran earthquake, etc
Flood	Russia flood, Texas flood, China flood, etc
Wildfire	Colorado wildfire, Arizona wildfire, New Jersey wildfire, etc
Airplane crash	Ukraina airplane crash, Taiwan airplane crash, etc
Court trial	David Westerfield, Andrea Yates, Robert Blake, etc
Kidnapping	Smantha Runnion, Elizabath Smart, Patrick Dennehy, etc
National Security	Mailbox pipebomb, Shoebomb, Dirty bomb, etc
Health	2002-West nile virus, 2003-West nile virus, SARS, etc

Table 7. Examples for selected topics and events

5   Experimental Results for Information Analysis

In this section, we present experimental results that demonstrate the effectiveness of the information analysis component. Section 5.1 illustrates our experimental setup. Experimental results are presented in Section 5.2.

5.1   Experimental Setup

For the empirical evaluation of the proposed clustering algorithm, approximately 3,000 news articles downloaded from CNN (http://www.cnn.com) are used. The total number of topics and events used in this research is 15 and 180, respectively. Thus, the maximum possible number of clusters we can obtain (at level 1) is 180. Note that the number of documents for events ranges from 1 to 151. Table 7 illustrates sample examples for topics and events.

The quality of a generated cluster hierarchy was determined by two metrics, precision and recall. Let T_r be a class on topic/event r.[9] Then, a cluster C_r is referred to as a topic r cluster if and only if the majority of subclusters for C_r belong to T_r. The precision and recall of the clustering at level i (where K_i is the number of clusters at level i) then can be defined as follows:

$$P_i = \frac{1}{K_i} \sum_{r=1}^{K_i} \frac{|C_r \cap T_r|}{|C_r|} \tag{11}$$

$$R_i = \frac{1}{K_i} \sum_{r=1}^{K_i} \frac{|C_r \cap T_r|}{|T_r|} \tag{12}$$

Thus, if there is large topic overlap within a cluster, then the precision will drop down. Precision and recall are relevant metrics in that they can measure "meaningful theme". That is, if a cluster (C) is about "Turkey earthquake", then C should contain all documents about 'Turkey earthquake". In addition, documents, which do not talk about 'Turkey earthquake", should not belong to C.

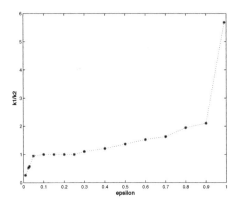

Fig. 5. Illustration of ϵ"'s sensitivity to clustering results

5.2   Experimental Results

For the purpose of comparison, we decided to use K-means clustering. However, since K-means is not suitable for incremental clustering, K-means clustering is

---

[9] A class is determined by ground truth dataset. Thus, a class on topic/event r contains all documents on r, and does not contain any other document on other topics or events. In contrast, a cluster is determined by clustering algorithms. Note that there exists 1-1 mapping between event and cluster at level 1 of hierarchy, and topic and cluster at level 2 of hierarchy.

performed retrospectively on datasets. In contrast, the proposed algorithm was tested on incremental datasets after learning IDF. Moreover, since we already knew the number of clusters at level 1 based on the ground-truth data, K could be fixed in advance. Furthermore, to overcome K-mean's sensitivity to initial seed selections, a seed p is selected with the condition that the chosen seeds are far from each other. Since we deal with document datasets, the intelligent seed selection[10] can be easily achieved by using an inverted index.

Parameterization The size of a neighborhood, which is determined by ϵ, influences clustering results. To observe the effect, we performed an experiment as follows: From 3,000 documents, we organized sample datasets, which consists of 500 documents in 50 clusters of different sizes. Then, while changing the value of ϵ, our clustering was conducted on the dataset.

In Figure 5, the x-axis represents the value of ϵ, and the y-axis represents the number of clusters in the result ($k1$) over the number of clusters determined by ground-truth data ($k2$). Thus, if the clustering algorithm guesses the exact number of clusters, then the value of y corresponds to one. As observed in Figure 5, we could find the best result when ϵ varies between 0.1 and 0.25, i.e., the algorithm guessed the exact number of clusters. If the value of ϵ was too small, then the algorithm found a few large-size clusters. In contrast, many small-size clusters were identified if the value ϵ is too large. Thus, the proposed algorithm might be considered as sensitive to the choice of ϵ. However, once the value of ϵ (i.e., $\epsilon = 0.2$) was fixed, the approximately right number of clusters were always obtained whenever we performed clustering on different datasets. Therefore, the number of clusters does not need to be given to our algorithm as an input parameter, which is a key advantage over partition-based clustering.

Ability to Identify Clusters with Same Density, But Different Shapes
To illustrate the simple example for the shapes of document clusters with the same density, approximately the same number of documents were randomly chosen from two different events (a wildfire event and a court trial event), and the document×term matrix on this dataset is decomposed by Singular Value Decomposition. By keeping the first two largest singular values, the dataset could be projected onto a 2D space corresponding to principal components. Figure 6 illustrates the plot of the documents. As shown, since the shape of document cluster can be arbitrary, a shape of document cluster cannot be assumed in advance (e.g., hyper-sphere in k-means).

To test the ability of identifying the different shapes of clusters, we organized datasets where each cluster consists of approximately the same number of documents (but as illustrated in Figure 6, each document cluster will have a different shape). As shown in Figure 7, the proposed algorithm outperforms the modified

---

[10] Two documents are mutually orthogonal if they share no terms. This holds true when the Cosine metric is used for the similarity measure.

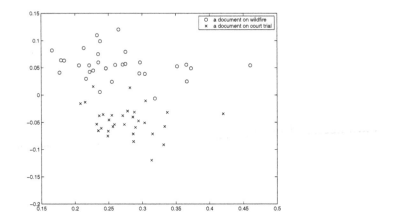

Fig. 6. Illustration of non-spherical document clusters

	Precision	Recall		Precision	Recall
Level 1	91.5%	90.3%	Level 1	83.1%	86.7%
Level 2	100%	76.4%			

(a) Proposed algorithm   (b) Modified K-means

Fig. 7. Comparison of the clustering algorithms on datasets-1. Datasets-1 consists of five different datasets where each cluster has approximately the same density. The values of precision and recall shown in this table are obtained by averaging the accuracy of the algorithm on each dataset

Precision	Recall
87.5%	88.6%

Precision	Recall
78.7%	79.5%

(a) Proposed algorithm (b) Modified k-means algorithm

Fig. 8. Comparison of the accuracy of clustering algorithms at level 1 on datasets-2. Datasets-2 consists of ten different datasets where each cluster has arbitrary numbers of documents. The values of precision and recall shown in this table are obtained by averaging the accuracy of the algorithm on each dataset

K-means algorithm in terms of precision and recall.[11] This is because the proposed algorithm measures similarity between a cluster and a neighborhood of a document while K-means clustering measures similarity between a cluster and a document. Note that 10% increase in accuracy is significant by considering the fact that we provided the correct the number of clusters (K) and choose the best initial seed points for K-means.

As illustrated in Figure 7, the recall of our algorithm decreases as the level increases. The main reason for this poor recall at level 2 is related to the characteristics of news articles. As discussed, a named entity (NE) plays a key role in defining who/when/where of an event. Hence, NE contributes to high quality clustering at level 1. However, at level 2, since the strength of topical terms are not very strong (unlike named entities), it was not easy to merge different event clusters (belonging to the same topic) into a same topical cluster.

Ability to Discover Clusters with Different Densities and Shapes Since the sizes of clusters can be of arbitrary numbers, clustering algorithms must be able to identify the clusters with wide variance in size. To test the ability of identifying clusters with different densities, we organized datasets where each dataset consists of document clusters with diverse densities. As shown in Figure 8, when the density of each cluster is not uniform, the accuracy of the modified K-means clustering algorithm degraded. In contrast, the accuracy of our algorithm remains similar. Therefore, based on the experimental results on datasets-1 and datasets-2, we can conclude that our algorithm has better ability to find arbitrary shapes of clusters with variable sizes than K-means clustering.

Event Confusion There are some events that we could not correctly separate. For example, on the wildfire topic, there exist different events, such as "Oregon wildfire", "Arizona wildfire", etc. However, at level 1, it was hard to separate those events into different clusters. Table 8 illustrates the reason for this event confusion at level 1. As shown, term frequency of topical terms (e.g., fire, firefighter, etc) is relatively higher than that of named entities (e.g., Colorado, Arizona, etc). Similarly, for the airplane crash topic, it was difficult to separate different airplane crash events since distinguishing lexical features like plane number has extremely low term frequency.

The capability of distinguishing different events on the same topic is important. One possible solution is to use temporal information. Rational behind this approach is based on the assumption that news articles on same event are temporally proximate, However, if two events occur during the same time interval, then this temporal information might not be helpful. Another approach is to use classification, i.e., training dataset is composed of multiple topic classes, and each class is composed of multiple events. After then, we learn the weight of

---

[11] We did not compare the modified k-means algorithm with ours at level 2. To do this, we also need to develop a feature selection algorithm to extend the modified K-means algorithm into a hierarchical version.

topic-specific terms and named entities [49]. However, this approach is not relevant since we cannot accommodate the dynamically changing topics. Therefore, we need further study for the event confusion.

6   Conclusion and Future Work

We presented the mining framework that is vital to intelligent information retrieval. An experimental prototype has been developed, implemented and tested to demonstrate the effectiveness of the proposed framework. In order to accommodate topics that change over time, we developed the incremental document clustering algorithm based on a neighborhood search. The presented clustering algorithm could identify news event clusters as well as topic clusters incrementally. We also showed that presented topic ontologies could characterize news topics at multiple levels of abstraction.

	Colorado wildfire	Num	Arizona wildfire	Num
1	fire	14.33	fire	17.68
2	forest	5.72	*rodeo*	4.76
3	firefighter	4.83	blaze	4.38
4	acre	3.94	firefighter	4.21
5	evacuate	3.77	burn	3.92
6	*hayman*	3.22	*arizona*	3.46
7	blaze	3.11	*paxon*	3.15
8	weather	3.06	acre	3.00
9	official	2.89	wildfire	3.00
10	national	2.83	*chediski*	2.89
11	burn	2.72	resident	2.61
12	area	2.66	center	2.46
13	wildfire	2.56	national	2.46
14	*denver*	2.43	area	2.46
15	*colorado*	2.33	evacuate	2.65

Table 8. Top 15 high term frequency words in Colorado wildfire and Arizona wildfire event. Num represents the average number of term occurrences per document in each event (without document length normalization). Terms with italic font carry event-specific information for each wildfire event

We intend to extend this work into the following five directions. First, although a document hierarchy can be obtained using unsupervised clustering, as shown in Aggarwal *et al.* [1], the cluster quality can be enhanced if a pre-existing knowledge base is exploited. That is, based on this priori knowledge, we can have some control while building a document hierarchy. Second, besides exploiting text data, we can utilize other information since Web news articles are composed of text, hyperlinks, and multimedia data. For example, as described in [25], both terms and hyperlinks (which point to related news articles or Web pages) can be used for feature selection. Third, coupling with WordNet [36], we plan to extend the topic ontology learning framework to accommodating rich semantic information extraction. To this end, we will annotate a topic ontology within Protégé [38, 54]. Forth, our clustering algorithm can be tested on other datasets like TDT corpus [53]. Finally, to strengthen our work in terms of generality, we are in the process of investigating the potential applicability of our method to earth science information streams.

7 Acknowledgement

This paper is based on our previous work [12], which was presented at the Second International Conference on Ontologies, DataBases, and Applications of Semantics for Large Scale Information Systems (ODBASE 2003), Catania, Sicily, Italy, November 2003. We would like to thank the audience and anonymous reviewers of ODBASE 2003 for their helpful comments. We also would like to appreciate anonymous reviewers of this special issue for their valuable comments. Finally, we would like to thank Jongeun Jun for helpful discussions on the clustering algorithm.

This research has been funded in part by the Integrated Media Systems Center, a National Science Foundation Engineering Research Center, Cooperative Agreement No. EEC-9529152.

References

[1] C.C. Aggarwal, S.C. Gates, and P.S. Yu. On the merits of using supervised clustering for building categorization systems. In *Proceedings of the 5th ACM SIGKDD International Conference on Knowledge Discovery and Data Mining*, 1999.

[2] E. Agirre, O. Ansa, E. Hovy, and D. Martinez. Enriching very large ontologies using the WWW. In *Proceedings of the ECAI Workshop on Ontology Learning*, 2000.

[3] R. Agrawal, C. Faloutsos, and A. Swami. Efficient similarity search in sequence database. In *Proceedings of International Conference of Foundations of Data Organization and Algorithms*, 1993.

[4] J. Allan, J. Carbonell, G. Doddington, J. Yamron, and Y. Yang. Topic detection and tracking: pilot study final report. In *Proceedings of the DARPA Broadcast News Transcription and Understanding Workshop*, 1998.

[5] J. Allan, V. Lavrenko, and H. Jin. First story detection in TDT is hard. In *Proceedings of the 9th ACM International Conference on Information and Knowledge Management*, 2000.

[6] N. Beckmann, H.P. Kriegel, R. Schneider, and B. Seeger. The R*-tree: an efficient and robust access method for points and rectangles. *ACM SIGMOD Record*, 19(2):322-331, 1990.

[7] S. Berchtold, D.A. Keim, and H.P. Kreigel. The X-tree: An index structure for high dimensional data. In *Proceedings of the 22nd International Conference on Very Large Data Bases*, 1996.

[8] M.W. Berry, S.T. Dumais, and G.W. O'Brien. Using linear algebra for intelligent information retrieval. *SIAM Review*, 37(4):573-595, 1995.

[9] P.S. Bradley, U. Fayyad, and C. Reina. Scaling clustering algorithms to large databases. In *Proceedings of the 4th ACM SIGKDD International Conference on Knowledge Discovery and Data Mining*, 1998.

[10] T. Brants, F. Chen, and A. Farahat. A system for new event detection. In *Proceedings of the 26th International ACM SIGIR International Conference on Research and Development in Information Retrieval*, 2003.

[11] K. Chan, and A.W. Fu. Efficient time series matching by wavelets. In *Proceedings of IEEE International Conference on Data Engineering*, 1999.

[12] S. Chung, and D. McLeod. Dynamic topic mining from news stream data. In *Proceedings of the 2nd International Conference on Ontologies, Databases, and Application of Semantics for Large Scale Information Systems*, 2003.

[13] R.O. Duda, P.E. Hart, and D.G. Stork. *Pattern Classification (2nd Ed.)*. Wiley, New York, 2001.

[14] D.M. Dunlavy, J. Conroy, and D.P. O'Leary. QCS: a tool for querying, clustering, and summarizing documents. In *Proceedings of Human Language Technology Conference*, 2003.

[15] L. Ertöz, M. Steinbach, and V. Kumar. Finding clusters of different sizes, shapes, and densities in noisy, high dimensional data. In *Proceedings of the 3rd SIAM International Conference on Data Mining*, 2003.

[16] U.M. Fayyad, C. Reina, and P.S. Bradley. Initialization of iterative refinement clustering algorithms. In *Proceedings of the 4th ACM SIGKDD International Conference on Knowledge Discovery and Data Mining*, 1998.

[17] E.J. Glover, D.M. Pennock, S. Lawrence, and R. Krovetz. Inferring hierarchical descriptions. In *Proceedings of the 2002 ACM CIKM International Conference on Information and Knowledge Management*, 2002.

[18] S. Guha, R. Rastogi, and K. Shim. CURE: An efficient clustering algorithm for large databases. In *Proceedings of the ACM SIGMOD International Conference on Management of Data*, 1998.

[19] S. Guha, R. Rastogi, and K. Shim. ROCK: A robust clustering algorithm for categorical attributes. In *Proceedings of the 15th International Conference on Data Engineering*, 1999.

[20] A. Guttman. R-Trees: A dynamic index structure for spatial searching. In *Proceedings of the ACM SIGMOD International Conference on Management of Data*, 1985.

[21] J. Han, and M, Kamber. *Data mining: concepts and techniques*. Morgan Kaufmann Publishers, 2000.

[22] V. Hatzivassiloglou, L. Gravano, and A. Maganti. An investigation of linguistic features and clustering algorithms for topical document clustering. In *Proceedings of the 23rd Annual International ACM SIGIR Conference on Research and Development in Information Retrieval*, 2000.

[23] P. J. Huber. *Robust Statistics*. Wiley, New York, 1981.

[24] R.A. Jarvis, and E.A. Patrick. Clustering using a similarity measure based on shared near neighbors. *IEEE Transactions on Computers*, C22, 1025-1034, 1973.

[25] T. Joachims, N. Cristianini, and J. Shawe-Taylor. Composite kernels for hypertext categorisation. In *Proceedings of the 18th International Conference on Machine Learning*, 2001.

[26] G. Karypis, E.H. Han, and V. Kumar. CHAMELEON: a hierarchical clustering algorithm using dynamic modeling. *IEEE Computer*, 32(8):68-75, 1999.

[27] L. Khan, and D. McLeod. Effective retrieval of audio information from annotated text using ontologies. In *Proceedings of ACM SIGKDD Workshop on Multimedia Data Mining*, 2000.

[28] L. Khan, and D. McLeod. Disambiguation of annotated text of audio using onologies. In *Proceeding of ACM SIGKDD Workshop on Text Mining*, 2000.

[29] L. Khan, D. McLeod, and E.H. Hovy. Retrieval effectiveness of an ontology-based model for information selection. *The VLDB Journal*, 13(1):71-85, 2004.

[30] B. Larsen, and C. Aone. Fast and effective text mining using linear-time document clustering. In *Proceedings of the 5th ACM SIGKDD International Conference on Knowledge Discovery and Data Mining*, 1999.

[31] X. Liu, Y. Gong, W. Xu, and S. Zhu. Document clustering with cluster refinement and model selection capabilities. In *Proceedings of the 25th ACM SIGIR International Conference on Research and Development in Information Retrieval*, 2002

[32] A. Maedche, and S. Staab. Ontology learning for the Semantic Web. *IEEE Intelligent Systems*, 16(2):72-79, 2001.

[33] A. McCallum, K. Nigam, and L.H. Ungar. Efficient clustering of high-dimensional data sets with application to reference matching. In *Proceedings of the 6th ACM SIGKDD International Conference on Knowledge Discovery and Data Mining*, 2000.

[34] K.R. McKeown, R. Barzilay, D. Evans, V. Hatzivassiloglou, J.L. Klavans, A. Nenkova, C. Sable, B. Schiffman, and S. Sigelman. Tracking and summarizing news on a daily basis with Columbia's Newsblaster. In *Proceedings of the Human Language Technology Conference*, 2002.

[35] I.D. Melamed. Automatic evaluation and uniform filter cascades for inducing n-best translation lexicons. In *Proceedings of the 3rd Workshop on Very Large Corpora*, 1995.

[36] G. Miller. Wordnet: An on-line lexical database. *International Journal of Lexicography*, 3(4):235-312, 1990.

[37] R.T. Ng, and J. Han. Efficient and effective clustering methods for spatial data mining. In *Proceedings of the 20th International Conference on Very Large Data Bases*, 1994.

[38] N.F. Noy, M. Sintek, S. Decker, M. Crubezy, R.W. Fergerson, and M.A. Musen. Creating Semantic Web contents with Protégé-2000. *IEEE Intelligent Systems*, 6(12):60-71, 2001.

[39] D. Pelleg, and A. Moore. X-means: Extending K-means with efficient estimation of the number of clusters. In *Proceedings of the 17th International Conference on Machine Learning*, 2000.

[40] M.F. Porter. An algorithm for suffix stripping. *Program*, 14(3):130-137, 1980.

[41] D.R. Radev, S. Goldensohn, Z. Zhang, and R.S. Raghavan. Newsinessence: a system for domain-independent, real-time news clustering and multi-document summarization. In *Proceedings of Human Language Technology Conference*, 2001.

[42] D.R. Radev, S. Goldensohn, Z. Zhang, and R.S. Raghavan. Interactive, domain-independent identification and summarization of topically related news. In *Proceedings of the 5th European Conference on Research and Advanced Technology for Digital Libraries*, 2001.

[43] L. Ralaivola, and F. d'Alché-Buc. Incremental support vector machine learning: a local approach. In *Proceedings of the Annual Conference of the European Neural Network Society*, 2001.

[44] G. Salton, and M.J. McGill. *Introduction to modern information retrieval*. McGraw-Hill, New York, 1983.

[45] M. Sanderson, and W.B. Croft. Deriving concept hierarchies from text. In *Proceedings of the 22nd Annual International ACM SIGIR Conference on Research and Development in Information Retrieval*, 1999.

[46] D. Song, and P. D. Bruza. Towards context sensitive information inference. *Journal of the American Society for Information Science and Technology*, 54(4):321-334, 2003.

[47] E.M. Voorhees. Query expansion using lexical-semantic relations. In *Proceedings of the 17th International ACM SIGIR Conference on Research and Development in Information Retrieval*, 1994.

[48] Y. Yang, J. Carbonell, R. Brown, T. Pierce, B.T. Archibald, and X. Liu. Learning approaches for detecting and tracking news events. *IEEE Intelligent Systems*, 14(4):32-43, 1999.

[49] Y. Yang, J. Zhang, J. Carbonell, and C. Jin. Topic-conditioned novelty detection. In *Proceedings of the 8th ACM SIGKDD International Conference on Knowledge Discovery and Data Mining*, 2002.

[50] L.A. Zadeh. Similarity relations and fuzzy orderings. *Information Sciences*, 3(2):177-200, 1971.

[51] T. Zhang, R. Ramakrishnan, and M. Livny. BIRCH: an efficient data clustering method for very large databases. In *Proceedings of the ACM SIGMOD International Conference on Management of Data*, 1996.

[52] Y. Zhao, and G. Karypis. Evaluations of hierarchical clustering algorithms for document datasets. In *Proceedings of the 11th ACM International Conference on Information and Knowledge Management*, 2002.

[53] Nist topic detection and tracking corpus. http://www.nist.gov/speech/tests/tdt/tdt98/index.htm, 1998.

[54] Protégé WordNet tab. http://protege.stanford.edu/plugins/wordnettab/

A Knowledge Network Approach for Implementing Active Virtual Marketplaces

Minsoo Lee[1], Stanley Y.W. Su[2], Herman Lam[2]

[1] Dept. Computer Science and Engineering, Ewha Womans University,
11-1 Daehyun-Dong, Seodaemoon-Ku, Seoul, Korea 120-750
mlee@ewha.ac.kr
[2] Database Systems Research and Development Center
University of Florida, Gainesville, Florida 32611, U.S.A
{su, hlam}@cise.ufl.edu

Abstract. The current Web technology is not suitable for representing knowledge nor sharing it among organizations over the Web. There is a rapidly increasing need for exchanging and linking knowledge over the Web, especially when several sellers and buyers come together on the Web to form a virtual marketplace. Virtual marketplaces are increasingly being required to become more intelligent and active, thus leading to an active virtual marketplace concept. This paper explains an infrastructure called the knowledge network that enables sharing of knowledge over the Web and thus effectively supports the formation of virtual marketplaces on the Web. The concept of an active virtual marketplace can be realized using this infrastructure by allowing buyers and sellers to effectively specify their knowledge in the form of events, triggers, and rules. The knowledge network can actively distribute and process these knowledge elements to help buyers and sellers to easily find each other. An example active virtual marketplace application has been developed using the knowledge network.

Keywords: virtual marketplace, knowledge network

1. Introduction

Virtual Marketplaces enable buyers and suppliers of products to meet together in cyberspace and exchange information about products. Buyers look for product items that are wanted while suppliers provide information regarding their available products. The virtual marketplace is becoming increasingly popular on the Web. However, the current technology still has certain limitations that make the virtual marketplace a passive meeting place where buyers and suppliers have to perform many manual tasks to find each other or obtain information from each other. We find the necessity of an active virtual marketplace where such operations can be automated and more intelligence could be built into the virtual marketplace.

---

[1] Contact author: Tel +82-2-3277-3401, Fax: +82-2-3277-2306

S. Spaccapietra et al. (Eds.): Journal on Data Semantics II, LNCS 3360, pp. 113-135, 2004.

We have previously developed the concept of knowledge networks in order to build an infrastructure that can embed intelligence into the Web [1]. Knowledge networks can link knowledge over the Web among publishers of knowledge and subscribers of knowledge. By linking knowledge it effectively enables real-time notification to subscribers of knowledge and also processing of knowledge.

Using the knowledge network and applying it to the virtual marketplace domain, we can easily and effectively include the knowledge of both buyers and sellers into the Web infrastructure and help each other find the right counterpart in a very active and automated fashion. We have developed such an application to demonstrate how the active virtual marketplace can be realized.

In the knowledge network, buyers and sellers can specify their knowledge in terms of events, triggers, and rules. Events enable buyers and sellers to monitor interesting things that happen within the virtual marketplace. Once an interesting thing happens, information is automatically passed in the form of events to buyers and sellers. Buyers and sellers can also populate the knowledge network with rules that are invoked by such events. The rules will carry out business tasks that are required by the buyers and sellers. Complex relationships among multiple events and multiple rules can also exist, which can be specified by triggers. The knowledge network can enhance the existing Web infrastructure by only adding special components to Web servers, and therefore is a simple yet powerful approach for implementing active virtual marketplaces on the Web.

The organization of this paper is as follows. Section 2 provides a survey of related work regarding virtual marketplaces and also rule systems and event notification architectures. Section 3 discusses the requirements for an active virtual marketplace. Section 4 explains the knowledge network concept. Section 5 discusses how the knowledge network can be built and deployed. Section 6 describes an active virtual marketplace application developed with the knowledge network. Section 7 deals with the implementation of the knowledge network. Section 8 gives the summary and conclusion.

2. Related Research

Virtual marketplaces have become very popular with the rise of the Internet. Virtual marketplaces have intermediaries that can reduce the gap between suppliers and consumers of products [2]. These intermediaries are currently in the form of Web sites that bring suppliers and consumers together. There have been large and small virtual marketplaces being formed in several industries such as the food industry, automobile industry, and service professionals in addition to the popular general auction sites. Ford, DaimlerChrysler, and General Motors have developed a business exchange, Ebay is very well-known for its vast number of products available for auction, handshake.com and servicelane.com provide a site for professional services [3].

The benefits of virtual marketplaces are improved process efficiencies, improved supply chain efficiencies, better control over the process, convenience, access to additional suppliers/buyers.

There are several limitations to the current technology that prohibit the virtual marketplace from becoming an active meeting place. Suppliers of products have to actively monitor incoming buyers and try to contact the buyers to see if they have any matching interests to make a deal. On the other hand, buyers have to seek the right supplier that can satisfy their requirements. The suppliers and buyers could be wasting a significant amount of time during this process even though they are concentrating on this single task and not being able to take on any other tasks. Furthermore, after they have found each other, many more tasks could be automated.

We suggest that this process can be automated by inputting the right knowledge from both the supplier and buyer into the virtual marketplace. The knowledge is modeled as events, triggers, and rules. The significant progress in past research regarding event and rule systems has provided a basis in our development of a new knowledge model.

The concept of rules was originally introduced in the research areas of artificial intelligence and expert systems. The rules were soon incorporated into databases to create a new category of databases, namely, active databases [4,5]. Event-Condition-Action (ECA) rules have been used in many of these systems. They are composed of three parts: event, condition, and action. The semantics of an ECA rule is, "When an event occurs, check the condition. If the condition is true, then execute the action." The event provides a finer control as to when to evaluate the condition and gives more active capabilities to the database systems. Rules can automatically perform security and integrity constraint checking, alert people of important situations, enforce business policies and regulations, etc.

WebRules [6] is a framework to use rules to integrate servers on the Internet. The WebRules server has a set of built-in events that can notify remote systems, and has a library of system calls that can be used in a rule to connect Web servers. However, it does not include concepts such as event and rule publishing or event filtering. WebLogic [7] also includes a basic form of rules, which are called actions. These actions need to be provided to the WebLogic server at the time when an application is registering for an event. These actions are actually specified with program codes rather than a high-level specification facility.

Several content-based event notification architectures have been recently proposed to provide an abstraction of the communication infrastructure on the Internet. These architectures focus on providing a scalable architecture for event delivery, as well as a mechanism to selectively subscribe to information. Siena [8] proposes a mechanism to maximize the expressiveness of a language to specify filters and patterns while not degrading the scalability. NeoNet [9] provides a rule-based message routing, queueing and formatting system. Keryx [10] is a language and platform independent infrastructure to distribute events on the Internet and is based on the publish-subscribe model. JMS [11] provides reliable, asynchronous communication between components in a distributed computing environment. CORBA Notification Service [12] uses an event channel concept and extends the Event Service by providing event filtering and quality of service.

Languages and models for specifying complex relationships among events have also been proposed by several researchers in the database area. HiPAC[13], Ode[14] are such systems that looked into the problem of relating multiple events and examining the semantics of the relationships. The events were classified into several different types, and operators that can show the relationship among multiple events were proposed. Efficient processing mechanisms that use tree-based pipelined data structures were also proposed. However, these systems focused on the problem in a single system context, and did not consider publish-subscribe mechanisms and distributed processing mechanisms in a Web environment. This composite event concept is incorporated into the trigger part of our knowledge model.

3. Requirements for an Active Virtual Marketplace

The currently implemented virtual marketplace configurations have significant limitations in terms of interactions among the participants of the marketplace. We identify the cause of such limitations as being manual operations that heavily burden the buyers, sellers, and coordinators of the marketplace. The following requirements need to be satisfied in order to make the marketplace more active.

(1) Automatic notification mechanisms need to be provided to alert buyers and sellers regarding new or changed information about their counter parties.

(2) Filtering mechanisms for accepting only the relevant information about their interested products and prices, or other specific purchase conditions need to be supported.

(3) An easy way to specify and establish business logic required by both the buyer and seller needs to be supported within the marketplace.

(4) A flexible way to connect notifications to various business logic pieces needs to be provided to encapsulate the complex transactions that occur between the buyers and sellers.

The active virtual marketplace can be realized by employing the knowledge network concept and adapt it to the requirements discussed above.

4. Overview of the Knowledge Network

The main goal of the knowledge network is to share the knowledge available on the Internet among the users of the Internet. This would promote efficient exchange of knowledge and the development of more organized and interconnected knowledge among individual expertise that is currently isolated from other Web sites and users.

4.1. Events, Triggers, and Rules

The knowledge network is composed not only of data elements but also knowledge elements which can be used to perform automatic reasoning and decision-making tasks. In this work, knowledge elements are presented by events, triggers, and rules. The events encapsulate timely information of what is happening on the Internet and makes the knowledge network actively responsive without human intervention. The rules express the decision-making factors allowing the intelligence of humans to be embedded into the knowledge network. The triggers model complex relationships among events and rules, checking histories of events and enabling various reasoning or activation sequences to reflect the complex decision making process. The detail syntax of events, triggers, and rules can be found in [1]. The knowledge network has a goal not just of sharing data but also sharing knowledge to make the Internet into a more active, collaborative, and intelligent infrastructure. Figure 1 shows an example of the Event-Trigger-Rule (ETR) model that is used for specifying knowledge in the knowledge network.

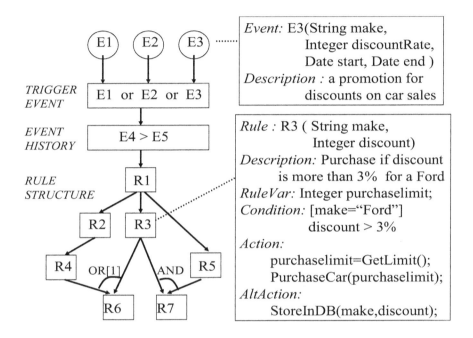

Figure 1. Event, Trigger, and Rule Example

The example shows the definition of an event named E3 within the box on the upper right hand side. The event notifies that a promotion for discounts on car sales is going on. It can carry data values in the form of event parameters such as the make of the car as a string type, the discount rate as an integer type, and the dates that the discount starts and ends.

A rule named R3 is shown within the box on the lower right hand side. The rule automatically initiates the purchasing transaction if it finds that the discount is more than 3% for a Ford. The rule accepts two parameters: a string that has the make information, and an integer that has the discount rate information. A Rule Variable named *purchaselimit* is used as a temporary local variable to be used within the rule body. Other types of rule variables such as persistent and existing type rule variables exist. The persistent type will persist the value of the variable and enables multiple rules to share a value beyond a single rule execution. The existing type references external servers modeled as objects. Rules can invoke methods on remote servers via the existing type variable. This makes the rules more powerful as they can act as the "glue" to several distributed systems. More details are provided in section 7.1 as well as in [1]. The rule has a Condition part that needs to be evaluated in order to decide whether to next execute the Action part or the Alternative Action part of the rule, or just skip the rule. If the Condition evaluates to true, the Action part is executed. If the Condition evaluates to false, the Alternative Action part is executed. If the guarded expression within the Condition evaluates to false, the rule is just skipped. The guarded expression is surrounded with brackets. It is used as a mechanism to first check basic essential conditions that are required for the rule execution to continue. In R3 the guarded expression checks if the make is a Ford and if it turns out that it is not a Ford, the rule execution will be immediately discontinued. However, if the make is a Ford and the discount is larger than 3%, the purchasing operation is carried out. Otherwise, the promotion information is just stored in a database.

The trigger is shown on the left hand side. The trigger is relating five events E1 to E5 with seven rules R1 to R7. The trigger has three parts: Trigger event, Event history, and Rule structure. The Trigger event part specifies the events that can initiate the processing of the trigger. The events are OR-ed, which means that any one of the events can initiate the processing of the trigger. The Event history checks for complex relationships among events that have occurred. Several event relationships such as different types of event sequences, timing constraints, number of occurrences, etc, are possible. The Event history in Figure 1 checks if event E4 has happened before event E5. The reason why the Triggering event and Event history were separated is because of the processing overhead of the Event history. If only the Event history were specified, then all events in the Event history need to be monitored and would create a significant amount of burden on processing the trigger. Therefore, we explicitly separate the Triggering event, and it becomes easy to monitor simple initiating events of the trigger while checking complex relationships can follow afterwards. The rules can be executed in various sequences as specified by the Rule structure. After R1 is executed, R2 and R3 are executed in parallel. OR-type and AND-type synchronization points exist. If any one of R3 or R4 finish, R6 can start. Only when both R3 and R5 finish, R7 can start.

The trigger structure can also support the formation of a generic event which is composed of a very complex structure of events. As an example, a company may define a generic event named "interesting event" which has a flexible meaning and can be raised by various types of source events in various combinations. The source events can be specified in the Trigger Event and Event history part in a flexible manner, while the Rule structure has a rule that posts the "interesting event".

4.2. Architectural Framework

The knowledge network can enhance active collaboration of Web servers and users on the Internet by providing a framework to (1) publish data, applications, constraints, events, and rules, (2) register for subscription of events and deliver events to subscribers, (3) define rules that are invoked by complex relationships among the subscribed events.

The framework to accomplish these tasks is based on the idea of providing a component that can be plugged into any standard Web server. This should allow the Web servers that need to collaborate to have a symmetric architecture. Another technology that is needed to support this framework is event, trigger, and rule processing capability being built into the component. This is the major part that should be developed in order to provide any type of intelligent, distributed and collaborative infrastructure. The idea of providing knowledge profiles for each user is also adopted to support a wide variety of users on the Internet who wish to have their own individually customized knowledge built into the applications.

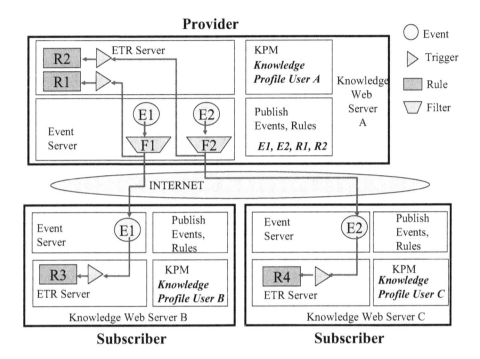

Figure 2. Architectural framework of the knowledge network.

The architectural framework of the knowledge network shown in Figure 2 is used to explain the key features of the knowledge network: publishing events and rules, event filters, push-based event delivery, knowledge profile, and processing of triggers and rules. In Figure 2, several Web servers are interconnected through the Internet. Each server is extended with several components that form the basis of the knowledge network. Only the extensions to the Web server are shown in the figure for simplicity. We refer to a Web server with these extensions as a knowledge Web server (KWS). Each KWS has an ETR Server which processes triggers and rules, an Event Server which processes events and filters, and a Knowledge Profile Manager (KPM) which manages the knowledge profiles. Assume that the knowledge Web server A takes the role of a data   provider who is user A and knowledge Web servers B and C are maintained by two different users, namely, user B and user C, who consume information from the knowledge Web server A. The users A, B, and C can connect to the sites KWS A, KWS B, and KWS C with a browser interface to the systems and the Internet.

Data providers can provide data and define events and rules, and publish them on web pages. Publishing of events will enable Web surfers to know what kind of data can be delivered to them in a timely manner. Interested Web surfers can register for the events and become subscribers of the event. Rules published by data providers can perform several operations on the knowledge Web server of the data provider. Subscribers of events can conveniently select these rules that will be executed remotely on the data provider's knowledge Web server when the subscribed event occurs. Figure 2 shows that the knowledge Web server A has published two events E1 and E2, and two rules R1 and R2. User B has subscribed to event E1 and linked it to rule R1, while user C has subscribed to event E2 and linked it to rule R2.

Event filter templates are provided by data providers to allow event subscribers to more precisely specify the subset of the event occurrences in which they are interested. The subscribers can give various conditions on the values that the event carries. Only those event instances that satisfy the condition will be delivered to the subscriber. By using event filters, only meaningful data will be provided to the subscribers. Thus, network traffic can be significantly reduced. Figure 2 shows that the event filter F1 is installed on event E1 by user B, while the event filter F2 is installed on event E2 by the user C.

In a knowledge network, events are delivered via a push-based mechanism to subscribers' knowledge Web servers. When the event occurs, the push mechanism is activated in order to deliver the event to a large number of knowledge Web servers in a timely fashion. This push-based mechanism can radically change the paradigm of how interactions on the Internet are performed. Moreover, the combination of event pushing with the event filtering creates a more powerful communication infrastructure for the knowledge network. Figure 2 shows the extension related to the push-based event delivery combined with the event filtering in each knowledge Web server.

The providers and subscribers of knowledge can specify and store their knowledge (i.e., events, triggers, and rules) in knowledge profiles. Each knowledge Web server is extended with a component that can provide a Web-based graphical user interface to the provider or subscriber of knowledge to edit their knowledge profile. The knowledge profile is persistently stored. The events, triggers, and rules stored in the knowledge profile are provided to other run-time components of the knowledge Web server. Figure 2 shows the knowledge profiles existing on different knowledge Web servers.

Triggers and rules are executed within the knowledge Web server when an event linked to it has occurred. Processing the triggers involves checking of complex relationships among event occurrences and also the scheduling of several rules. Rules can activate various operations on the Web server. The execution of a rule may again cause new events to occur, resulting in a chained execution of rules. Figure 2 shows the processing components for triggers and rules residing within the knowledge Web servers. Knowledge Web server B will execute rule R3 upon receiving filtered event E1, and knowledge Web server C will execute rule R4 upon receiving filtered event E2.

5. Building and Deploying the Knowledge Network

The knowledge network is constructed through a process involving a series of steps that need to be followed by the providers and subscribers participating in the knowledge network. This section explains each of the steps in the order they occur.

Figure 3 shows an example for a single provider and single subscriber participating in the construction of the knowledge network. This simplified view of the construction process is used as the example to be explained throughout this section.

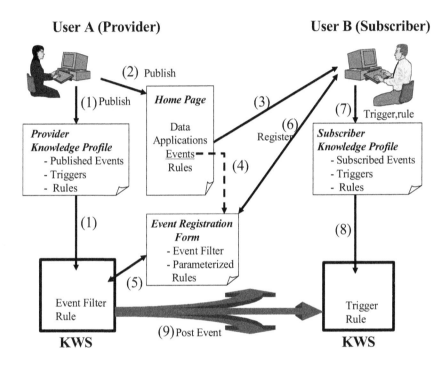

Figure 3. Steps for constructing the knowledge network.

5.1. Publishing Data, Applications, Events, and Rules

The knowledge publishing is shown as steps (1) and (2) in Figure 3. Currently, a user (or organization), say A, that has data and applications (i.e., methods that may be connected to a database in his/her home directory) can publish this data and application on his/her home page. Using the knowledge network concept, user A can also publish the events that can be raised from his/her own data and applications and allow other Web surfers to subscribe to those events. The definitions of the events are input into the knowledge profile to enable the knowledge Web server to process the events. All other knowledge elements described in this section are also input into the knowledge profile. User A can easily hookup the event to his/her home page afterwards.

An event filtering mechanism may also be provided by user A. Subscribers will later on give some value ranges for the filters during the event registration step (to be explained in Section 5.2), and when the event is being posted, the system checks if the event attribute values satisfy these given value ranges prior to sending out the event to the subscriber. The type of filters that can be defined on the event attributes are equal, range, greater (or less) than, single value selection, multiple value selection. The type of filter decides how the event filtering form will be displayed to the subscriber. The equal type means that the subscriber should specify the exact value of the event attribute, which is of interest to the subscriber. This will be displayed as a single blank box to the subscriber requesting input. The range type means that the subscriber should specify the minimum and maximum values for the event attribute which is of interest to the subscriber. Two blank boxes indicating the maximum and minimum value will be displayed to the subscriber for the range to be input. The greater (or less) than type requires the subscriber to provide a lower bound (or upper bound) of the event attribute. This results in a single blank box being displayed to the subscriber requesting a lower bound or upper bound value to be input. The single selection type allows the subscriber to select one of the values that the provider has pre-defined. This results in a drop-down box, which includes all of the candidate values. The multiple selection type is similar to the single selection operator except that it allows the subscriber to select multiple values rather than just a single value, meaning that the subscriber can receive events that have attribute values falling into any of the multiple selected values. The multiple selection type is displayed as multiple radio buttons that can be individually selected and unselected.

Rules that are applied to user A's data can also be published for use by various applications that require meta-data (e.g., in e-commerce applications.) Several parameterized rules that can be triggered by user A's own events may also be published. The subscriber of user A's event can link the event to the parameterized rules during event registration so that automatic rule processing can be conducted on the provider site (i.e., user A's site) with the guarantee that these operations are authorized and safe for user A's own Web server.

5.2. Event Registration

Another user, say B, is surfing on the web and discovers the homepage of user A and finds an event of interest. User B then accesses the event registration form and registers for an event that user A has published on his/her home page. In a more advanced automated scenario, users do not need to surf on the Web to find out about newly added events but can automatically be informed by registering for an event named "AddedNewEvent" on the Web sites. User B may subscribe to the event to be sent out either as an e-mail notification or a pushed event to his/her knowledge Web server. At the time of registration, user B may also provide values that are to be used later on for filtering out irrelevant events. If some parameterized rules linked to the subscribed event are supported by the event provider, the user B may select some rules to be executed on the event provider's site. An example of such a rule could be changing user B's subscription information (i.e., discontinue subscription of an event after some specified number of postings) automatically after sending the event. The event registration steps are shown as steps (3) to (6) in Figure 3. After user B performs this registration, the event that occurs later on will be filtered and then either be sent out as an e-mail notification or be posted to the knowledge Web server on which the user B has his/her own knowledge profile. The knowledge profile should contain the events that the user B has subscribed to as well as the triggers and rules that are defined for the event. User B can also define additional triggers and rules that are to be processed at his/her own knowledge Web server when an event notification has reached the knowledge Web server. This is further described in the following subsection.

5.3. Trigger and Rule Specification

After subscribing to an event, user B may then access the Knowledge Profile Manager - a module which manages the user's knowledge profile (event subscription, trigger and rule definition information) - of his/her own knowledge Web server and specify the additional triggers and rules that should be executed upon the occurrences of the events he/she has subscribed to. Several events that user B has subscribed to may be linked to a set of rules, forming composite events and structures of rules. In Figure 3, these steps are shown as (7) and (8).

5.4. Event Posting, Filtering, and Rule Execution

Service providers will later generate events that first go through a filtering process to identify the relevant subscribers of the event. Once the subscribers are identified, rules on the provider's site can be executed. These rules are remotely executable rules, which are intended to allow remote users to have a limited capability to execute units of code on the provider's site. The event is then posted either as an e-mail message to the subscriber or an event notification to the subscriber's knowledge Web server. If the subscriber has some triggers and rules defined on his/her own knowledge Web server linked to the event, the event will trigger the execution of these rules which may perform some operations within the subscriber's web server and/or generate another event that can be again posted to another site. This is step (9) in Figure 3.

6. Active Virtual Marketplace Implementation

The virtual marketplace is currently one of the most rapidly growing application areas on the Internet. The knowledge network concept can be used to further enhance the virtual marketplace and business-to-business e-commerce by adding active capabilities and intelligence to the Internet.

6.1. The IntelliBiz Company

We demonstrate our concept by implementing an example company named IntelliBiz. The IntelliBiz company performs the Business-to-Business e-commerce service by connecting suppliers of products and/or services to buyers who are seeking these products and/or services. They publish a list of suppliers and buyers on their company's home pages categorized by the products and services. A new supplier can go through a supplier registration process and give information about the types of product or service the company provides along with the company contact information. New buyers go through a separate registration process and give information about the product or service for which they are seeking. IntelliBiz provides the services to allow businesses to easily find each other and forms a virtual marketplace of products and services at the business level.

The IntelliBiz company has several types of events to which the suppliers or buyers can subscribe. The description of these events and the supported filters are as follows:

- NewSupplier (String ID, String e-mail, String URL, String product, Range price): This event is posted when a new supplier registers with the IntelliBiz company. The information about the supplier is encapsulated in the event parameters. Buyers can subscribe to this event to obtain the information about the new suppliers. Filters on this event are supported for the product and price attributes.
- NewBuyer (String ID, String e-mail, String URL, String product, Range price): This event is posted when a new buyer registers with the IntelliBiz company. The event parameters encapsulate the buyer information. Suppliers can subscribe to this event to obtain this important information about newly registered buyers in a timely manner. Filters on this event are supported for the product and price attributes.
- RFQ (String ID, String BuyerURL, String product, String quantity, String delivery_date): This event represents an RFQ (Request For Quote) which is generated by a buyer who is looking for a specific product and wants to collect quotes from the suppliers registered with IntelliBiz. This event is originally generated and posted by a buyer to the IntelliBiz company. The IntelliBiz company will then post this event to any of the suppliers who have subscribed to this event through IntelliBiz. Filters on this event are supported for the product attribute.

The IntelliBiz company also has the following parameterized rules (provider-side rule) that the subscribers of the events can make use of while registering for the subscription of the event.

- NotifyBuyer(String SupplierID, String SupplierE-mail, String SupplierURL) : This rule will send an e-mail notification to a new buyer to introduce a new supplier. A supplier can select this rule to be installed when the supplier subscribes to the NewBuyer event. The parameter within this rule is the buyer's e-mail address to be used to send the e-mail notification. This rule is later invoked when a new buyer comes in and performs the registration task which posts the NewBuyer event.
- NotifySupplier(String BuyerID, String BuyerE-mail, String BuyerURL) : This rule does exactly the same thing as the NotifyBuyer rule except that the buyer and the supplier roles are reversed. This rule will send an e-mail notification to a new

supplier to introduce a buyer. A buyer can select this rule to be installed when the buyer subscribes to the NewSupplier event. This rule is later invoked when a new supplier comes in and performs the registration task which posts the NewSupplier event.

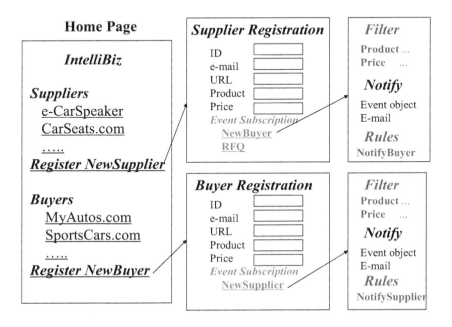

Figure 4. The IntelliBiz home page and registration forms.

The home page and the registration forms for the buyers and suppliers are shown in Figure 4. The event registration forms for the NewBuyer event and NewSupplier event are also shown.

6.2. The Suppliers and Buyers

In our scenario, we assume that there are two suppliers, two buyers and the IntelliBiz company. All of these companies have their own web sites.

The suppliers are as follows:

- e-CarSpeakers : This Internet company specializes in selling audio speakers for cars.
- CarSeats.com : This company sells car seats over the Internet.

The buyers are as follows:

- MyAutos.com : This company is a new manufacturer of economic class family sedans.
- SportsCars.com : This company is a sports car manufacturer.

The subscribed events and filters along with the triggers and rules that are defined for each of the suppliers are as follows:

The e-CarSpeakers company subscribes to the two events NewBuyer and RFQ. The filter installed for the NewBuyer event checks for the product to be speakers and also restricts the price range to be more than $300. The NotifyBuyer rule is also selected on the provider side. On the e-CarSpeakers site, the trigger relates the NewBuyer event to the AlertMarketing rule. The AlertMarketing rule will store the buyer information into the database and also alert the marketing department about the new buyer. The RFQ event is not only subscribed on the IntelliBiz site but also from other potential web sites that can post the event to the e-CarSpeakers company. The company filters out all but the product being speakers and having a quantity constraint of more than 20 speakers. The RFQ event is tied to the GenQuote rule on the e-CarSpeakers web site. The GenQuote rule will generate the quote accordingly and post the QuoteEvent to whoever generated the RFQ event. The GenQuote rule will extract the buyer's URL from the RFQ event and use it to post the QuoteEvent back to the buyer.

Explanations of the CarSeats.com events, triggers, and rules are similar to the e-CarSpeakers web site except that, for the NewBuyer event, it does not perform any operation on its web site. Using the knowledge network, the suppliers can effectively contact those buyers of interest with the events and filtering concepts and further initiate local operations such as alerting people and invoking applications within their companies via rules.

Table 1. Subscription information of supplier e-CarSpeakers.

IntelliBiz Site (Publisher)			e-CarSpeakers Site (Subscriber)	
Subscribed Event	Event Filter	Provider Rule	Trigger [Event](Rule)	Rule
NewBuyer	(Product= Speaker) AND (Price. morethan (300))	Notify Buyer	[NewBuyer] (AlertMarketing)	AlertMarketing C: true; A: Store in DB; Alert Marketing dept.;
RFQ (also exist on other sites)	(Product= Speaker) AND (Quantity> 20)		[RFQ] (GenQuote)	GenQuote C: true A:GenerateQuote; Post QuoteEvent;

Table 2. Subscription information of supplier CarSeats.com.

IntelliBiz Site (Publisher)			CarSeats.com Site (Subscriber)	
Subscribed Event	Event Filter	Provider Rule	Trigger [Event](Rule)	Rule
NewBuyer	(Product= Seats) AND (Price. lessthan (300))	Notify Buyer		
RFQ (also exist on other sites)	(Product= Seats) AND (Quantity> 100)		[RFQ] (GenQuote)	GenQuote C: true A: Generate Quote; Post QuoteEvent;

Table 3. Subscription information of buyer MyAutos.com.

IntelliBiz Site / any Site (Publisher)			MyAutos.com Site (Subscriber)	
Subscribed Event	Event Filter	Provider Rule	Trigger [Event](Rule)	Rule
New Supplier (IntelliBiz site)	(Product= Speaker) AND (Price. lessthan (500))	Notify Supplier	[NewSupplier] (EvalSupplier)	EvalSupplier C: Credibility = good; A: Save in DB; Post RFQ to Supplier;
Quote Event (any site)			[QuoteEvent] (ProcessQuote)	ProcessQuote C: [Count>10] Quote=best A: Post AcceptQuote;

Table 4. Subscription information of buyer SportsCars.com.

IntelliBiz Site / any Site (Publisher)			SportsCars.com Site (Subscriber)	
Subscribed Event	Event Filter	Provider Rule	Trigger [TriggerEvent] (EventHistory) <Rule>	Rule
New Supplier (IntelliBiz site)	(Product= Seats) AND (Price. lessthan (300))	Notify Supplier		
Quote Event (any site)			[QuoteEvent] (QE1 AND QE2) <ProcessQuote>	ProcessQuote C: true; A: Compare with QE1 and QE2;
			[QuoteEvent] ( ) <SaveRule>	SaveRule C: true; A: Save in DB;

The subscribed events and filters along with the triggers and rules that are defined for each of the buyers are as follows. The MyAutos.com company subscribes to the two events NewSupplier and QuoteEvent. The QuoteEvent can come from any website participating in a quote submission. When the NewSupplier event is posted, the MyAutos.com has put a filter that checks if the product is a speaker and also if the price is less than $500. If an event satisfying this filter is posted, the provider side rule NotifySupplier is invoked and then the event is delivered to the MyAutos.com web site. The MyAutos.com company is very cautious about posting its RFQs and only wants to post it individually to the suppliers that have good credit rather than posting its RFQ through the IntelliBiz web site and receiving many quotes from relatively small companies. Therefore, the NewSupplier event is linked to the EvalSupplier rule, which performs a credit check and then proceeds to send out an RFQ individually to the supplier. The capability of defining rules on each of the local web sites allows personal information or policies to be kept secure and undisclosed. The QuoteEvent is an event that is posted in response to the RFQ encapsulating a quote that is generated by a supplier. The QuoteEvent is linked to the ProcessQuote rule through a trigger. The ProcessQuote rule will check the number of quotes and see if it is the best quote received. If it is the best quote, then the quote accepting process is initiated.

The SportsCars.com web site has similar events, triggers and rules except that for the QuoteEvent it has two triggers. The first trigger also includes an event history expression - denoted as EH - and checks if two important quotes QE1 and QE2 have arrived. If they both have arrived, the quote comparison can be done by the ProcessQuote rule. Otherwise the quote is just saved in the database via the SaveRule.

6.3. The Big Picture

An overall diagram, which puts all of these knowledge elements together, is shown in Figure 5. The links in the figure show how the events are posted and the triggers and rules are executed on each of the supplier and buyer sites. The filters (which were described in detail in the previous section) are not shown in order to simplify the diagram. The figure shows how the IntelliBiz web site links the buyers and the suppliers through the knowledge network.

As shown in the above scenario, the knowledge network provides an ideal infrastructure for collaboration and for adding knowledge into the web to make it more intelligent and applicable to the emerging areas of Internet applications such as virtual marketplaces and e-commerce applications.

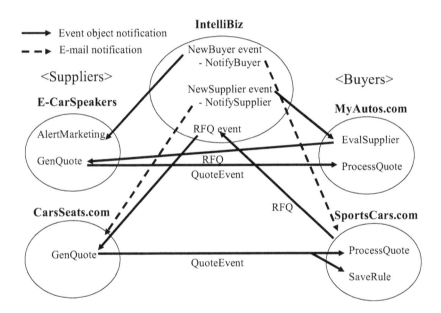

Figure 5. The Business-to-Business e-commerce scenario.

7. Knowledge Network Modules

The Event Server, ETR Server, Knowledge Profile Manager components, which compose the knowledge Web Server were developed using Java (JDK 1.4). Applet, servlet and RMI technology were used to implement the components. The popular Apache Web Server and Tomcat servlet engine were used as the basic existing infrastructure, which we extended with our newly developed components.

The core component is the ETR Server, which can process events, triggers and rules. The following subsections describe the implementation of the ETR Server, Event Server and Knowledge Profile Manager in detail.

7.1. ETR Server

The ETR Server has many key features that are not supported by other rule systems. They are:

- The ETR Server is developed in Java and is thus deployable on any platform.
- Processing of complex event relationships and rule sequences is possible. This includes checking events happening in a certain order, the occurrence of all (or any) of the events. Rules can be executed in a sequential, synchronized, or parallel fashion.
- The ETR Server can extract the parameters delivered via the events and distribute them to the appropriate rules. This eliminates the need for rules to be tightly coupled with event types.
- The ETR Server has an extensible interface that enables it to receive events from various communication infrastructures.
- The ETR Server supports dynamic changing of rules. Rules can be modified during run-time; i.e., rule instances in the previously defined form can be running while instances of the newly modified rule can be created and executed. This is implemented with the dynamic class loading capability of Java.
- Rules are grouped and can be activated or deactivated as a group.
- Events posted in synchronous mode or asynchronous mode is supported by the ETR Server. Synchronous and asynchronous modes of events are supported by building in a return value for the triggers. When a synchronous event is posted to a KWS, the relevant trigger is identified and will complete the execution and return a value to the site that posted the event. Thus the source site of the event will wait until the trigger execution is completed. The synchronous event has a limitation that the event can only be related to a single trigger on the KWS due to its waiting semantics. When an asynchronous event is posted to a KWS, there is no value that is returned to the source site of the event. Therefore the source site of an asynchronous event need not wait for the trigger execution to complete. This allows multiple triggers to be tied to an event and is considered more realistic and suitable for the Internet.
- The ETR Server can process various built-in rule variable types that are useful for different applications. There are temporary type, persistent type, and existing type rule variables. The temporary type is used just like a local variable in a program and can store a value while the rule is being executed. It can contain a constant value used within the rule body, or temporarily store return values from method executions and pass them as parameters to other method calls. The persistent type has an assigned identifier when it is declared. The identifier is used to initialize the rule variable from a persistent storage area as well as save it into the shared persistent storage. When rules need to communicate among each other, the persistent rule variable can be used to share common values through the persistent

store. In some cases, the same rule can use the persistent value to execute multiple times beyond a single rule execution in such cases where counting is needed. The existing type is used to reference RMI server objects on the system. The declaration of the reference type requires the server name to be provided. The existing type can be used within the rule body to invoke methods on the servers and can tie several servers through the rule body. The existing type enables external servers and libraries to be linked into the rule language other than standard Java calls. These three types of rule variables are converted to the appropriate Java calls when compiling the rules to produce the Java codes.

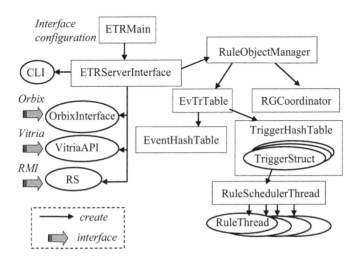

Figure 6. Architecture of the ETR Server

Figure 6 illustrates the architecture of the ETR Server. The Java class name of the modules are shown. The classes on the left show the interfaces currently supported for the communication infrastructure. RMI, Orbix, and Vitria's Communicator are currently supported. The RuleObjectManager is the entry point to the core ETR Server classes. There exist two hash tables: event hash table and the trigger hash table to store the mappings to/from triggering events and triggers. Each trigger element in the trigger hash table also contains a complex structure called TriggerStruct, which contains the event history and rule sequence information. The event history is processed by the Event History Processor. TriggerStruct data structure stores information about predecessors and successors of each rule specified in the trigger. Scalability issues can be solved by the RuleScheduler which uses this data structure to schedule the multiple rules via threads. The RGCoordinator manages the rule group information.

In order to minimize the overhead on monitoring and processing events, the Knowledge network uses a push-based event delivery mechanism. Events will be actively notified to subscribers rather than subscribers needing to poll the source to identify events. However when composite events such as chained events (i.e., event 1 is based on event 2 while event 2 is again based on event 3) are defined, the overhead on monitoring and processing events becomes nontrivial even in push-based event delivery systems. A source event will be pushed to another site, which in turn will identify a trigger and invoke a rule to post another event to another site. Therefore identifying the relevant triggers for an event needs to be very efficient. The ETR Server in the Knowledge network incorporates a very efficient special dual hash table to identify relevant triggers of events and can minimize the overhead. A more severe overhead is experienced when multiple types of events distributed over the Web are inter-related in a more complex way than a chained relationship. The trigger can be used to specify the complex relationships among events. However, this processing involves historical events to be compared against each other and therefore an event graph is used to speed up the comparison among historical event occurrences maintained in an event base. The event graph eliminates the need to scan a large part of the event base. The trigger is also designed to reduce the monitoring overhead by splitting the trigger into two parts: the trigger event and event history. The trigger event is an OR-ed expression of events and can minimize checking of complex historical conditions by allowing the event history to be evaluated only when an event specified in the trigger event occurs. In this way, the monitoring and processing of complex events becomes very efficient in the Knowledge network.

7.2. Event Server

The event is implemented as a Java class in the Event Server. When the event is delivered over the Internet, depending on the delivery mechanism it may be converted to an XML format. This is true when HTTP is used for communication.

The Event Server consists of the following 4 key modules :

- A module to receive events : This module is implemented as a servlet or RMI server to receive events through HTTP or RMI. It then forwards the event to the ETR server through RMI. The Event server on the system has a configured port that the RMI server is listening to in order to catch events happening on its local site. The subscribers' mechanism to monitor when an event occurs is simplified by employing a push-based event delivery to the subscribers. Therefore, subscribers will perform subsequent operations only when an event is pushed to its site. A servlet and RMI server that are part of the Event Server listen to certain ports on the Knowledge Web server to receive the pushed event.
- A module to deliver events : This module accepts requests to send events over the Internet through HTTP or RMI. Once a generated event goes through the event filtering module and identifies the appropriate subscribers, the delivering module will post the event to the destination.
- A module to filter events : This module keeps the event subscription information along with the event filters that have been defined. The event filters are kept in three kinds of data structures : inverted index, modified 2-3 tree, Range Table. This information is persistently stored.
- A module to process event registration : This module automatically generates event subscription forms that are shown to event subscribers during the event registration time. Events and their filters are stored in XML format and are processed with XSL to create the HTML forms. This module is implemented as a servlet.

Scalability of filtering are achieved by the efficient filtering data structures while the delivery mechanism can be improved by using an event multicasting scheme.

The above four key modules cooperatively form the basis of the communication infrastructure of the knowledge network.

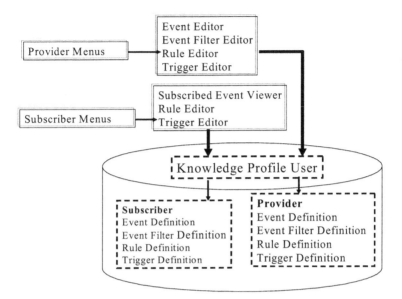

Figure 7. The Knowledge Profile Manager GUI menus and storage

7.3. Knowledge Profile Manager

The Knowledge Profile Manager is implemented as an applet, servlet and RMI server combination. The front end of the Knowledge Profile Manager is developed as an applet. The applet enables users to access menus for defining and viewing events, triggers, and rules. Two different menus such as the Provider menu and the Subscriber menu are available as shown in Figure 7. The backend is formed as a servlet and talks to an RMI server that is used to persistently store the knowledge information.

8. Conclusion

In this paper, we have discussed the concept and an implementation of an active virtual marketplace. The active virtual marketplace can be realized by adapting the knowledge network infrastructure. The knowledge network extends the existing Internet-Web infrastructure by adding event and rule services as a part of the information infrastructure. Events, rules, and triggers, which relate events to the evaluation of event history and the activation of rules, can be used to capture human and enterprise knowledge in the Internet, making the Internet an active knowledge network instead of a passive data network. The event, event filter, event history, and rule processing capabilities of the knowledge network offer very powerful and useful services to enable the timely delivery of relevant data and the activation of operations that are necessary for the realization of an active virtual marketplace application.

A few future research issues are identified as follows. First, security issues need to be further investigated due to the executable characteristics of rules on the provider (i.e., virtual marketplace coordinator) site. Rules can have potentially damaging effects if the proper authorization and security issues are not clearly specified. This is especially important when financial hazards could occur for virtual marketplaces. Second, an event ontology is required to effectively make the infrastructure more scalable for a global marketplace. The event definitions may be controllable within a limited size group of nodes. However, when the target platform becomes the whole Internet, ontology issues need to be resolved. One way to practically solve this problem would be to provide an ontology server for specific business domains rather than supporting the entire business domain. Third, dynamic change of events need to be looked into. Although we support dynamic change of rules in our framework, events may also need to be modified in a dynamic way. The event parameters can change when the event semantics are refined and thus the event subscribers would have to accommodate such changes. This dynamic change of events could make use of the event notification mechanism by defining an event such as EventChanged event which carries modified event definitions to the subscribers and rules could take actions to inform administrators or disable the relevant triggers. Fourth, interconnecting rules in this way could have a potential to contradict each other or have infinitely looping effects among the buyers and sellers or coordinators in the virtual marketplace. Therefore, a validation mechanism for global rule chaining could be devised by adding distributed deadlock monitors into the infrastructure. Fifth, an enhancement on scalability is needed. Current scalability features are built into the rule scheduling and event filtering mechanisms. However, event notifications can also be very time-consuming. Therefore, rather than using point-to-point delivery as in our prototype, hierarchical broadcasting or multicasting techniques for event delivery need to be investigated.

References

1. M. Lee, S.Y.W. Su, and H. Lam. Event and Rule Services for Achieving a Web-based Knowledge Network. Technical Report, UF CISE TR00-002, University of Florida (2000).
2. Beat F. Schmid and Dorian Selz. Requirements for electronic markets architecture. *EM –* Electronic *Markets*, 7(1), 1997.
3. Lawrence J. Magid, Wednesday, March 22, 2000 Los Angeles Times, March 22, 2000, http://www.larrysworld.com/articles/sb_b2bvirtual.htm
4. U. Dayal, B.T. Blaustein, A.P. Buchmann, et al. The HiPAC Project: Combining Active Databases and Timing Constraints. In ACM SIGMOD Record, Vol. 17(1), March (1988) 51-70.
5. J. Widom, (ed.). Active Database Systems: Triggers and Rules for Advanced Database Processing. Morgan Kaufmann, San Francisco, California (1996).

6. I. Ben-Shaul and S. Ifergan. WebRule: An Event-based Framework for Active Collaboration among Web Servers. In Computer Networks and ISDN Systems, Vol. 29(8-13), October (1997) 1029-1040.

7. BEA, WebLogic Events, http://www4.weblogic.com/docs/techoverview/ em.html

8 A. Carzaniga, D.S. Rosenblum, and A.L. Wolf. Achieving Expressiveness and Scalability in an Internet-Scale Event Notification Service. In Proc. of the 19th ACM Symposium on Principles of Distributed Computing (PODC2000), Portland, OR, July (2000) 219-227.

9. NEONet, http://www.neonsoft.com/products/NEONet.html

10.S. Brandt and A. Kristensen. Web Push as an Internet Notification Service. W3C Workshop on Push Technology. http://keryxsoft.hpl.hp.com/doc/ins.html, Boston, MA, September (1997).

11.Sun Microsystems. Java Message Service API, http://java.sun.com/products/jms/, January 22 (2001).

12.Object Management Group (OMG), CORBA Notification Service, specification version 1.0. June 20 (2000).

13. Dayal, U., Blaustein, B.T., Buchmann, A.P., Chakravarthy, U.S., Hsu, M., Ledin, R., McCarthy, D.R., Rosenthal, A., Sarin, S.K., Carey, M.J., Livny, M., Jauhari, R. The HiPAC Project: Combining Active Databases and Timing Constraints. ACM Sigmod Record 17(1):51-70, (1988).

14. Gehani, N.H., Jagadish H.V. ODE as an Active Database: Constraints and Triggers. Proc. of the 17th. VLDB Conference, Barcelona, Catalonia, Spain, 327-336, (1991).

15.G. Banavar, M. Kaplan, K. Shaw, R.E. Strom, D.C. Sturman, and W. Tao. Information Flow Based Event Distribution Middleware. In Proc. of Electronic Commerce and Web-based Applications Workshop at the International Conference on Distributed Computing Systems (ICDCS99), Austin, TX, May 31 - June 4 (1999).

16. M. Franklin, S. Zdonik. A Framework for Scalable Dissemination-Based Systems. OOPSLA 1997, Proc. ACM SIGPLAN, Atlanta, Georgia, 94-105, October (1997).

Stream Integration Techniques for Grid Monitoring

Andy Cooke, Alasdair J.G. Gray, and Werner Nutt

School of Mathematical and Computer Sciences,
Heriot-Watt University, Edinburgh, UK

Abstract. Grids are distributed systems that provide access to computational resources in a transparent fashion. Providing information about the status of the Grid itself is called Grid monitoring. As an approach to this problem, we present the Relational Grid Monitoring Architecture (R-GMA), which tackles Grid monitoring as an information integration problem.

A novel feature of R-GMA is its support for integrating stream data via a simple "local as view" approach. We describe the infrastructure that R-GMA provides for publishing and querying monitoring data. In this context, we discuss the semantics of continuous queries, provide characterisations of query plans, and present an algorithm for computing such plans.

The concepts and mechanisms offered by R-GMA are general and can be applied in other areas where there is a need for publishing and querying information in a distributed fashion.

1 Introduction

Data integration systems allow a user to access several, heterogeneous data sources as if they were one *virtual* database. This is generally achieved by presenting a single global schema at which the user poses queries. A query is "translated" by a *mediator* component into one or more queries over the individual data sources. Each data source is related to the global schema by some predefined mapping. The data collected from the individual sources, in response to the user's query, are then combined together to form the answer set.

Data integration has been a popular topic in the literature. The semantics of query answering has been discussed [19, 17, 34], and several data integration systems have been described [5, 20]. More recently, researchers have considered how to support integrity constraints on a global schema [4]. However, all this body of work has been focused on *static data* sources such as databases and web pages. In this paper, we discuss data integration techniques for a set of distributed data streams.

The concept of a *data stream* is useful when we are primarily interested in how a data source *changes over time*. Data streams appear in many situations, e.g. stock market prices, sensor data, monitoring information. Recently, there has been a lot of research focus on data streams and management systems for them

S. Spaccapietra et al. (Eds.): Journal on Data Semantics II, LNCS 3360, pp. 136–175, 2004.

[2]. However, to the best of our knowledge there has been no work previously conducted on integrating distributed data streams.

A *Grid* is a collection of distributed computational resources which have been pooled to present users with a single, virtual supercomputer. In order to be able to behave as a supercomputer, components of the Grid need to be able to find out the status of other Grid components. The gathering of status information falls into the fields of fabric monitoring and network monitoring. The problem of locating and delivering this status information is known as *Grid monitoring*.

It is easily seen that a Grid monitoring system requires facilities for publishing distributed data. However, this data comes in two varieties: (i) static data which does not change regularly, e.g. the software installed on a particular computing cluster, and (ii) stream data which changes often in a short period of time, e.g. the memory load of a particular computing element. A system that supports Grid monitoring should provide a global view of the data and be able to answer queries about the current state and the history of streams as well as continuous queries, which ask for an answer stream. It needs to be scalable to allow thousands of nodes to publish, and it must be resilient if any node fails. There are also issues of privacy of data that need to be addressed.

In collaboration with the European Union's DataGrid project (2001–2004) [9], we have been involved in the development of the Relational Grid Monitoring Architecture (R-GMA) as a framework for realising a Grid monitoring system. A distinguishing feature of R-GMA is that it approaches Grid monitoring as a data integration task: combining existing techniques for static data integration with techniques that we have developed for integrating data streams. This allows users to query a global schema to retrieve the data they are interested in. The system will seamlessly locate all the data of interest and return it as an answer to the query.

DataGrid's aim was to build and deploy middleware for a Grid that will allow three major user groups to process and analyse the results of their scientific experiments: (i) high energy physicists who want to distribute and analyse the vast amounts of data that will be produced by the Large Hadron Collider at CERN, (ii) biologists who need to process medical images as part of the exploitation of genomes, and (iii) scientists of the European Space Agency's Earth Observation project who are analysing images of atmospheric ozone.

During the past two years, we have implemented a working R-GMA system within DataGrid. Our aim was to develop functionality that had a firm theoretical basis and that was flexible enough to quickly respond to user requirements as they became clearer. We will describe the status of our implementation at the end of the DataGrid project. R-GMA has an open-source licence and can be downloaded from [10].

The main contribution of this paper is a formal framework for developing techniques to integrate distributed data streams. A characteristic feature of the framework is that it allows one to set up so-called *republishers*, which are analogous to materialised views in that they are defined by queries over the global schema and make the answers to those queries available for further processing.

Such republishers can make answering queries over distributed stream data more efficient. For the case of selection queries over distributed streams, we present algorithms to compute execution plans that take advantage of views. Based on our framework, we show that the plans have formal properties like soundness and completeness. We have addressed these topics in the context of a Grid monitoring system. However, our approach is general and can be used wherever there is a need to publish and query distributed stream data.

The rest of the paper is structured as follows. In Section 2 we give an overview of Grid computing, outline the requirements of a Grid monitoring system and discuss how far existing techniques and systems meet these requirements. Then, in Section 3, we present an idealised architecture of a data integration system for both static and stream data in the context of Grid monitoring: this abstracts from the idiosyncrasies of the actual R-GMA implementation. Republishers allow queries to be answered more efficiently, but make query planning more involved. We define the semantics of stream queries in R-GMA in Section 4, develop characterisations for query plans in the presence of republishers in Section 5, and present an algorithm for computing query plans in Section 6. We discuss the state of the current implementation and the experiences with it in Section 7. Finally, we present our conclusions in Section 8.

2 Grid Monitoring: Overview and Requirements

We shall now present the idea of Grid computing and describe the components of a Grid. We explain what is meant by Grid monitoring and identify requirements for a Grid monitoring system.

2.1 Grids

A *Grid* is a collection of connected, geographically distributed computing resources belonging to several different organisations. Typically the resources are a mix of computers, storage devices, network bandwidth and specialised equipment, such as supercomputers or databases. A Grid provides instantaneous access to files, remote computers, software and specialist equipment [12]. From a user's point of view, a Grid is a single virtual supercomputer.

In the late 90s, the concept of a Grid emerged as a new model for pooling computational resources across organisations and making them available in a transparent fashion, using communication networks [12]. Since then, there has been a growing number of projects to construct Grids for different tasks. They include the NASA Information Power Grid [18] and TeraGrid [3] in the US, and CrossGrid [7] and DataGrid [9] in Europe. The Globus group [15] is developing the Globus Toolkit, a suite of middleware components, which are being widely used as a platform for building Grids.

To make a Grid behave as a virtual computer, various components are required that mimic the behaviour of a computer's operating system. The components of DataGrid, and their interactions, can be seen in Fig. 1 and are similar to those presented in [13]:

User Interface: allows a human user to submit and track jobs, e.g. "analyse the data from a physics experiment, and store the result".

Resource Broker: controls the submission of jobs, finds suitable available resources and allocates them to the job.

Logging and Bookkeeping: tracks the progress of jobs, informs users when jobs are completed, which resources were used, and how much they will be charged for the job.

Storage Element (SE): provides access to physical storage devices for storing data files.

Replica Catalogue: tracks where data is stored and replicates data files as required.

Computing Element (CE): provides access to a cluster of CPUs, and manages the jobs that run on these.

Monitoring System: monitors the state of the components of the Grid and makes this data available to other components.

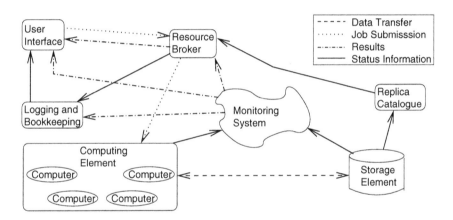

Fig. 1. The major components of DataGrid.

2.2   Grid Monitoring Requirements

The purpose of a Grid monitoring system is to make information about the status of a Grid available to users and to other components of the Grid. This is separated from the task of capturing monitoring information, which is performed locally at the computing element, storage element or between network nodes. For example, network monitoring measurements can be made using the PingER tool [23] to measure the throughput between two network nodes. The results of these local monitoring tasks are then made available across the Grid by the Grid monitoring system.

As a basis for discussing the requirements that such a system should meet, we consider the following use cases:

1. A resource broker needs to quickly (within 10 seconds) locate a computing element (CE) that has 5 CPUs available, each with at least 200 MB of memory. The CE should have the right software installed, and the user must be authorised to use it. The throughput to an SE needs to be greater than 500 Mbps.
2. A visualisation tool that is used by users to monitor the progress of their jobs needs to be updated whenever the status of a job changes.
3. Network administrators need to interrogate the past state of the network so that typical behaviour can be ascertained and anomalies identified.

Publishing Data. There are many different kinds of information about a Grid, which come from numerous sources. The following are examples:

– Measurements of network throughput, e.g. made by sending a `ping` message across the network and publishing the runtime (use cases 1 and 3 above);
– Job progress statistics, either generated by annotated programs or by a resource broker (use case 2);
– Details about the topologies of the different networks connected (use cases 1 and 3);
– Details about the applications, licences, etc., available at each resource (use case 1).

This monitoring data can be classified into two types based on the frequency with which it changes and depending on the way in which it is queried:

Static data (pools): This is data that does not change regularly or data that does not change for the duration of a query, e.g. data that is being held in a database management system with concurrency control. Typical examples are data about the operating system on a CE, or the total space on an SE (use case 1).

Dynamic data (streams): This is data that can be thought of as continually changing, e.g. the memory usage of a CE (use case 1), or data that leads to new query results as soon as it is available, for example the status of a job (use case 2).

A core requirement, then, of a Grid monitoring system is that it should allow both static and streaming data to be published. The act of publishing involves two tasks: (i) advertising the data that is available, and (ii) answering requests for that data.

Locating Data. Data about Grid components will be scattered across the Grid, and the monitoring system must provide mechanisms for users of the Grid to locate data sources.

In addition, users need a *global view* over these data sources, in order to understand relationships between the data and to query it.

Queries with Different Temporal Characteristics. A monitoring system should support queries posed over data streams, over data pools, or over a mix of these (use case 1).

It should be possible to ask about the state of a stream right now (a *latest-state* query—use case 1), continuously from now on (a *continuous* query—use case 2), or in the past (a *history* query—use case 3).

Up-to-date answers should be returned quickly, e.g. in use case 1 the resource broker requires that the data is no more than a few seconds old. To be accepted by users, the query language should capture most of the common use cases, but should not force a user to learn too many new concepts.

Scalability, Robustness, and Performance. A Grid is potentially very large: DataGrid's testbed contains hundreds of resources each producing monitoring information. In the normal use of a Grid, the fabric will be unreliable: network connections will fail and resources will become inaccessible.

It is important that the monitoring system can *scale*. It needs to be able to handle a large number of sources, publishing potentially large amounts of data. Likewise there will be a large number of users of monitoring information, both humans and grid components, who require correct answers in a timely manner. The monitoring system should not become a performance bottleneck for the entire Grid. It should be able to cope with large numbers of queries received at the same time.

The monitoring system itself should be resilient to failure of any of its components, otherwise the whole Grid could fail along with it. The monitoring system cannot have any sort of central control as resources will be contributed by organisations that are independent of each other.

Security. An information source must be able to control who can "see" its data and this must also be respected by the monitoring system. Users should be able to identify themselves so that they can make use of the resources that they are entitled to. Resources should be able to prevent access by users who are not authorised.

2.3   Possible Approaches for a Grid Monitoring System

We now discuss the fields of data stream management systems and semantic matchmaking for which several systems and prototypes exist. Here we will examine whether these could be suitable for Grid monitoring.

Data Stream Processing. Data streams show up in many different situations where dynamically changing data can be collected, e.g. stock market prices, sensor data, monitoring information. Recently, the idea of a centralised data stream management system (DSMS) has been developed, and some preliminary systems have been implemented, such as STREAM [2], Aurora [6], Tribeca [31],

Telegraph [28] and AIMS [29]. They support querying and management of relations, akin to a relational database management system, only these relations
may be either streaming or static.

These existing DSMS do not meet all the requirements of a Grid monitoring
system (Section 2.2). The centralised systems developed today would not cope
dynamically with the creation and removal of geographically distributed streams
nor coordinate the communication of data from sources to clients. This central
point would become a single point of failure as all information sources and clients
of the systems would need to interact with it.

Some work is now being carried out to distribute the query processing of a
DSMS over a cluster of machines. One such distributed DSMS is the D-CAPE
system [32]. However, this is still tightly coupled and essentially a centralised
DSMS.

Another interesting contribution to the processing of data streams is the
dQUOB project [26]. In dQUOB, precompiled trigger queries, called "quoblets",
are inserted into the distributed data streams. These quoblets then filter the
stream at, or near, the source and perform some processing on the data contained. However, as the queries must be precompiled they cannot easily handle
the ad hoc one-off queries found in Grid monitoring. There is also no support
for querying the latest-state or the history of a stream as required of a Grid
monitoring system.

Semantic Matchmaking. In the area of web services, and multi agent systems, there is a need to match service requests with service descriptions. These
service descriptions, and likewise requests, include information about the processing performed by the service, the parameters taken as inputs and the results
provided as output. However, since web services cover a wide area of domains,
e.g. train tickets, air travel, etc, it is not possible, or even desirable, to agree on
one standardised vocabulary. As such, ontologies are used to relate terms from
differing domains which leads to approximate matches being found for service
requests. These techniques have been deployed in systems [21, 25].

The problem domain of Grid monitoring differs from that of matching service
descriptions. In Grid monitoring we are dealing with one fixed domain, so it
is possible to fix a single, standardised vocabulary. Thus we do not need to
reason about how closely related terms are in an ontology and can retrieve exact
semantic matches for requests of monitoring data.

2.4   Existing Grid Monitoring Systems

Several Grid monitoring systems have been developed to this date: AutoPilot [27], CODE [30], and the Monitoring and Discovery Service (MDS) [8], to
name some of them. MDS, being part of the Globus Toolkit [15], is the most
widely known among these systems.

Monitoring and Discovery Service (MDS). The main components of MDS
are *information providers,* which publish monitoring data at Grid locations, and

aggregate directories, which collect them and make them available for querying. Aggregate directories can be organised in hierarchies, with intermediaries that forward their data to other directories at higher levels.

Also, data is organised hierarchically in a structure that provides a name space, a data model, wire protocols and querying capabilities. MDS exists currently in its third incarnation. Previous versions were based on the LDAP data model and query language. The latest version is based on XML and supports the XPath query language.

Although the hierarchical architecture makes it *scalable*, MDS does not meet other requirements outlined in Section 2.2. Firstly, hierarchical query languages have limitations. For one, the hierarchy must be designed with popular queries in mind. Moreover, there is no support for users who want to relate data from different sections of the hierarchy—they must process these queries themselves.

Secondly, to be able to offer a global view of the Grid to users, a hierarchy of aggregate directories must be set up manually—information providers and intermediary directories need to know which directory further up the hierarchy to register with. The system does not automate this, nor does it recover if any component in the hierarchy fails.

Lastly, MDS only supports latest-state queries with no assurance that the answers are up-to-date. It is claimed that users can create archives of historical information by (i) storing the various latest-state values that have been published via MDS in a database and by (ii) providing an interface to allow the system to access the database. However, this approach would require considerable effort on the side of the user.

3   The R-GMA Approach

The R-GMA approach differs from those discussed before by the fact that it perceives Grid monitoring as a data integration problem. The Grid community has proposed the Grid Monitoring Architecture as a general architecture for a Grid monitoring system. However, this architecture does not specify a data model, nor does it say how queries are to be answered. We have extended this architecture by choosing the relational data model, and by applying ideas that originated in the area of data integration. In this section we present an idealised architecture. While this is guiding the implementation work, the actual R-GMA system as deployed in DataGrid differs from it in several ways. Details of the current implementation of R-GMA can be found in Section 7.

3.1   The Grid Monitoring Architecture

The Grid Monitoring Architecture (GMA) was proposed by Tierney *et al.* [33] and has been recommended by the Global Grid Forum [14] for its scalability. It is a simple architecture comprising three main types of actors:

Producers: Sources of data on the Grid, e.g. a sensor, or a description of a network topology.

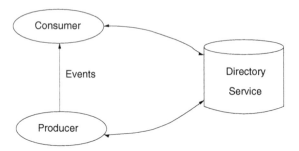

Fig. 2. The components of the GMA and their interactions

Consumers: Users of data available on the Grid, e.g. a resource broker, or a
system administrator wanting to find out about the utilisation of a Grid
resource.
Directory Service: A special purpose component that stores details of producers and consumers to allow consumers to locate relevant producers of
data.

The interaction of these actors is schematically depicted in Fig. 2. A producer
informs the directory service of the kind of data it has to offer. A consumer
contacts the directory service to discover which producers have data relevant
to its query. A communication link is then set up directly with each producer
to acquire data. Consumers may also register with the directory service. This
allows new producers to notify any consumers that have relevant queries.

Intermediary components may be set up that consist of both a consumer and
a producer. Intermediaries may be used to forward, broadcast, filter, aggregate
or archive data from other producers. The intermediary then makes this data
available to other consumers from a single point in the Grid.

By separating the tasks of information discovery, enquiry, and publication,
the GMA is *scalable*. However, it does not define a data model, query language,
or a protocol for data transmission. Nor does it say what information should be
stored in the directory service. There are no details of how the directory service
should perform the task of matching producers with consumers.

3.2   R-GMA as a Virtual Database

R-GMA builds upon the GMA proposal by choosing the relational data model.
Components playing the part of a consumer need to be able to locate and retrieve
data of interest (Section 2.2). R-GMA achieves this by presenting a "virtual
database" into which all monitoring data appears to flow. As in a real database,
the data in the virtual database conforms to a relational schema. It is this *global
schema* that allows consumers to locate data of interest.

Consumers describe the monitoring data that they are interested in by posing
queries against the global schema. The data is provided by a number of producers

who each have a *local schema*. R-GMA uses the idea of a mediator [35] to match a consumer's request for data with the advertisements of data registered by producers.

In order for R-GMA to be able to present the illusion of a virtual database, extra components are needed. These components, along with their interactions, are shown in Fig. 3. In the rest of this section, we shall introduce each component, and explain the rationale behind its design: consumers, producers, consumer and producer agents, schema, republishers and registry.

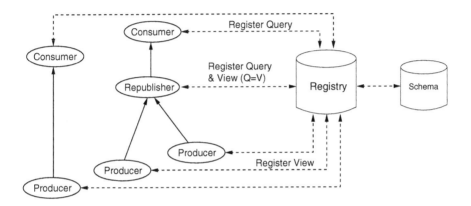

Fig. 3. Components of R-GMA

3.3 Roles and Agents

R-GMA takes up the consumer and producer metaphors of the GMA and refines them. An R-GMA installation allows clients, which may be Grid components or applications running on the Grid, to *play the role* of an information *producer* or a *consumer*.

Producers. In order that both data pools and streams can be published, two producer roles should be supported: a *database producer* and a *stream producer*. A database producer publishes a collection of relations maintained in a relational database. A stream producer publishes a collection of streams, each of which complies with the schema of a specific relation. We refer to these static or streamed relations as the *local relations* of a producer.

A producer advertises its local relations by describing them as simple views on the global schema. In the current implementation of R-GMA, the views can only be selections.

Consumers. A consumer is defined by a relational query. If the query is posed over stream relations, then the consumer has to declare whether it is to be

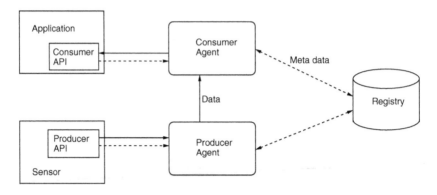

Fig. 4. Roles and agents of R-GMA.

interpreted as a continuous, a history or a latest-state query (see Section 2.2). Once the execution of a continuous query has started, the consumer receives the answer as a stream of tuples.

Agents. R-GMA provides *agents* that help clients to play their roles. The interactions of producers and consumers with their agents is illustrated in Fig 4. To play a role, an application uses an API, which in turn communicates with a remote agent. All of the functionality required to play the role is provided by the agent. Agents are realised using Java servlet technology, and are hosted in web servers. Details are discussed in Section 7.

3.4   The Schema

To interact with each other, producers and consumers need a common *language* and *vocabulary*, in which producers can describe the information they supply and consumers the information for which they have a demand. In R-GMA, both the language for announcing supply and the one for specifying demand—that is, the query language—are essentially fragments of SQL. The vocabulary consists of relations and attributes that make up a global schema, which is stored in R-GMA's *schema* component.

Ideally the global schema distinguishes between two kinds of relations, *static* and *stream* relations. The two sets are disjoint. The global schema contains a core of relations that exist during the entire lifetime of an installation. In addition, producers can introduce new relations to describe their data, and withdraw them again if they stop publishing.

The attributes of a relation have types as in SQL. In addition to its declared attributes, every stream relation has an additional attribute timestamp, which is of a type DateTime and records the the time a tuple was published.

For both kinds of relations, a subset of the attributes can be singled out as the *primary key*. Primary keys are interpreted as usual: if two tuples agree on the key attributes and the timestamp, they must also agree on the remaining attributes. However, since data are published by independent producers, the constraint cannot be enforced.

For stream relations, the keys play an additional semantic role. The key attributes specify the parameters of a reading, i.e. they identify "where" and "how" a reading was taken. The rest of the attributes, except the timestamp, are the *measurement attributes*, i.e. the attributes that state "what" the current reading is.

For instance, R-GMA's schema contains the core relation ntp for publishing readings of the throughput of network links. The relation has the schema

ntp(from, to, tool, psize, latency, timestamp),

which records the time it took (according to some particular tool) to transport packets of a specific size from one node to another. All attributes except latency make up the primary key of ntp.

Intuitively, a specific set of values for the key attributes of a stream relation identify a *channel* along which measurements are communicated. For example, for the ntp relation with the tuple

('hw', 'ral', 'ping', 256, 93, 2004-03-17 14:12:35),

measuring a latency of 93 ms for a 256 byte ping message between Heriot-Watt University and Rutherford Appleton Laboratories on Wednesday 17 March 2004 at 2:12 pm, the channel is identified by the values

('hw', 'ral', 'ping', 256).

Consumers pose queries over the global schema. For example, suppose we are interested to know how long it will take to copy the file myData, containing experimental data, from the storage elements where it is stored to the cluster workerNode where it is to be processed. Suppose also the global schema contains the ntp relation defined above and a static file allocation table

fat(site, file),

which tracks which files are stored at which sites.

Using these relations we can gather the required information with the SQL-like query

```
SELECT LATEST N.from, N.psize, N.latency
FROM   ntp as N, fat as F
WHERE  N.from = F.site and
       F.file = 'myData' and
       N.to = 'workerNode' and
       N.tool = 'ping',
```

which asks for the sites where the file is stored and the most up-to-date information about the network throughput, based on the ping tool, from those sites to the cluster that will perform the processing. The query uses the keyword "LATEST", which in R-GMA indicates that this is a latest-state query (see Section 3.5 for more details on temporal query types). This information can then be used to calculate which will be the fastest site to transfer the file from.

Similarly, producers are able to describe their local relations as views on the global schema. In Halevy's terminology [17], this means that R-GMA takes a "local as view" approach to data integration.

3.5   Producers and Consumers: Semantics

At present, R-GMA requires that producers declare their content using views *without projections*. Thus, each producer contributes a set of tuples to each global relation. This allows us to give an intuitive semantics to an R-GMA installation: a static relation is interpreted as the union of the contributions published by the database producers; a stream relation is interpreted as a global stream obtained by merging the streams of all the stream producers.

A *static query* is interpreted over the collection of all static relations, while a *continuous query* is conceptually posed over the virtual global stream. An *history query* refers to all tuples that have ever been published in the stream. Finally, a *latest-state query* posed at time t_0 refers to the set of tuples obtained by choosing from each active channel the last tuple published before or at time t_0.

Actually, the semantics of stream relations is not as well-defined as it may seem because it does not specify an order for the tuples in the global stream. We do not guarantee a specific order on the entire global stream. However, we require that global streams are *weakly ordered*, that is, for a given channel the order of tuples in the global stream is consistent with the timestamps. This property ensures that aggregation queries on streams that group tuples according to channels have a well-defined semantics. As we shall see later on, it also facilitates switching between query plans. We explain in Sections 5 and 6 how one can enforce this constraint.

We are aware that our semantics of stream relations causes difficulties for some kinds of queries, for instance, aggregate queries over sliding windows where the set of grouping attributes is a strict subset of the keys. In such a case, different orderings of a stream can give rise to different query answers. We have not yet dealt with this issue.

Among the three temporal interpretations of stream queries, only continuous queries are supported by default by a stream producer agent. However, when a stream producer is created, the agent can be instructed to maintain a pool with the history and/or the latest-state of the stream. This would enable it to answer queries of the respective type. The creation of these pools is optional because their maintenance will impact on the performance of the stream producer agent.

3.6   Republishers

Republishers in R-GMA resemble materialised views in a database system. A republisher is defined by one or more queries over the global schema and publishes the answers to those queries. The queries either have to be all continuous or all one-time queries. Republishers correspond also to the intermediaries in the GMA. Their main usage is to reduce the cost of certain query types, like continuous queries over streams, or to set up an infrastructure that enables queries of that type in the first place, like latest-state or history queries.

A republisher combines the characteristics of a consumer and a producer. Due to the redundancy of information created by republishers, there are often several possibilities to answer a query. Section 6 describes how this is taken into account in the construction of query execution plans for simple stream queries.

In principle, two types of republisher are conceivable, corresponding to the distinction between static and stream relations. However, the current implementation of R-GMA supports only stream republishers.

Stream Republishers. Stream republishers pose a continuous query and output the answer stream. All stream republishers can answer continuous queries. In addition, similar to a stream producer agent, a stream republisher agent can be configured to maintain also a pool of latest-state values or a history so that it can answer also latest-state and history queries.

Since both input and output are streams, one can build *hierarchies* of stream republishers over several levels. An important usage for such hierarchies is to bundle small flows of data into larger ones and thus reduce communication cost.

Stream producers often publish data obtained from sensors, such as the throughput of a network link measured with a specific tool. While such primary flows of data, to elaborate on the metaphor, tend to be trickles, with stream republishers they can be combined into streams proper. For instance, stream republishers may be used to first collect data about the network traffic from one site and then, at the next level up, between the sites belonging to an entire organisation participating in a Grid. Thus a consumer asking for network throughput on all links from a particular site need only contact the republisher for that site or for the organisation instead of all the individual stream producers.

Database Republishers. A database republisher will pose a one-time query at a set of published databases and make the answer available as a *materialised view*. This is useful for pre-computing union and join queries where the source relations are distributed across the Grid.

Applications of R-GMA in DataGrid have shown a clear need for this functionality. It has been met so far by periodically publishing static relations as streams and by using a stream republisher with latest-state pool to collect the union of those relations. This approach is bound to become unfeasible as the size of applications increases. Instead, view maintenance techniques will be needed to propagate only changes of the underlying data instead of the full data sets.

3.7   The Registry

We refer to producers and republishers together as *publishers*. Consumer agents need to find publishers that can contribute to answering their query. This is facilitated by R-GMA's *registry*, which records all publishers and consumers that exist at any given point in time. Publishers and consumers send a heartbeat to the registry at predefined intervals to maintain their registration.

When a new publisher is created, its agent contacts the registry to inform it about the type of that publisher and, if it is a stream publisher, whether it maintains latest-state or history pools. If the publisher is a producer, the agent registers its local relations together with the views on the global schema that describe their content. If it is a republisher, the agent registers its queries. Similarly, when a consumer is created, the consumer's agent contacts the registry with the consumer's query.

The registry cooperates with the consumer agent in constructing a query plan. It identifies publishers that can contribute to the answers of that query, called the *relevant* publishers. In the current implementation, the registry informs the agent of *all* relevant publishers. Due to the existence of republishers, there may be some redundancy among the relevant publishers. In the future, the registry may exploit this to reduce the amount of information sent to the agent. It could do so by informing the agent only of the publishers that contribute maximally to the query, called *maximal* relevant publishers, while ignoring those that are subsumed by a maximal one. Based on the list of publishers it has received, the agent constructs a query plan. (In Section 6 we discuss how to choose maximal relevant publishers and how to create plans for the case of continuous selection queries over streams.)

When a consumer registers a continuous query, R-GMA ensures that during the entire lifetime of the consumer it can receive all the data the query asks for. At present, whenever a new producer registers, the registry identifies the consumers to which this producer is relevant and notifies their agents. Then the agent integrates the new producer into its query plan. A refined approach would consist in informing a consumer only about a new producer if the producer is not subsumed by a relevant republisher (see Section 6 for further details). Consumer agents need to be informed as well when a republisher goes offline because then the consumer may miss data that it has received via that republisher. Similarly, the registry has to contact a consumer agent if a new relevant republisher is created and when a producer goes offline.

4   A Formal Model of Stream Queries in R-GMA

Most often, applications seeking information require the latest-state or the history of several stream relations to be joined and aggregated. As an example, consider the query presented in Section 3.4 where the consumer is interested in calculating how long it will take to transfer their experimental data from a storage element where it is stored, to the cluster which will process it. Such a query can be processed if we exploit republishers for the relations ntp and fat based at each site. Suppose there are n sites $site_1, \ldots, site_n$. Each of these site republishers would pose a query of the form

```
SELECT *
FROM    ntp
WHERE from = site_i,
```

which can be represented in relational algebra as $\sigma_{from=site_i}(\mathsf{ntp})$. Similarly, for the relation fat the republisher would hold the view $\sigma_{site=site_i}(\mathsf{fat})$. Then the query of Section 3.4 can be processed by posing it locally to each site republisher and taking the union of the answers. This is due to the fact that the query only joins ntp and fat tuples that agree on the site attribute.

The query could equally be answered by a republisher that had the full fat relation available and that collected together all of the ping measurements of the ntp relation, i.e. a republisher that poses the query

$$\sigma_{tool='ping'}(\mathsf{ntp}).$$

A consumer agent could discover automatically that queries like the one in the example can be answered locally. If a query is monotonic, the answers generated by merging the local answers are always correct. For such a query, the agent would only have to make sure that no answers are lost if this approach is taken. In fact, this can be detected by satisfiability checks involving the join conditions of the query and the selection conditions of the views held by the republishers.

Queries can be answered efficiently if a hierarchy of stream republishers has been set up to collect the data needed. As shown in the example above, by using the pools maintained by the republishers, complex latest-state and history queries can also be answered.

For the monitoring applications we have encountered so far it is sufficient if consumers and republishers pose simple continuous queries that are selections over a single relation. Although this is a very restricted form of query, its semantics in a data integration scenario like R-GMA's is not straightforward.

In this and the subsequent sections we introduce a formalism to define the meaning of simple stream queries that are posed against a global schema, while data are provided by stream producers and republishers. Since data can only be obtained from publishers, a global query has to be translated into a plan, that is, a query over the local stream relations of the publishers. Part of the difficulty of the problem stems from the fact that a republisher offers a stream of data, but at the same time has to run a plan to acquire its data.

Fig. 5 shows a consumer, producers, and a hierarchy of republishers for the throughput relation ntp. For each component, the query or descriptive view, respectively, is indicated by a condition involving the attributes of ntp. The bold lines leading to each republisher indicate how data can flow through the hierarchy, while the dashed lines leading to the consumer represent publishers that are relevant to the consumer query. We will refer to the situation depicted in the figure to illustrate the query plans that our techniques will generate.

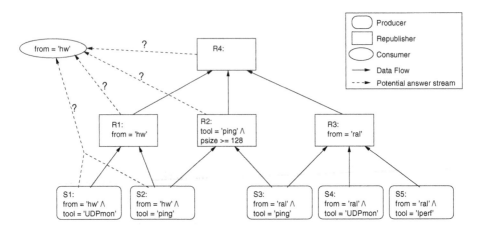

Fig. 5. A hierarchy of stream republishers for ntp.

In the present section we define a formal framework for publishing and querying distributed streams with the help of a global schema. This will be used in Section 5 to develop characterisations of query plans. In Section 6 we discuss how to compute query plans for consumers and republishers.

4.1 Streams and Their Properties

We formalise data streams as finite or infinite sequences of tuples. To capture the idea that a stream consists of readings, each of which is taken at a specific point in time, we assume that one attribute of each stream tuple is a timestamp.

More precisely, suppose that T is the set of all tuples. Then a stream s is a partial function from the natural numbers $\mathbb{N}$ to T,

$$s \colon \mathbb{N} \hookrightarrow T,$$

such that, if $s(n)$ defined for some $n \in \mathbb{N}$, the tuple $s(m)$ is defined for all $m < n$. Thus, $s(n)$ denotes the nth tuple of s. We write $s(n) = \bot$ if the nth tuple of s is undefined. A special case is the empty stream, also denoted as $\bot$, which is undefined for every $n \in \mathbb{N}$.

We have chosen to model data streams in this way as it allows different tuples to have the same timestamp and tuples to arrive in an order independent of their timestamp. Thus, we have no requirements about how regularly a reading can be taken nor do we require that readings are published in chronological order.

Suppose r is a relation with a relation schema, specifying a type for each attribute. We define as usual when a tuple satisfies the schema. A stream satisfies the schema if all its tuples satisfy it. We assume from now on that a relation schema is declared for every stream and that the stream satisfies its *local* schema.

Properties of Data Streams. As in Section 3, we assume that the attributes of a stream relation are split into three parts: key attributes, measurement attributes and the timestamp.

We specify the following shorthands for the subtuples of $s(n)$ relating to these three parts:

$s^\kappa(n)$ for the values of the key attributes;
$s^\mu(n)$ for the values of the measurement attributes;
$s^\tau(n)$ for the timestamp of $s(n)$.

We use this notation to formalise the channels of a stream. We say that a stream s_1 is a *substream* of s_2 if s_1 can be obtained from s_2 by deleting zero or more tuples from s_2. A *channel* of s is a maximal substream whose tuples agree on the key attributes of s. For every tuple t occurring in s, where t^κ is the subtuple of t that contains the values of the key attributes, the substream of s consisting of the tuples with $s^\kappa(n) = t^\kappa$ is the *channel* of t^κ.

The following properties of streams are central to our discussion of the semantics of stream queries.

Duplicate Freeness: A stream s is *duplicate free* if for all m, n with $m \neq n$ we have that $s(m) \neq s(n)$, that is, if no tuple occurs twice in s.

Weak Order: A stream s is *weakly ordered* if for all m, n with $s^\kappa(m) = s^\kappa(n)$ and $m < n$ we have that $s^\tau(m) < s^\tau(n)$. This means that in every channel of s, tuples appear in the order of their timestamps. Note that this definition is equivalent to requiring that for all m, n with $s^\kappa(m) = s^\kappa(n)$ and $s^\tau(m) < s^\tau(n)$ we have that $m < n$.

Channel Disjointness: Two streams s_1 and s_2 are *channel disjoint* if for all m, n we have that $s_1^\kappa(m) \neq s_2^\kappa(n)$, that is, if s_1 and s_2 have no channels in common.

Operations on Streams. We define two simple operations on streams. Let s be a stream and suppose that C is a condition involving attributes of the schema of s, constants, operators "=", "$\leq$", "$\geq$", and boolean connectives. Then the *selection* $\sigma_C(s)$ of s is the stream that consists of the tuples in s that satisfy C where those tuples appear in the same order as they do in s.

Let $s_1, \ldots, s_n$ be streams for relations with compatible schemas. A stream s is a *union* of $s_1, \ldots, s_n$ if s can be obtained by merging these streams, i.e. , if each s_i contributes all its tuples to s, and the tuples of s_i occur in s in the same order as they do in s_i.

Note that the result of a selection is unique, while this is not the case for a union. Note also that (i) streams resulting from these operations are weakly ordered if the argument streams are, and that (ii) the result of a union is duplicate free it the argument streams are mutually disjoint.

4.2   Stream Producers

A *stream producer* is a component that is capable of producing a data stream. Every stream producer has a local relation schema. We denote both, stream producers and their local relations, with the letter S.

Local Queries over Stream Producers. We want to pose queries over stream producers. We call such queries *local queries* as opposed to *global queries*, which are posed over a global schema.

The queries we consider are unions of selections of the form

$$Q = \sigma_{C_1}(S_1) \uplus \ldots \uplus \sigma_{C_m}(S_m), \tag{1}$$

where $S_1, \ldots, S_m$ are distinct stream producers whose schemas are mutually compatible. A special case is the empty union, written ε.

To define the semantics of such a query, we have to associate a stream to each producer. A *stream assignment* over a set of producers is a mapping $\mathcal{I}$ that associates to each producer S a stream $S^\mathcal{I}$ that is compatible with the schema of S. A stream s is an *answer* for Q w.r.t. $\mathcal{I}$ if s is a union of the selections $\sigma_{C_1}(S_1^\mathcal{I}), \ldots, \sigma_{C_m}(S_m^\mathcal{I})$. We remind the reader that an answer is not uniquely defined, since there is more than one way to merge the selections $\sigma_{C_i}(S_i^\mathcal{I})$. The empty union ε has only one answer, namely the empty stream $\perp$.

Producer Configurations. We want to formalise collections of stream producers as they can be created in R-GMA. We assume there is a *global schema* $\mathcal{G}$, which is a collection of stream relations. A *producer configuration* consists of a finite set $\mathcal{S}$ of stream producers and a mapping v that associates to each producer $S \in \mathcal{S}$ a query v_S over the global schema $\mathcal{G}$ such that v_S is compatible with the schema of S. If no confusion arises we will also denote the producer configuration with the letter $\mathcal{S}$. In R-GMA, producer configurations are represented in the schema and the registry.

We call v_S the *descriptive view* of the producer S. In this paper we limit ourselves to descriptive views that are selections, that is, they have the form $\sigma_D(r)$ where D is a condition and r is a global relation.

To keep things simple we require, if S is described by the view $\sigma_D(r)$, that S and r have the same attributes and the same type and key constraints. We also require that the condition D in $\sigma_D(r)$ involves *only key attributes* of r. Thus, the view restricts the channels of a producer, but not the possible measurements of the readings.

Instances of Producer Configurations. A producer configuration is similar to a database schema. It contains declarations and constraints, but no data. We want to define which streams are the possible instances of such a configuration.

We say that a stream s is *sound* w.r.t. a query $\sigma_D(r)$ over the global schema if the schema of s is compatible with the schema of r and if every tuple $s(n)$ satisfies the view condition D.

An assignment $\mathcal{I}$ for the producers in a configuration $\mathcal{S}$ is an *instance* of $\mathcal{S}$ if for every $S \in \mathcal{S}$ the stream $S^{\mathcal{I}}$ is (i) sound w.r.t. the descriptive view $v(S)$, (ii) duplicate free and (iii) weakly ordered and if, moreover, (iv) distinct producers have channel disjoint streams.

4.3   Global Queries and Query Plans

Consumer components in R-GMA pose queries over the global schema and receive a stream of answers. The only queries over the global schema that we consider in this section are selections of the form

$$q = \sigma_C(r),$$

where r is a global relation.[1] Since the relation r does not refer to an existing stream it is not straightforward what the answer to such a query should be.

Intuitively, we understand that query q is posed against a virtual stream, made up of all the small streams contributed by the producers. We say that a producer S *produces for* the relation r if S is described by a view over r. If $\mathcal{I}$ is a producer instance then an *answer* for q w.r.t. $\mathcal{I}$ is a duplicate free and weakly ordered stream that consists of those tuples satisfying C that occur in streams $S^{\mathcal{I}}$ of producers S which produce for r. Note that, according to our definition, there can be infinitely many different answer streams for a query q. Any two answer streams consist of the same tuples, but differ regarding the order in which they appear.

Note also that we have not postulated that tuples occur in the same order as in the original producer streams. We only require that the tuples of a channel appear in the same order as in the stream of the publishing stream producer. This makes it possible for streams to be split and then re-merged during processing.

Since global queries cannot be answered directly, they need to be translated into local queries. We say that a local query Q is a *plan* for a global query q if for every producer instance $\mathcal{I}$ we have that all answer streams for Q w.r.t. $\mathcal{I}$ are also answer streams for q w.r.t. $\mathcal{I}$.

The following proposition gives a characterisation of plans that use only stream producers.

Proposition 1 (Plans Using Producers). *Let* $Q = \sigma_{C_1}(S_1) \uplus \ldots \uplus \sigma_{C_m}(S_m)$ *be a local query where each S_i is described by a view $\sigma_{D_i}(r)$ and let $q = \sigma_C(r)$ be a global query. Then Q is a plan for q if and only if the following holds:*

1. for each $i \in 1..m$ we have that

$$C_i \wedge D_i \models C \qquad and \qquad C \wedge D_i \models C_i; \tag{2}$$

2. every stream producer S with a descriptive view $\sigma_D(r)$ such that $C \wedge D$ is satisfiable occurs as some S_i.

---

[1] It would be straightforward to generalise our work to unions and projections, although it would complicate the presentation.

Proof. The first condition ensures that any producer occurring in Q contributes only tuples satisfying the query and that it contributes all such tuples that it can possibly produce. The second condition ensures that any producer that can possibly contribute occurs in the plan.

Since by assumption all S_i are distinct and the streams of distinct producers are channel disjoint, all answers of Q are duplicate free. Also, by the definition of union of streams, all answers are weakly ordered.   □

The proposition can be immediately translated into an algorithm to compute plans. For instance, in the scenario of Fig. 5, it would yield the plan $Q = \sigma_{true}(\mathsf{S1}) \uplus \sigma_{true}(\mathsf{S2})$. We discuss in Section 6 how to compute plans in the presence of republishers.

5   Query Plans Using Republishers

We introduce republishers and generalise query plans accordingly. Then we develop characteristic criteria that allow one to check whether a local query over arbitrary publishers is a plan for a glolal query.

5.1   Republishers and Queries over Republishers

A *republisher* R is a component that is defined by a global query $q_R = \sigma_D(r)$. For a given instance $\mathcal{I}$ of a producer configuration the republisher outputs a stream that is an answer to q_R w.r.t. $\mathcal{I}$. The descriptive view $v(R)$ of a republisher is identical to the defining query q_R. A *republisher configuration* $\mathcal{R}$ is a set of republishers.

Publisher Configurations. Since both producers and republishers publish streams, we refer to them collectively as *publishers*. Ultimately, we want to answer global queries using arbitrary publishers.

We define a *publisher configuration* as a pair $\mathcal{P} = (\mathcal{S}, \mathcal{R})$ consisting of a producer and a republisher configuration. By abuse of notation, we shall identify $\mathcal{P}$ with the set $\mathcal{S} \cup \mathcal{R}$.

A stream assignment $\mathcal{J}$ for publishers in $\mathcal{P}$ is an *instance* of $\mathcal{P}$ if (i) the restriction $\mathcal{J}_{|\mathcal{S}}$ of $\mathcal{J}$ to $\mathcal{S}$ is an instance of $\mathcal{S}$ and if (ii) for every republisher R the stream $R^{\mathcal{J}}$ is an answer for the global query q_R w.r.t. $\mathcal{J}_{|\mathcal{S}}$. Thus, an instance $\mathcal{J}$ is "essentially" determined by $\mathcal{J}_{|\mathcal{S}}$. Note that $R^{\mathcal{J}}$ being an answer for a global query implies that $R^{\mathcal{J}}$ is duplicate free and weakly ordered.

Local Queries over Publishers. In the presence of republishers we generalise our local queries, which had the form (1), in such a way as to allow them to be posed over arbitrary publishers. Thus, general local queries have the form

$$Q = \sigma_{C_1}(P_1) \uplus \ldots \uplus \sigma_{C_m}(P_m), \tag{3}$$

where $P_1, \ldots, P_m$ are distinct publishers.

A stream s is an *answer* for Q w.r.t. $\mathcal{J}$ if s is a union of the selections $\sigma_{C_1}(P_1^{\mathcal{J}}), \ldots, \sigma_{C_m}(P_m^{\mathcal{J}})$.

Similarly as before, we say that a local query Q as in Equation (3) is a *plan* for a global query q if for all instances $\mathcal{J}$, every answer for Q is an answer for q.

We are interested in characterising when a local query over a publisher configuration is a plan for a global query. Republishers add to the difficulty of this task because they introduce redundancy. As a consequence, answers to such a query need not be duplicate free or weakly ordered.

5.2   Properties of Plans

We first identify the characteristic properties of plans. They are defined in terms of the properties of the answers to a query.

Consider a fixed publisher configuration $\mathcal{P}$ and let Q be a query over $\mathcal{P}$ as in Equation (3). We say that Q is *duplicate free* if for all instances $\mathcal{J}$ of $\mathcal{P}$ all answer streams for Q w.r.t. $\mathcal{J}$ are duplicate free. In a similar way, we define when Q is *weakly ordered*. Let q be a global query. We say that Q is *sound* for q if for all instances $\mathcal{J}$ of $\mathcal{P}$ all answer streams for Q w.r.t. $\mathcal{J}$ are sound for q. A stream s is *complete* for q w.r.t. a producer instance $\mathcal{I}$ if every tuple in an answer stream for q w.r.t. $\mathcal{I}$ occurs also in s. We say that Q is *complete* for q if for all instances $\mathcal{J}$ all answer streams for Q w.r.t. $\mathcal{J}$ are complete for q w.r.t. $\mathcal{J}_{|S}$.

Clearly Q is a plan for q if and only if Q is (i) sound for q, (ii) complete for q, (iii) duplicate free, and (iv) weakly ordered. For soundness and completeness one would expect characterisations similar to those in Propostion 1. However, with republishers there is the difficulty that the descriptive views do not accurately describe which data a republisher offers in a given configuration. For instance, a republisher may always publish the empty stream if the configuration does not contain any producers whose views are compatible with the republisher's query.

Given a publisher configuration $\mathcal{P}$, we derive for every republisher R, defined by the query $\sigma_D(r)$, a new condition D' as follows. Let $S_1, \ldots, S_n$ be all producers for r in $\mathcal{P}$, where $v(S_i) = \sigma_{E_i}(r)$. Then we define

$$D' = D \wedge \left(\bigvee_{i=1}^{n} E_i \right).$$

Intuitively, D' describes which of the tuples that can actually be produced in $\mathcal{P}$ will be republished by $\mathcal{R}$. We call $v'(R) := \sigma_{D'}(r)$ the *relativisation* of $v(R)$ w.r.t. $\mathcal{P}$. For a producer S we define the relativisation $v'(S)$ to be equal to $v(S)$. Note that an empty disjunction is equivalent to *false* and therefore the relativised condition for a republisher that does not have producers is *false*.

5.3   Soundness

First, we give a characterisation of soundness.

Theorem 1. *Let $\mathcal{P}$ be a publisher configuration, $q = \sigma_C(r)$ a global query, and*

$$Q = \sigma_{C_1}(P_1) \uplus \cdots \uplus \sigma_{C_m}(P_m) \tag{4}$$

be local query over $\mathcal{P}$. Suppose that the descriptive view of P_i is $v(P_i) = \sigma_{D_i}(r)$ and that the relativisation is $v'(P_i) = \sigma_{D'_i}(r)$. Then Q is sound for q if and only if for each $i \in 1..m$ we have that

$$C_i \wedge D'_i \models C. \tag{5}$$

Proof. Clearly, if Equation (5) holds, then every tuple in an answer to $\sigma_{C_i}(r)$ over $\mathcal{P}$ satisfies C, and so does every tuple in an answer to Q over $\mathcal{P}$.

Conversely, if Equation (5) does not hold, then there is a tuple t that satisfies some C_i and D'_i, but not C. Since the argument is simpler if P_i is a producer, we assume without loss of generality that P_i is a republisher.

Since t satisfies D'_i, there is a producer S with $v(S) = \sigma_E(r)$ such that t satisfies D_i and E. Let $\mathcal{J}$ be an instance where the stream $S^{\mathcal{J}}$ contains t. Then the stream $P_i^{\mathcal{J}}$ contains t as well, because $P_i^{\mathcal{J}}$ is an answer for $\sigma_{D_i}(r)$. Then t is in every answer stream for $\sigma_{C_i}(P_i)$ and therefore in every answer stream for Q w.r.t. $\mathcal{J}$. However, t does not occur in any answer stream for Q because t does not satisfy C. $\qquad\square$

It is easy to see that the criterion of the theorem above can be weakened to a sufficient one if instead of Equation (5) we require that for each $i \in 1..m$ we have

$$C_i \wedge D_i \models C, \tag{6}$$

where D_i is the original condition in the descriptive view of P_i.

5.4   Completeness

To characterise completeness, we distinguish between the producers and the republishers in a local query. The reason is that the stream of a republisher is always complete for its descriptive view while this need not be the case for a producer.

Let Q be a query as in Equation (4) and suppose that $R_1, \ldots, R_k$ are the republishers and $S_1, \ldots, S_l$ the stream producers among $P_1, \ldots, P_m$. Then we can write the query as $Q = Q^{\mathbf{R}} \uplus Q^{\mathbf{S}}$ where

$$Q^{\mathbf{R}} = \sigma_{C_1}(R_1) \uplus \cdots \uplus \sigma_{C_k}(R_k) \tag{7}$$

$$Q^{\mathbf{S}} = \sigma_{C'_1}(S_1) \uplus \cdots \uplus \sigma_{C'_l}(S_l). \tag{8}$$

Suppose that the republishers have the descriptive views $v(R_i) = \sigma_{D_i}(r)$.

We define a condition $C_Q^{\mathbf{R}}$, which summarises the conditions in the selections of the republisher part $Q^{\mathbf{R}}$ of Q, as follows:

$$C_Q^{\mathbf{R}} = \bigvee_{j=1}^{k} (C_j \wedge D_j). \tag{9}$$

Theorem 2. *Let $\mathcal{P}$ be a publisher configuration, $q = \sigma_C(r)$ a global query, and $Q = Q^{\mathbf{R}} \uplus Q^{\mathbf{S}}$ a local query where $Q^{\mathbf{R}}$ and $Q^{\mathbf{S}}$ are as in Equations (7) and (8). Then Q is* complete *for q if and only if for every stream producer $S \in \mathcal{P}$, where S is described by the view $\sigma_E(r)$, one of the two following statements hold:*

1. *$S = S_i$ for some producer S_i in $Q^{\mathbf{S}}$ and*

$$C \wedge E \models C_Q^{\mathbf{R}} \vee C_i'; \tag{10}$$

2. *S does not occur in $Q^{\mathbf{S}}$ and*

$$C \wedge E \models C_Q^{\mathbf{R}}. \tag{11}$$

Proof. We only give a sketch. A full proof is not difficult but tedious.

To see that the criterion is sufficient note that any tuple in an answer for q must satisfy C and must originate from some producer for r with view condition E. Let S be such a producer. A tuple returned by Q can occur either as an element of an answer for $Q^{\mathbf{R}}$ or as an element of an answer for $Q^{\mathbf{S}}$. If S is present in Q, then Equation (10) guarantees that a tuple produced by S is either returned by $Q^{\mathbf{R}}$ or by $Q^{\mathbf{S}}$. If S is not present in Q, then Equation (11) guarantees that a tuple produced by S is returned by $Q^{\mathbf{R}}$.

To see that the criterion is necessary, assume that there is producer S for which none of the two statements holds. Suppose that S occurs in $Q^{\mathbf{S}}$. Then there is a tuple t such that t satisfies $C \wedge E$, but satisfies neither $C_Q^{\mathbf{R}}$ nor C_i'. There exists an instance $\mathcal{J}$ of $\mathcal{P}$ such that t occurs in the stream $S^{\mathcal{J}}$. Every answer for q w.r.t. $\mathcal{J}$ contains t. However, t does not occur in any answer for Q w.r.t. $\mathcal{J}$. With a similar argument one can show that t does not occur in any answer for Q if S does not occur in $Q^{\mathbf{S}}$. In summary, this proves that Q is not complete for q. $\qquad\square$

5.5   Duplicate Freeness

Next, we give a characterisation of duplicate freeness.

Theorem 3. *Suppose $\mathcal{P}$ is a publisher configuration and Q a local union query over publishers $P_1, \ldots, P_m$ as in Equation (3). Suppose that the relativised descriptive view of each P_i is $v'(P_i) = \sigma_{D_i'}(r)$. Then Q is* duplicate free *if and only if the condition*

$$(C_i \wedge D_i') \wedge (C_j \wedge D_j') \tag{12}$$

is unsatisfiable for each republisher P_i and publisher P_j where $i \neq j$.

Proof. If the statement is true, then for any instance $\mathcal{J}$, the streams $\sigma_{C_i}(P_i^{\mathcal{J}})$ are mutually disjoint and every answer of Q is duplicate free because the streams $\sigma_{C_i}(P_i^{\mathcal{J}})$ are duplicate free.

If the statement is not true, then there are i and j with $i \neq j$ and a tuple t such that t satisfies both $C_i \wedge D_i'$ and $C_j \wedge D_j'$. Suppose that P_i is a republisher and P_j is a producer. Consider an instance $\mathcal{J}$ where t occurs in the stream $P_j^{\mathcal{J}}$ of the producer P_j. Since P_i is a republisher, t occurs also in the stream $P_j^{\mathcal{J}}$. Finally, since t satisfies both C_i and C_j, the tuple occurs in both streams, $\sigma_{C_i}(P_i^{\mathcal{J}})$ and $\sigma_{C_j}(P_j^{\mathcal{J}})$. Hence, there is an answer to Q where the tuple t occurs twice.

If both P_i and P_j are republishers, one can show that there is a producer S with view $\sigma_E(r)$ such that $D_i \wedge D_j \wedge E$ is satisfiable. Then one chooses a satisfying tuple t and considers an instance $\mathcal{J}$ where $S^{\mathcal{J}}$ contains t. The rest of the argument is analogous to the first case.   □

Similar to Theorem 1, we can turn the criterion of the above theorem into a sufficient one if we replace in Equation (12) the relativised conditions D_i' by the view conditions D_i, that is, if we require that

$$(C_i \wedge D_i) \wedge (C_j \wedge D_j) \tag{13}$$

is unsatisfiable for each republisher P_i and publisher P_j where $i \neq j$.

5.6   Weak Order

The following lemma gives a semantic characterisation of weakly ordered queries.

Lemma 1. *Let $\mathcal{P}$ be a publisher configuration and $Q = \sigma_{C_1}(P_1) \uplus \cdots \uplus \sigma_{C_m}(P_m)$ be a local query. Then Q is weakly ordered if and only if for all publishers P_i, P_j with $i \neq j$ occurring in Q and for every instance $\mathcal{J}$ of $\mathcal{P}$ the following holds:*

If t and t' are tuples occurring in the two streams $\sigma_{C_i}(P_i^{\mathcal{J}})$ and $\sigma_{C_j}(P_j^{\mathcal{J}})$, respectively, then t and t' disagree on their key attributes.

The lemma holds because otherwise the two streams in question could be merged in such a way that t and t' occur in an order that disagrees with their timestamps. The lemma excludes, for instance, the possibility to use two republishers $R_{>10}$ and $R_{\leq 10}$ with views $\sigma_{\mathsf{latency}>10}(\mathsf{ntp})$ and $\sigma_{\mathsf{latency}\leq 10}(\mathsf{ntp})$, respectively, for answering the query $\sigma_{\mathsf{true}}(\mathsf{ntp})$. The reason is that, latency being a measurement attribute, some tuples of a given channel could end up being republished by $R_{>10}$ and others by $R_{\leq 10}$.

Since in the end, we are interested in characterising plans for global queries, we ask next when a local query is weakly ordered *and* complete for some global query q. Considering these two properties together has the advantage that it leads to a characterisation in terms of the individual disjuncts that make up a union query.

Lemma 2. *Let $\mathcal{P}$ be a publisher configuration and $Q = \sigma_{C_1}(P_1) \uplus \cdots \uplus \sigma_{C_m}(P_m)$ be a local query. Suppose that Q is complete for the global query $\sigma_C(r)$. Then Q is weakly ordered if and only if for every publisher P_i occurring in Q and every instance $\mathcal{J}$ of $\mathcal{P}$ the following holds:*

If the stream $\sigma_{C_i}(P_i^{\mathcal{J}})$ contains some tuple t that satisfies C, then this stream contains every tuple t' that is generated by a producer for r such that t' satisfies C and t' agrees with t on the key attributes.

This lemma follows immediately from the preceding one: if it is impossible for two publishers to publish tuples from the same channel, then all tuples of one channel must come from the same publisher.

Lemma 2 can be formalised in logic. We write the condition C of query q as $C(x,y)$, where x stands for the vector of key attributes of r, which identifies a channel, and y for the non-key attributes. Similarly, we write the conditions C_i in query Q and D'_i in the relativised descriptive views as $C_i(x,y)$ and $D'_i(x,y)$ and we abbreviate the conjunction $C_i(x,y) \wedge D'_i(x,y)$ as $F_i(x,y)$.

Theorem 4. *Let $\mathcal{P}$ be a publisher configuration, Q a local query over $\mathcal{P}$, where $Q^{\mathbf{R}} = \sigma_{C_1}(R_1) \uplus \cdots \uplus \sigma_{C_k}(R_k)$, and $q = \sigma_C(r)$ a global query. Suppose that Q is complete for q w.r.t. $\mathcal{P}$. Then Q is weakly ordered if and only if for all $i \in 1..k$ we have*

$$\exists y.\,(C(x,y) \wedge F_i(x,y)) \models \forall y.\,(C(x,y) \rightarrow F_i(x,y)). \tag{14}$$

Proof. Suppose that Equation (14) holds for all $i \in 1..k$. Consider an instance $\mathcal{J}$ of $\mathcal{P}$. We want to show the claim using Lemma 2.

Suppose that $t = (t_x, t_y)$ is a tuple in the stream $\sigma_{C_i}(R_i^{\mathcal{J}})$ obtained from a republisher R_i. Then t_x satisfies $\exists y.\,(C(x,y) \wedge F_i(x,y))$. By Equation (14), it follows that t_x also satisfies $\forall y.\,(C(x,y) \rightarrow F_i(x,y))$. Let $t' = (t_x, t'_y)$ be a tuple that is generated by a producer for r and agrees with t on the key attributes. Suppose that t' satisfies C. Then, since t_x satisfies $\forall y.\,(C(x,y) \rightarrow F_i(x,y))$, it follows that t' also satisfies F_i. Hence, t' occurs also in the stream $\sigma_{C_i}(R_i^{\mathcal{J}})$.

Since producer streams do not share channels, Lemma 2 yields the sufficiency of the criterion.

We now show the necessity. Suppose that Equation (14) does not hold for some $i \in 1..k$. Then there is a tuple $t = (t_x, t_y)$ that satisfies $C \wedge F_i$ and a tuple $t' = (t_x, t'_y)$ such that t' satisfies C, but not F_i. By definition of F_i, the tuple t satisfies C_i, D_i, and some condition E for a stream producer S with descriptive view $\sigma_E(r)$. We construct an instance $\mathcal{J}$ where both t and t' occur in the stream of S. Then t occurs in every answer to $\sigma_{D_i}(r)$, the defining query of R_i, and thus in $R_i^{\mathcal{J}}$. Moreover, t occurs in the stream $\sigma_{C_i}(R_i^{\mathcal{J}})$. However, since t' does not satisfy F_i, it does not occur in that stream. Hence, by Lemma 2 it follows that Q is not weakly ordered. □

We note that the proof above would go through as well if we changed Equation (14) into

$$\exists y.\,(C(x,y) \wedge C_i(x,y) \wedge D'_i(x,y)) \models \forall y.\,(C(x,y) \rightarrow C_i(x,y) \wedge D_i(x,y)),$$

that is, if we replace D'_i by D_i on the right hand side of the entailment. This formulation, however, is less concise.

Let us review that part of the proof above that shows the sufficiency of the fact that Equation (14) holds for all $i \in 1..k$ for the claim of Theorem 4. It turns out that it goes through as well if we define

$$F_i(x,y) = C_i(x,y) \wedge D_i(x,y), \tag{15}$$

that is, if we replace relativised by original view conditions. Thus, Equation (15) leads to a simpler albeit sufficient criterion for weak order.

The entailment in Equation (14) of Theorem 4 is in general difficult to check because of the universal quantifier. However, it can be simplified if in queries and in descriptive views the conditions on key and on non-key attributes are decoupled, that is, if every condition $C(x, y)$ can be written equivalently as $C^\kappa(x) \wedge C^\mu(y)$ (and analogously C_i and D_i, and therefore also F_i). This restriction is likely not to cause difficulties in practice.

Theorem 5. *Suppose* $C(x, y) \equiv C^\kappa(x) \wedge C^\mu(y)$ *and* $F_i(x, y) \equiv F_i^\kappa(x) \wedge F_i^\mu(y)$. *Then*

$$\exists y.\, (C(x, y) \wedge F_i(x, y)) \models \forall y.\, (C(x, y) \rightarrow F_i(x, y))$$

holds if and only if one of the following holds:

1. $C^\kappa(x) \wedge F_i^\kappa(x)$ *is unsatisfiable;*
2. $C^\mu(y) \wedge F_i^\mu(y)$ *is unsatisfiable;*
3. $C^\mu(y) \models F_i^\mu(y)$.

We omit the proof of the theorem, since it is elementary, but tedious. Again, we obtain a sufficient criterion if in the definition of the F_i we replace the relativised view conditions by the original ones.

The theorems in this subsection contain characterisations that allow us to verify whether a local query is a plan for a global query. As we have seen, the characterisations can be simplified to yield sufficient criteria for soundness, duplicate freeness and weak order.

In the next section we discuss how the characterisations can be used to compute query plans over a publisher configuration. Specifically, these techniques can be used to realise hierarchies of republishers where republishers consume from other republishers.

6   Computing Query Plans

Based on the characterisations in the previous section, there is a straightforward approach to constructing a plan Q for a global query $q = \sigma_C(r)$. If $S_1, \ldots, S_n$ is a sequence comprising all stream producers in a configuration $\mathcal{P}$ that publish for relation r, then by Proposition 1 the query

$$\sigma_C(S_1) \uplus \cdots \uplus \sigma_C(S_n) \tag{16}$$

is a plan for q. This plan, however, may access a higher number of publishers than necessary because it does not make use of republishers. The question arises when a publisher is potentially useful for a query.

General Assumption. *We assume from now on that in global queries and descriptive views the conditions on key and non-key attributes are decoupled, that is, every condition C can be equivalently rewritten as $C^\kappa \wedge C^\mu$, where C^κ involves only key attributes and C^μ involves only non-key attributes.*

6.1   Relevant Publishers

We want to find out which publishers can potentially contribute to a query plan.

We say that a publisher P is *strongly relevant* for a query q w.r.t. to a configuration $\mathcal{P}$ if there is a plan Q for q that contains a disjunct $\sigma_{C'}(P)$ such that for some instance $\mathcal{J}$ of $\mathcal{P}$ the stream $\sigma_{C'}(P^{\mathcal{J}})$ is non-empty.

Proposition 2 (Strong Relevance). *Let $\mathcal{P}$ be a publisher configuration and P a publisher with view $\sigma_D(r)$, where $D = D^\kappa \wedge D^\mu$, and where D' is the relativised view condition. Let $q = \sigma_C(r)$ be a global query where $C = C^\kappa \wedge C^\mu$. Then P is strongly relevant for q w.r.t. $\mathcal{P}$ if and only if*

1. *$C \wedge D'$ is satisfiable, and*
2. *$C^\mu \models D^\mu$.*

Proof. If P is strongly relevant, then Statement 1 holds because P contributes some tuple to q and Statement 2 holds by Theorem 4 because the plan containing P is complete and weakly ordered.

Conversely, suppose the two statements hold. If P is a producer we construct an instance where P produces a tuple satisfying C. Then P can be part of a plan as in Equation (16). Because of Statement 1 there is an instance where P contributes at least one tuple to the answer of the plan.

If P is a republisher, we consider the query $Q = \sigma_C(P) \uplus \sigma_{C'}(S_1) \uplus \cdots \uplus \sigma_{C'}(S_n)$, where $S_1, \ldots, S_n$ are all producers for r in $\mathcal{P}$ and $C' = C \wedge \neg D$. Then it is easy to check that Q is duplicate free and sound and complete for q. Moreover, because of Statement 2, Q is weakly ordered. Finally, Statement 1 allows us to construct an instance of $\mathcal{P}$ where P actually contributes to Q.   □

Criterion 1 of Proposition 2 involves relativised views. In practice, this is hard to check because there may be a large number of producers in a configuration and producers may come and go. We therefore generalise the criterion in such a way that it depends solely on the publisher and the query. We say that a publisher P with view $\sigma_D(r)$, where $D = D^\kappa \wedge D^\mu$, is *relevant* for a query $\sigma_C(r)$ with $C = C^\kappa \wedge C^\mu$ if it has the following two properties:

1. $C \wedge D$ is satisfiable   (Consistency);
2. $C^\mu \models D^\mu$ (Measurement Entailment).

Intuitively, the first property states that P can potentially contribute values for *some* channels requested by q, while the second states that for those channels *all* measurements requested by q are offered by P.

Clearly, strong relevance implies relevance. Also, a relevant republisher may become strongly relevant if the right producers are added to the current configuration.

Consider the scenario in Fig. 5. Let $q = \sigma_{\text{from}='\text{hw}'}(\text{ntp})$ be the query of the consumer. Then S1, S2, R1, R2 and R4 are the relevant publishers for q. They are also strongly relevant.

6.2 Subsumption of Publishers

In principle, there is a wide range of possibilities to construct query plans in the presence of republishers. We want to give preference to republishers over producers, since one of the main reasons for setting up republishers is to support more efficient query answering. Among the republishers, we want to prefer those that can contribute as many channels as possible to a query. In order to be able to rank publishers we introduce a subsumption relationship.

We say that a stream s_1 is *subsumed* by a stream s_2 if for every channel c_1 in s_1 there is a channel c_2 in s_2 such that c_2 is a substream of c_1. A publisher P is *subsumed* by a republisher R w.r.t. a configuration $\mathcal{P}$, if for every instance $\mathcal{J}$ of $\mathcal{P}$ the stream $P^{\mathcal{J}}$ is subsumed by $R^{\mathcal{J}}$. Since $\mathcal{P}$ is usually clear from the context, we denote this simply as $P \preceq R$. We say that P is *strictly subsumed* by R and write $P \prec R$ if P is subsumed by R but not vice versa.

The definition entails that if P has the view $\sigma_{D^\kappa \wedge D^\mu}(r)$ and R the view $\sigma_{E^\kappa \wedge E^\mu}(r)$, then P is subsumed by R if and only if

$$D^\kappa \models E^\kappa \qquad \text{and} \qquad E^\mu \models D^\mu. \tag{17}$$

Consider a query $q = \sigma_C(r)$, where $C = C^\kappa \wedge C^\mu$. We want to rank relevant publishers for q also according to the channels they can contribute to q. If P is a relevant publisher for q and R a relevant republisher, then we say that P is *subsumed by R w.r.t. q*, and write $P \preceq_q R$, if for every instance $\mathcal{J}$ of $\mathcal{P}$ the stream $\sigma_C(P^{\mathcal{J}})$ is subsumed by $\sigma_C(R^{\mathcal{J}})$. We write $P \prec_q R$ to express that P is strictly subsumed by R w.r.t. q.

If the descriptive view of P is $\sigma_{D^\kappa \wedge D^\mu}(r)$ and the one of R is $\sigma_{E^\kappa \wedge E^\mu}(r)$, then $P \preceq_q R$ if and only if

$$D^\kappa \wedge C^\kappa \models E^\kappa. \tag{18}$$

The property $C^\mu \wedge E^\mu \models C^\mu \wedge D^\mu$ is always satisfied, since the relevance of R and P implies that $C^\mu \models E^\mu$ and $C^\mu \models D^\mu$.

In the scenario of Fig. 5, among the relevant publishers for q we have the subsumption relationships S1 $\prec_q$ R1, S2 $\prec_q$ R1, R2 $\prec_q$ R1, R1 $\preceq_q$ R4, and R4 $\preceq_q$ R1.

6.3 Plans Using Maximal Relevant Republishers

We present a method for constructing query plans that consist of publishers that are maximal with regard to the subsumption relation "$\preceq_q$". We suppose that the publisher configuration and the query $q = \sigma_C(r)$ are fixed.

A relevant publisher is *maximal* if it is not strictly subsumed by another relevant publisher. Let M_q be the set of maximal relevant publishers for q. We partition M_q into the subsets $M_q^{\mathbf{S}}$ and $M_q^{\mathbf{R}}$, consisting of stream producers and republishers, respectively.

We write $P_1 \sim_q P_2$ if $P_1 \preceq_q P_2$ and $P_2 \preceq_q P_1$. Note that a producer is never equivalent to another publisher because it cannot subsume the other publisher. Thus, the relation "$\sim_q$" is an equivalence relation on the set of republishers $M_q^{\mathbf{R}}$

and we say that R_1 is *equivalent to* R_2 *w.r.t.* q if $R_1 \sim_q R_2$. We denote the equivalence class of a republisher R w.r.t. q as $[R]_q$. Clearly, if P_1 and P_2 are two distinct maximal relevant publishers, and $P_1 \preceq_q P_2$, then $P_1 \sim_q P_2$.

We call

$$\mathcal{M}_q^{\mathbf{R}} = \left\{ [R]_q \mid R \in M_q^{\mathbf{R}} \right\}$$

the *meta query plan* for q. The set $\mathcal{M}_q^{\mathbf{R}}$ consists of equivalence classes of maximal relevant republishers. A sequence $\langle R_1, \ldots, R_k \rangle$ of republishers that is obtained by choosing one representative from each class of republishers in $\mathcal{M}_q^{\mathbf{R}}$ is called a *supplier sequence* for q.

Let $\langle R_1, \ldots, R_k \rangle$ be a supplier sequence for q and $S_1, \ldots, S_l$ be the stream producers in $M_q^{\mathbf{S}}$. Suppose the descriptive views of the R_i have the conditions D_i. We define the *canonical republisher query* for the sequence as

$$Q^{\mathbf{R}} = \sigma_{C_1}(R_1) \uplus \cdots \uplus \sigma_{C_k}(R_k), \tag{19}$$

where $C_1 = C$ and $C_i = C \wedge \neg(D_1 \vee \cdots \vee D_{i-1})$ for $i \in 2..k$. Moreover, we define the *canonical stream producer query* as

$$Q^{\mathbf{S}} = \sigma_{C_1'}(S_1) \uplus \cdots \uplus \sigma_{C_l'}(S_l), \tag{20}$$

where $C_j' = C \wedge \neg(D_1 \vee \ldots \vee D_k)$ for $j \in 1..l$.

The selection conditions on the disjuncts in $Q^{\mathbf{R}}$ ensure that R_i only contributes channels that no $R_{i'}$ with $i' < i$ can deliver, and the ones in $Q^{\mathbf{S}}$ that producers only contribute channels that cannot be delivered by the republishers.

Note that the conditions C_i depend on the order of republishers in the sequence, but once the order is fixed, they do not depend on which republisher is chosen from an equivalence class. This is due to the fact that for relevant republishers R and R' with descriptive conditions D and D', respectively, we have that $R \sim_q R'$ if and only if $C \wedge D$ is equivalent to $C \wedge D'$, that is, if and only if $C \wedge \neg D$ is equivalent to $C \wedge \neg D'$. Similarly, for all supplier sequences the conditions C_j' are the same up to equivalence.

Theorem 6. *Let q be a global query a $Q^{\mathbf{R}}$ and $Q^{\mathbf{S}}$ be the canonical republisher query and stream producer query for some supplier sequence for q. Then*

$$Q = Q^{\mathbf{R}} \uplus Q^{\mathbf{S}} \tag{21}$$

is a plan for q.

Proof. We only sketch the proof. To prove that Q is a plan, we have to show that Q is sound and complete for q, duplicate free and weakly ordered.

The conditions in the selections of Q satisfy Equation (6) and thus ensure soundness. They also satisfy Equation (13) and thus ensure duplicate freeness. Completeness is guaranteed because Q satisfies the properties stated in Theorem 2 because maximal republishers are chosen for Q, together with producers that are not subsumed by a republisher. Finally, Q is weakly ordered because the republishers used in Q are relevant and thus satisfy the Measurement Entailment Property. □

Continuing the discussion of the example in Fig. 5, we see that R1 and R4 are the maximal relevant publishers for the consumer query. Since both republishers are equivalent w.r.t. q, the local queries $\sigma_{from='hw'}(R1)$ and $\sigma_{from='hw'}(R4)$ are both plans for q.

As another example, let us consider the query $q' = \sigma_{true}(ntp)$, by which the top level republisher is defined. For this query, all publishers are relevant (except R4, for which we do the planning). Moreover, subsumption and subsumption w.r.t. q' coincide. There are three maximal publishers, R1, R2, R3, none of which is equivalent to another publisher. Thus $\langle R1, R2, R3 \rangle$ is a supplier sequence, and the corresponding plan is

$$\sigma_{true}(R1) \uplus \sigma_{from \neq 'hw'}(R2) \uplus \sigma_{from \neq 'hw' \wedge (tool \neq 'ping' \vee psize < 128)}(R3).$$

Computing plans that use maximal republishers involves satisfiability and entailment checks. Clearly, this makes the task intractable in the worst case if we admit arbitrary conditions. However, if conditions in queries and views are of the restricted form that R-GMA supports currently, namely conjunctions

$$attr_1\ op_1\ val_1 \wedge \ldots \wedge attr_n\ op_n\ val_n,$$

where $op_i \in \{<, \leq, =, \geq, >\}$, then both satisfiability and entailment checks are polynomial. They remain polynomial if one allows for slightly more general conditions by admitting also comparisons between attributes of the form "$attr_1\ op\ attr_2$" or limited disjunctions of the form "$attr$ in $\{val_1, \ldots, val_n\}$".

We foresee that the technique presented above will be the basis for planning consumer queries in R-GMA. For planning republisher queries, however, some modifications are needed to ensure that plans do not introduce cyclic dependencies between republishers. To avoid checking for possible cycles whenever a new republisher query is planned, it seems more feasible not to consider all republishers relevant to the query, but only those that are strictly subsumed with respect to the general subsumption relationship.

In an implementation, the responsibility for planning can be divided between registry and consumer agents. A possible way to do this is for the registry to hand the list of maximal publishers over to the consumer agent, which then decides which republisher in each class to contact. Such an approach could also reduce the communication between registry and consumer agent because an agent would only need to be notified of new producers that are not subsumed by the republishers in the meta query plan.

6.4   Irredundant Plans

A natural question to ask about the planning technique presented in the previous section is how good the plans it produces are. A way to approach this question is to ask whether or not the plans contain redundancies. To simplify the discussion, we focus only on redundancies among republishers.

We say that a local query Q *covers* a global query $q = \sigma_C(r)$ w.r.t. a publisher configuration if Q is complete for q and for every relevant republisher P for q we have

$$C \wedge D \models C_Q^{\mathbf{R}}, \tag{22}$$

where D is the condition in the descriptive view of R and $C_Q^{\mathbf{R}}$ is defined as in Equation (9). While completeness requires a query to "cover" all relevant producers, a covering query has to "cover" also all relevant republishers. Plans based on maximal republishers as introduced in the preceding subsection are always covering by construction.

Given q, a covering query Q using republishers $R_1, \ldots, R_k$ is *irredundant* if there is no covering query Q' that uses only a strict subset of $R_1, \ldots, R_k$.

We say that a condition is *simple* if it is a conjunction of comparisons of the form "*attr op val*", where *op* is one of $\leq, <, =, >$, or $\geq$. A global query is simple if its condition is simple. A configuration is *simple* if all its descriptive views are simple. A local query is *simple* if all its disjuncts have simple conditions.

Proposition 3 (Irredundancy is NP-hard). *Checking whether a covering query is irredundant is* NP-*hard. This is still the case if we consider only local queries, global queries, and configurations that are simple.*

Proof. We prove the claim by a reduction of the irredundancy problem for propositional clauses. A set of clauses Γ is said to be irredundant if there is no clause $\gamma \in \Gamma$ such that $\Gamma \models \gamma$. Irredundancy of clause sets is known to be NP-complete [22].

Suppose Γ is a clause set and $p_1, \ldots, p_n$ are the propositional atoms occurring in Γ. Let r be a relation with key attributes $a_1, \ldots, a_n$, ranging over the rational numbers. We define conditions G_i as $a_i > 0$ and $\bar{G}_i$ as $a_i \leq 0$. For every clause $\gamma \in \Gamma$ we define D_γ as the conjunction of all G_i such that $\neg p_i \in \gamma$ and all $\bar{G}_i$ such that $p_i \in \gamma$.

For each γ, let R_γ be a republisher defined by the query $\sigma_{D_\gamma}(r)$ and let $\mathcal{P}$ be the configuration consisting of all republishers R_γ. Let $q = \sigma_{true}(r)$ and let Q be the union of all $\sigma_{true}(R_\gamma)$ where $\gamma \in \Gamma$. Then Q is clearly covering q w.r.t. $\mathcal{P}$. Moreover Q is irredundant if and only if for all $\gamma \in \Gamma$ we have that

$$D_\gamma \not\models \bigvee_{\gamma' \in \Gamma \setminus \{\gamma\}} D_{\gamma'},$$

which holds if and only if $\bigwedge_{\gamma' \in \Gamma \setminus \{\gamma\}} \neg D_{\gamma'} \not\models \neg D_\gamma$. Now, it is easy see that this is the case if and only if $\bigwedge_{\gamma' \in \Gamma \setminus \{\gamma\}} \gamma' \not\models \gamma$ for all $\gamma \in \Gamma$, that is, if Γ is irredundant. $\square$

We note without proof that there are situations where all plans based on maximal relevant republishers are irreducible. Let us a call a set of operators *one-sided* if it is a two-element subset of $\{<, \leq, =\}$ or $\{>, \geq, =\}$. If all conditions in queries and views are simple and built up from a one-sided set of operators ranging over the rational numbers, then plans of the form (21) are irreducible. The reason is that if D, E, and E' are such conditions, then we have that $D \models E \vee E'$ holds if and only if $D \models E$ or $D \models E'$ holds.

6.5   Open Problems

We have set up a framework to model distributed streams that are queried via a global schema. A feature of the approach are so-called stream republishers, a view-like mechanism that allows one to create new streams that are defined by a continuous query. We have restricted the form of queries to enable us to concentrate on semantic issues, such as the meaning of a query or characteristic properties of query plans. The restrictions are reflecting the current requirements of the R-GMA Grid monitoring system, to the development of which we are contributing.

Even in this restricted framework there are a number of open issues that we have not addressed in the current paper. The most important one is how to switch from one plan to another. In its simplest form it involves replacing a republisher by an equivalent one, for instance, when a republisher experiences a failure. A slightly more difficult task is to replace a republisher by the producers that feed into it or vice versa. In doing so it is crucial that no tuples are lost and no duplicates are introduced into the answer stream.

To achieve this a consumer agent has to know where to stop consuming from old input streams and where to start consuming from new ones. We envisage protocols that make the switch on a channel by channel basis and exploit the fact that channels are weakly ordered: For each publisher in a plan, the consumer agent remembers the timestamp of the last tuple from each channel that it has received. Then it can switch that channel to a new supplier as soon as it receives from it a tuple that the old one has already delivered. Tricky situations may arise if a component fails during such a transition period.

In our discussion we have assumed that the publisher configuration is fixed. In reality, however, it changes continuously, as publishers come and go. This requires plan modification techniques that subject existing plans to changes that are as small as possible.

7   R-GMA Implementation

We have been collaborating with the European Union's DataGrid project to implement the architecture and techniques presented in this paper. By the end of the DataGrid project, a working R-GMA system had been deployed on a testbed containing 25 sites and was attracting a growing user base. In this section, we describe this implementation and indicate some of the ways the system is being used.

The system continues to be developed in a follow-on project Enabling Grids for E-Science in Europe (EGEE) [11]. One of the aims of EGEE is to prepare Grid middleware components developed in DataGrid, including R-GMA, for use in a much larger Grid being set up to support physicists working with the Large Hadron Collider (LHC) at CERN.

7.1   Overall Approach

The Grid components that play the role of producer or consumer in R-GMA are applications that are coded in several programming languages. To support these R-GMA offers APIs in C, C++, Java, Perl and Python. As it would not make sense to duplicate all of the core functionality of R-GMA in each of these languages, these APIs communicate with agents. The agents are realised using servlet technology and are hosted by web servers.

Through the approach of APIs and agents we hope to impose as small a load on the Grid components as possible. This is because the agent is responsible for all R-GMA specific functionality, e.g. answering queries posed by consumers. The load imposed on the Grid component is that of making the measurement, which is the responsibility of the fabric or network monitor, and passing the measurement to the agent.

We have seen in Section 2 that the system should be resilient to failures in the network. R-GMA achieves this by using a simple heartbeat registration protocol. Heartbeats are sent from API to agent and from agent to registry. If a problem occurs and heartbeats fail to arrive within some time interval, the receiver can assume that the sender is no longer around. The use of heartbeats does consume some network bandwidth from the Grid but this is kept low by (i) using suitable time intervals for the heartbeats and (ii) not requiring a heartbeat to be sent if a tuple has been sent instead.

Another requirement, that the system should not have a single point of failure, was not met by the end of DataGrid. Work was started on protocols for replicating the registry and schema. However, this had not been finalised by the end of the DataGrid project and is continuing in the EGEE project.

7.2   Use of R-GMA Components in DataGrid

In DataGrid, R-GMA was mainly used for publishing network monitoring data and for providing information on resources for resource brokers. In addition, it was tested for monitoring batch jobs.

Schema. R-GMA ships with a set of core relations that describe the components of a Grid and how they are related to each other. These relations are derived from a conceptual model called GLUE [16], which was defined by a number of Grid projects, including DataGrid. Users may also introduce new relations into the global schema.

To keep the system simple, R-GMA currently only supports publication of stream relations. Nevertheless, care was taken when designing the schema to separate data that changes rapidly (such as the number of free CPUs of a computing element) from more static data (e.g. lists specifying access rights of users).

Producers. As the schema only supports stream relations, R-GMA currently offers just a stream producer API for publishing data. All stream producers can answer continuous queries. In addition, the user can configure the agent to maintain the history or the latest state of the stream in a database.

In DataGrid, one use of stream producers was to periodically publish information about Grid resources for resource brokers. Dynamically changing relations were published every 30 seconds, whereas static relations were resent every hour. Fortunately, the volume of static information was moderate, as the testbed was small, and so this approach worked. However, as EGEE's testbed grows in size, mechanisms may be needed that forward only changes to "static" data sets.

Consumers. The consumer API allows users to pose continuous, latest-state and history queries in SQL. In principle, arbitrary one-time queries can be posed. However, these can only be answered if a republisher for all the tables in the query can be located. Select-project queries, on the other hand, can always be answered by contacting all of the relevant producers.

Resource brokers have complex latest-state queries. In DataGrid's testbed, each resource broker was provided with a dedicated republisher. A consumer agent acting on behalf of a resource broker then has a choice. The closest republisher is always chosen for query answering, but if that cannot be contacted for some reason, then the agent automatically switches to using another republisher.

Republishers. Stream republishers have proved useful in DataGrid, for both query answering and for archiving. However, the system does not currently support the republisher hierarchies discussed earlier. There has not been a need for these so far, as DataGrid's testbed was small.

A use case for republisher hierarchies is emerging in the EGEE project. A job submissions accounting service is needed for the LHC Grid that logs all of the jobs that run on the Grid. Data about jobs that run at individual sites is to be collected into site databases, whereas a global history is needed in a central database. Such a system could be easily configured if R-GMA supported republisher hierarchies. Also, if global republishers stream from site republishers, then it becomes easier to automatically recommence a stream that is interrupted by network failure, as the site republisher maintains a history in a database.

Registry. Currently, publishers can only register views over single relations with conditions that are conjunctions of equalities of the form "*attr* = *val*". In this simple case, views can be stored in a structured form in a relational database and the satisfiability and entailment tests for finding relevant publishers can be expressed as SQL queries.

For large Grids, support for views involving aggregation might prove useful. Republishers could then republish summaries of streams rather than whole streams, and so the volume of information flowing through a hierarchy of republishers would be reduced.

8   Conclusions

We have developed techniques for integrating data streams published by distributed data sources. This has been motivated by the Grid monitoring problem. We will now consider how well our approach addresses the issues.

8.1   Grid Monitoring as a Setting for Stream Integration

We begin by considering how closely Grid monitoring matches the abstract setting of a data integration system. Grid monitoring involves publishing data from many independent sources and querying it in a transparent manner. These are characteristics of a typical information integration setting. A number of challenges that complicate other information integration problems do not exist here, though.

Since Grids are dynamic environments where the data of interest is relatively short lived, it is not necessary to deal with legacy data. Moreover, components of a Grid obey certain naming conventions to be interoperable. This vastly simplifies the task of matching of entities in different sources when joining information and eliminates the need for sophisticated matching algorithms. Thus, in a nutshell, the case of Grid monitoring is close to the abstract settings that have been considered in theoretical work on information integration, which makes it an ideal candidate for applying these techniques [19].

8.2   R-GMA as a Grid Monitoring System

Together with the European Union's DataGrid project, we have developed and implemented R-GMA. We will now consider whether R-GMA meets the requirements identified in Section 2.2 for Grid Monitoring.

Through the role of a producer, Grid components can publish their monitoring data. The approach adopted in the architecture allows for both static and stream data to be published. However, the current implementation only allows for stream data. The schema provides a global view of all the monitoring data available. Grid components interested in monitoring data can locate and retrieve that data through the role of a consumer. This is achieved by posing a query over the global schema. The actual task of locating and retrieving the data is automated by the consumer's agent and the registry. By separating out the tasks of locating and retrieving data, the system should scale effectively.

The use of different types of temporal queries allows a user of the system to retrieve data of differing temporal characteristics: the latest-state query allows a user to find the most recent values of each measurement, the history query allows for the retrieval of previously published data and the continuous query provides consumers with a mechanism for being informed whenever a change in state occurs.

As stated in Section 7, the scalability and robustness of R-GMA is currently very limited due to the registry being a single point of failure. To overcome this, it is planned that the registry should be replicated. Also, R-GMA has a very limited security model: at present it relies on the fact that the user has authenticated themselves to the Grid and thus is authorised to use the Grid. In the future, we envision providing a more fine grained approach through the use of security views. This would allow publishers to declare who is allowed to "see" their data.

8.3   R-GMA Compared with Other Grid Monitoring Systems

Several Grid monitoring systems exist, as stated in Section 2.4, The most notable being the Monitoring and Discovery Service (MDS) which ships with the Globus Toolkit. We will now consider how R-GMA compares with MDS.

MDS and R-GMA approach the Grid monitoring problem in two different ways. MDS uses a hierarchical data model with a static name space. While this is able to capture the components of a Grid well, the use of a hierarchical model imposes limitations on queries that can be posed at MDS, as stated in Section 2.4. The use of a static name space means that new concepts cannot be easily added. Also, MDS can only answer latest-state queries.

On the other hand R-GMA uses the relational model. While it is not straightforward to design a suitable relational schema to model the components of a Grid there are several benefits: (i) arbitrary queries can be posed as the name space does not need to be designed with queries in mind; (ii) new concepts can be added to the schema by simply adding a new relation. Also, due to the republishers in R-GMA, continuous, latest-state and history queries can all be answered.

8.4   Integration Techniques

In R-GMA, consumers of monitoring information pose queries in terms of a global schema and publish their data as views on that schema. Although the current implementation of R-GMA makes only limited use of advanced data integration techniques, such as query rewriting using views, there will be a need for them as the Grids on which R-GMA is being used grow.

Query rewriting using views translates a global query into a query over a distributed set of sources, which has to be executed by a distributed query processor. Such facilities are now being made available in the public domain by the OGSA-DAI project although the code has not yet reached production quality [24].

Another future improvement of the system would be to allow more complex continuous queries. This would require additional constructs in the query language for expressing aggregates and joins over streams. Some work exists on stream query languages such as CQL [1] for expressing these more complex queries. Currently, it is unkown how to process such queries in an integration environment.

The R-GMA approach also raises new research questions. Most notably, since monitoring data often comes in streams, formal models for integrating data streams are needed. In the present paper we have defined a framework for approaching this task and applied it to a simple type of continuous queries. The generalisation to more expressive queries will be a topic of future work.

Acknowledgement

The work reported in this paper was supported by the British EPSRC under the grants GR/R74932/01 (Distributed Information Services for the Grid) and GR/SS44839/01 (MAGIK-I). The R-GMA architecture was developed jointly with the members of Work Package 3 in the European Union's DataGrid.

References

[1] A. Arasu and J. Widom S. Babu. CQL: A language for continuous queries over streams and relations. In *10th International Workshop on Database Programming Languages*, pages 1–19, Potsdam (Germany), September 2003. Springer-Verlag.

[2] B. Babcock, S. Babu, M. Datar, R. Motwani, and J. Widom. Models and issues in data stream systems. In *Proc. 21st Symposium on Principles of Database Systems*, pages 1–16, Madison (Wisconsin, USA), May 2002. ACM Press.

[3] F. Berman. From TeraGrid to Knowledge Grid. *Communications of the ACM*, 44(11):27–28, 2001.

[4] A. Calì, D. Lembo, and R. Rosati. Query rewriting and answering under constraints in data integration systems. In G. Gottlob and T. Walsh, editors, *Proc. 18th International Joint Conference on Artificial Intelligence*, pages 16–21, Acapulco (Mexico), August 2003. Morgan Kaufmann Publishers.

[5] A. Calì, S. De Nigris, D. Lembo, G. Messineo, R. Rosati, and M. Ruzzi. DIS@DIS: A system for semantic data integration under integrity constraints. In *Proc. 4th International Conference on Web Information Systems Engineering*, pages 335–339, Rome (Italy), December 2003. IEEE Computer Society.

[6] D. Carney, U. Cetintemel, M. Cherniack, C. Convey, S. Lee, G. Seidman, M. Stonebraker, N. Tatbul, and S. Zdonik. Monitoring streams—a new class of data management applications. In *Proc. 28th International Conference on Very Large Data Bases*, pages 215–226. Morgan Kaufmann Publishers, September 2002.

[7] The CrossGrid Project. http://www.crossgrid.org, July 2004.

[8] K. Czajkowski, S. Fitzgerald, I. Foster, and C. Kesselman. Grid information services for distributed resource sharing. In *10th International Symposium on High Performance Distributed Computing*, pages 181–194, San Francisco (California, USA), June 2001. IEEE Computer Society.

[9] The DataGrid Project. http://www.eu-datagrid.org, July 2004.

[10] DataGrid WP3 Information and Monitoring Services. http://hepunx.rl.ac.uk/edg/wp3/, July 2004.

[11] Enabling Grids for E-science in Europe. http://public.eu-egee.org/, July 2004.

[12] I. Foster and C. Kesselman. *The Grid: Blueprint for a New Computing Infrastructure*, chapter 2: Computational Grids, pages 15–51. Morgan Kaufmann, 1999.

[13] I. Foster, C. Kesselman, and S. Tuecke. The anatomy of the Grid: Enabling scalable virtual organization. *The International Journal of High Performance Computing Applications*, 15(3):200–222, 2001.

[14] Global Grid Forum. http://www.ggf.org, July 2004.

[15] Globus Toolkit. http://www.globus.org, July 2004.

[16] High Energy Nuclear Physics InterGrid Collaboration Board. http://www.hicb.org/glue/glue.htm, July 2004.

[17] A. Halevy. Answering queries using views: A survey. *The VLDB Journal*, 10(4):270–294, 2001.

[18] W.E. Johnston, D. Gannon, and B. Nitzberg. Grids as production computing environments: The engineering aspects of NASA's Information Power Grid. In *8th International Symposium on High Performance Distributed Computing*, pages 197–204, Redondo Beach (California, USA), August 1999. IEEE Computer Society.

[19] M. Lenzerini. Data integration: A theoretical perspective. In *Proc. 21st Symposium on Principles of Database Systems*, pages 233–246, Madison (Wisconsin, USA), May 2002. ACM Press.

[20] A.Y. Levy, A. Rajaraman, and J.J. Ordille. The world wide web as a collection of views: Query processing in the Information Manifold. In *Proc. Workshop on Materialized Views: Techniques and Applications*, pages 43–55, Montreal (Canada), June 1996.

[21] L. Li and I. Horrocks. A software framework for matchmaking based on semantic web technology. In *Proc. 12th International World Wide Web Conference*, pages 331–339, Budapest (Hungary), May 2003. ACM Press.

[22] P. Liberatore. The complexity of checking redundancy of CNF propositional formulae. In *Proc. 15th European Conference on Artificial Intelligence*, pages 262–266. IEEE, IOS Press, July 2002.

[23] W. Matthews and L. Cottrel. The pinger project. http://www-iepm.slac.stanford.edu/pinger/, July 2004.

[24] Open Grid Services Architecture–Data Access and Integration (OGSA-DAI). http://www.ogsadai.org.uk, July 2004.

[25] M. Paolucci, T. Kawamura, T.R. Payne, and K.P. Sycara. Semantic matching of web services capabilities. In *Proc. International Semantic Web Conference*, volume 2342 of *Lecture Notes in Computer Science*, pages 335–339, Chia (Sardinia, Italy), June 2002. Springer-Verlag.

[26] B. Plale and K. Schwan. Dynamic querying of streaming data with the dQUOB system. *IEEE Transactions on Parallel and Distributed Systems*, 14(3):422–432, April 2003.

[27] R.L. Ribler, J.S. Vetter, H. Simitci, and D.A. Reed. Autopilot: Adaptive control of distributed applications. In *7th International Symposium on High Performance Distributed Computing*, pages 172–179, Chicago (Illinois, USA), August 1998. IEEE Computer Society.

[28] M.A. Shah, S. Madden, M.J. Franklin, and J.M. Hellerstein. Java support for data-intensive systems: Experiences building the Telegraph dataflow system. *SIGMOD Record*, 30(4):103–114, 2001.

[29] C. Shahabi. AIMS: an Immersidata management system. In *Proc. 1st Biennial Conference on Innovative Data Systems Research*, Asilomar (California, USA), January 2003. Online Proceedings.

[30] W. Smith. A system for monitoring and management of computational Grids. In *Proc. 31st International Conference on Parallel Processing*, Vancouver (Canada), August 2002. IEEE Computer Society.

[31] M. Sullivan. Tribeca: A stream database manager for network traffic analysis. In *Proc. 22nd International Conference on Very Large Data Bases*, page 594, Bombay (India), September 1996. Morgan Kaufmann Publishers.

[32] T. Sutherland and E.A. Rundensteiner. D-CAPE: A self-tuning continuous query plan distribution architecture. Technical Report WPI-CS-TR-04-18, Worcester Polytechnic Institute, Worcester (Mass., USA), April 2004.

[33] B. Tierney, R. Aydt, D. Gunter, W. Smith, M. Swany, V. Taylor, and R. Wolski. A Grid monitoring architecture. Global Grid Forum Performance Working Group, March 2000. Revised January 2002.

[34] J.D. Ullman. Information integration using logical views. In *Proc. 6th International Conference on Database Theory*, volume 1186 of *Lecture Notes in Computer Science*, pages 19–40, Delphi (Greece), January 1997. Springer-Verlag.

[35] G. Wiederhold. Mediators in the architecture of future information systems. *IEEE Computer*, 25(3):38–49, March 1992.

Information Release Control: A Learning-Based Architecture*

Claudio Bettini[1], X. Sean Wang[2], and Sushil Jajodia[3]

[1] DICo, University of Milan, Italy, and
Center for Secure Information Systems, George Mason University, Virginia
bettini@dico.unimi.it
[2] Department of Computer Science, University of Vermont, Vermont, and
Center for Secure Information Systems, George Mason University, Virginia
xywang@cs.uvm.edu
[3] Center for Secure Information Systems, George Mason University, Virginia
jajodia@gmu.edu

Abstract. Modern information system applications involve collaboration in the form of information flow through organization boundaries. Indeed, organizations have vast amounts of information that is shared with other organizations and even the general public for various purposes. In addition to the standard network-level protections, systems usually use some access control mechanisms to protect data. However, access control systems are not designed to deal with deliberate and accidental release of information, to which the user has the authority to access but is not supposed to be released. Moreover, effective access control assumes a perfect categorization of information, which is increasingly difficult in a complex information system. Information release control is viewed as complementary to access control, and aims at restricting the outgoing information flow at the boundary of information systems. This paper presents a general architectural view of a release control system, and discusses the integration in the proposed architecture of a module for learning release control constraints. Continuous learning is applied to adjust the release control constraints in order to reduce both mistakenly released and mistakenly restricted documents. The paper describes in detail the process of learning keyword-based release control constraints.

1 Introduction

The complexity of modern information environments has been growing dramatically in the last decades. Database-centered systems as well as document-centered systems have evolved into heterogeneous environments where structured, semi-structured, and unstructured data from different sources are being exchanged, mostly through Internet technologies, within and across protected domains. Exchanged data takes the form of

---

* This paper is a revised and extended version of the one appeared in the Proceedings of the Sixth IFIP TC-11 WG 11.5 Working Conference on Integrity and Internal Control in Information Systems, 2003.

S. Spaccapietra et al. (Eds.): Journal on Data Semantics II, LNCS 3360, pp. 176–198, 2004.

public web pages, financial reports, technical white papers, biographies of personnel, memos, etc. Furthermore, the knowledge workers of the organizations send out messages for collaboration purposes. Security plays an important role in these environments in the form of secure communication, reliable authentication, and access controls. However, these security measures are not sufficient; security models and techniques are needed that can rapidly and effectively evolve to keep pace with the increasing complexity.

Traditionally, access control has been used to restrict users to limited views of available data. Although early access control models were devised for structured data, they are being extended to deal with XML data. However, access control is not always sufficient to secure complex information environments. Threats may come, for example, from incorrect categorization of information or users, derivation of inferences from legally obtained data, unauthorized exchanges of information between users, and combining data obtained from different internal sources. Indeed, according to Wiederhold [Wie00], the partitioning of the information into cells in order to appropriately restrict the access is often under-emphasized and requires a highly reliable categorization of all information to those cells. It is in the management of that categorization where many failures occur. In other words, if some information is miss-categorized, which is highly likely in a complex organization, it is possible for the sensitive information to be released to unauthorized users. A more serious threat to sensitive information comes from careless or malicious *insiders*, individuals or organizational entities with authorized access to the system. This type of threats are potentially very damaging since the access control rules (on which organizations rely heavily) are not effective. Insider threats need to be countered using several different methods, from intrusion analysis to information forensics.

In addition to the aforementioned security considerations, some legal concerns of information release need to be addressed. Depending on the category of information, an organization may wish to append disclaimers, copyright and other legal notices, and even watermarks.

In this paper we investigate Information Release Control, a complementary approach to current access control mechanisms, based on checking data not before they are extracted from data sources, but when they are being released across a gate representing a critical security boundary. The checking process is not based simply on source/destination addresses as in current firewall systems, or on simple ``dirty word" matching as in current filtering software, but on a deeper content analysis based on release constraints. We believe that release control will soon become an important component for securing and managing information of an organization. From a technical perspective, our approach is based on the specification and enforcement of release constraints. Within each constraint we separate the specification of sensitive data from the way it is matched against any outgoing document. We call the set of sensitive data *controlled items*, and the way these items are checked *matching rules*. This separation leads to more convenient management of the release control system to fit the ever-changing organizational security and legal needs, and facilitates the application and testing of new algorithms for the matching process.

The definition of a framework for release control, includes (i) the specification of appropriate formalisms to represent controlled items and matching rules, (ii) the development of techniques and tools to help security officers in the definition of release constraints, and (iii) the design and implementation of efficient matching algorithms that are capable of dealing with different matching rules and data formats. In this paper, we focus on the issues (i) and (ii). Regarding (i), we present an architectural view of the release control system, and we define a formal framework for the specification of release constraints, including the proposal of a formal language to define release constraints for XML documents. The language syntax has been devised to satisfy a list of expressiveness requirements for the representation within matching rules of relationships between controlled items and other data in XML documents. Regarding (ii), we discuss the role that learning techniques could play in the definition of release control constraints, illustrating how they can actually be applied for learning keyword-based release control constraints.

To determine what needs to be controlled at the release point, in addition to the definition of those release constraints derived from experience or high-level requirements, security officers may query the data store. We call this the "manual" method. For example, access control rules are usually adopted to restrict the access to the data store [JSSS01]. When some data have restricted access, it is likely that the release of such data should be checked. In addition, information that might be inferred through integrity constraints from restricted data should also be automatically added to the release constraints store. Furthermore, data that are similar to such restricted data may also need to be checked at the release point. Due to the involved complexity of these tasks, "automated tools" are necessary.

In the proposed learning-based approach, the security officer can give an initial sample set of documents, including both "cleared for release" documents and "restricted" documents. The system will try to learn an initial set of release control constraints from the given sample set and from pre-defined *template rules*. As the time goes by, when more and more documents are released and restricted (some of the releasing and restricting are certified by the security officer), the learning process will periodically adjust the release control constraints to do a better job: reducing the mistakenly released documents as well as the mistakenly restricted documents.

The remainder of the paper is organized as follows. In Section 2, we describe the release control architecture. In Section 3 we give a formal foundation for specifying release control constraints. We also describe a language that can be used to represent release control constraints on XML documents. In Section 4, we describe how the architecture could benefit from the integration of a learning module, and in Section 5, we give a specific example of learning keyword-based release control constraints. We discuss related work in Section 6 and conclude the paper in Section 7.

2   Release Control Architecture

The release control architecture is based on three basic components: (i) the flow of documents that are going to be released, (ii) a Data Store from which the documents are extracted/derived, and (iii) a Release Control System monitored by a security officer. Figure 1 illustrates these components and their internal structure, ignoring at this level the machinery needed for the learning process.

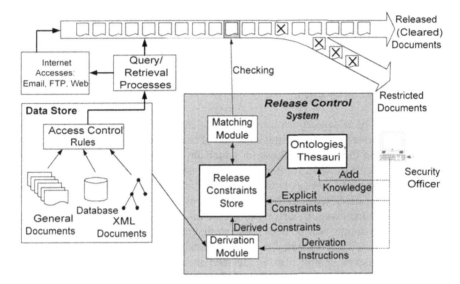

Figure 1. General architecture for release control.

The Data Store can include different types of data sources like standard relational databases, XML or other document type repositories. Documents to be released may be obtained through queries on different data sources in the Data Store as well as through access to internet/intranet services. Databases in the Data Store as well as other sources can be assumed to be protected by usual access control systems.

The main modules in the Release Control System are the *Release Constraints Store* and the *Matching Module*. The first module is the repository of release constraints and includes constraints explicitly inserted by the security officer, constraints derived from the data store with processes guided by the security officer, and constraints derived from examples of restricted and released documents by a learning process, which will be explained later in this section. An example of derivation of constraints from the data store is using the information about access control rules in order to derive sensible associations of terms directly or indirectly bounded to items whose access is forbidden by those rules. Ontologies and thesauri can also be used to derive new release constraints by identifying "semantic" similarities to the given ones. As will be described in detail in Section 3, each Release Constraint (*RC*) is a pair consisting of a list of controlled items (*CI*) and a matching rule (*R*), with the first identifying "sensitive" items (e.g., keywords) and the second specifying how these items should appear in the documents for the document to be restricted.

Optimization modules (not depicted in the figure) will operate on the Release Constraints Store. For example, the set of Release Constraints can be reduced considering the subsumption relationships along the hierarchies of matching rules and controlled items.

Example 1. Consider a corporate database that includes data about Employee's salaries and assume an internal policy prohibits the release of the salary of Mr. Woo, which is currently *75k*. Suppose a release constraint implementing this policy says that each tuple in the outgoing data should not contain the strings *Woo* and *75k*, while a second release constraint, possibly related to other policies, says that the string *Woo* should not appear anywhere in the outgoing data. In this case the first release constraint can be disregarded.

Given a set of release constraints in the Release Constraints Store, the Matching Module is responsible for checking each one of them against the outgoing documents, and for blocking the release of those for which any of the constraints is satisfied. If we assume documents in XML form, the module must contain a matching algorithm with a XML parsing component. A basic version of the algorithm may consider an explicit listing of controlled items in each release constraint, and hence, it will perform keyword-based matching. Clearly, appropriate indexing on the keywords appearing in the release constraints will be necessary, so that all applicable release constraints are efficiently selected upon reading one of the sensitive keyword in the outgoing data. Efficient techniques should also be devised in order to keep track of the current position within the list of controlled items in each release constraint. More sophisticated versions of the algorithm will consider working with compact representations of the controlled items (possibly in the form of queries).

A caching system may be devised to avoid reconsidering a document for which a decision on its release has already been made and the document has not changed since it was last considered. Clearly, such a system may be tuned to consider temporal aspects as well as differences among the users asking for release.

3   Formal Framework

For a uniform treatment, we assume the data to be checked before release is in XML format (the underlying data may be a table resulting from a database query, semistructured data or a full text document). The data are checked against a number of release constraints.

3.1   Release Constraints

A *release constraint* (*RC*) is a pair $\langle R, CI \rangle$, where R is a *matching rule* and *CI* a set of *controlled items*.

Each RC is evaluated against the data being released and it prevents its release if satisfied. Formally, each *RC* gives a mapping that assigns each document with a label in {**Restrict, Release**}. A document *Doc* can be released if for each release constraint *RC, RC(Doc)* = **Release**, i.e., in the data, the controlled items do not appear in the way given by the corresponding matching rules.

The set *CI* of controlled items is a set of tuples of the form $\langle A_1{:}a_1, A_2{:}a_2, ..., A_n{:}a_n \rangle$, where A_j are variable symbols and a_j their values. Values can range over several simple domains (including integer, string, Boolean, etc.) or even complex domains (admitting single-valued, multi-valued, or possibly structured attribute values). Variable symbols may actually denote attribute names as well as paths in the document structure. In the simplest case, variable symbols are omitted and each tuple is a list of keywords.

Syntactically, the attribute part *A* of each pair can be specified by an XPath expression, while the value part *a* can be specified by a regular expression if it is a string (e.g., to denote any word starting with a certain prefix) or, in the case it is a numerical value, it can be specified by a simple condition (op, k) with $op \in \{<, =, >, \leq, \geq\}$ and *k* being a number (e.g., to denote all values greater than or equal to a certain constant).

The matching rule *R* specifies how a document should be checked against the controlled items. As an example, when the data to be checked are answers from a database query, they can be represented as a sequence of tuples. Then, a simple matching rule may check if one of these tuples contains the attribute values specified in one of the tuples in the set of controlled items. In the case of data containing unstructured text, the rule may specify, for example, that the words in each tuple of the set of controlled items should not appear together in any *k*-words portion of the text, where *k* is a parameter defined by the specific rule. In other words, the set of controlled items essentially lists the pairs attribute-value involved in a release constraint, while the matching rule specifies their relationships.

Example 2. Continuing Example 1, we consider a corporate database that includes data about Employee's salaries and an internal policy that prohibits the release of the salary of Mr. Woo. The administrator will set up a *RC* with *CI* = {⟨*Employee:Woo, Salary:75,000*⟩} and *R* equal to the simple rule on relational query results checking all the query results being released for tuples containing the attribute values specified in *CI*. In this case, the system will check each tuple returned, as part of a database query result, making sure the values *Woo* and *75,000* do not appear in it.

Note that this is a conceptual model of release constraints. In practice, controlled items will have compact representations, in the form of SQL queries, general XQuery expressions including predicates, strings with meta-characters, or other representations.

The above formal model can be easily extended to represent overriding constraints. Their purpose is to handle exceptions when matching controlled items against outgoing documents. For example, suppose an organization is very concerned with the release of information related to electronic chips, which may be denoted by many terms, as e.g., "computer chips", "cellular phone chips", ... , or simply "chips". In this case, the security officer may set up a release constraint where the keyword "chip" is the controlled item, with a matching rule such that each document containing the keyword will be restricted. This policy clearly leads to over-restricting the information flow with undesired consequences and complaints from the users. For example, it will prevent the organization even to release documents where the word "chip" is part of the sequence "chocolate chip", which should clearly be released. Technically, in order to accommodate overriding constraints, we allow negative terms in controlled items, in the form $\neg A{:}a$. Example 3 below shows a set of controlled items with a negative term.

3.2   A Language for Matching Rules on XML Documents

The description of matching rules requires a formal language that depends on the format of outgoing documents. Since we consider XML documents, we first identified a list of expressiveness properties, which we consider necessary for our task.

1. The language should be able to express the maximum distance between all pairs of values as a pre-determined upper bound. In terms of XML this may be the number of edges in the XML tree that separate the nodes storing the values.
2. The language should be able to express the presence of certain nodes (with particular labels, semantic tagging, degree, type, e.g., leaf, root, etc.) in the path between the pair of nodes for which we consider the distance in the XML structure.
3. The language should be able to express relationships between nodes. Example of relationships include the difference in depth in the XML tree, the difference in the semantic tagging possibly attached to the nodes, the presence of a common ancestor with a specific tag, relationships between node attributes, etc.
4. The language should be able to discriminate the order of the values in the XML structure. The order may be particularly relevant in overriding. In our chocolate-chip example above, the word 'chocolate' must appear before the word 'chip'.

Based upon the above expressiveness requirements, we propose a formal language for matching rules; the language expressions can be divided into *cardinality rules* and *node-relation* rules. Each matching rule is represented as a conjunction of a cardinality rule and one or more node-relation rules.[1]

Definition 1. A *cardinality rule* has the form *NumVal* $\geq k$ where k is a positive integer and *NumVal* is a language keyword denoting the number of different values specified in the controlled items that should be observed in the document.

Hence, a cardinality rule specifies that the number of these values must be at least k, not considering negative terms in the controlled items representing overriding

---

[1] Alternative matching rules (disjunctive behavior) can be established by adding more release control rules with the same controlled items.

conditions. If no cardinality rule is given, a default cardinality rule is assumed with $k=1$; this is the most conservative choice.

Example 3. Given a set of controlled items ($A_1:a_1$, $\neg A_2:a_2$, $A_3:a_4$, $A_4:a_4$), a cardinality rule *NumVal* ≥ 2 would restrict any document that would contain at least two of the positive controlled items; i.e., either $A_1:a_1$ and $A_3:a_3$, or $A_1:a_1$ and $A_4:a_4$ or $A_3:a_3$ and $A_4:a_4$, but not containing $A_2:a_2$. In the case of XML documents, by containment of $A:a$ we mean the presence of a node/attribute identified by A and having text/value a.

In order to formally characterize node-relation rules, we define first *atomic distance formulas* and *atomic node formulas*. A set of nodes is identified in outgoing XML documents for each controlled item. For example, when the attribute part A is empty, for each controlled item value a, a node N is part of the set identified in the document if a is exactly the content of the XML element represented by N. Intuitively, node-relation rules specify properties on these nodes.

In the definitions, the notation $|P(N)|$ stands for the length of the path P in the XML tree of the document from the root to node N. Clearly, when N is the root node of the XML document, $|P(N)| = 0$.

The language also allows paths to be specified relatively to other paths by applying the following operators:

- $P_1 \cap P_2$ (Path Intersection)

- $P_1 - P_2$ (Path Difference)

- *Prefix$_k$*(P) (Path Prefix of length k)

- *Suffix$_k$*(P) (Path Suffix of length k)

Definition 2. An *atomic distance formula* has the form:

- $|P_1|$ *op* $|P_2|$, where P_1, P_2 are paths in the XML document tree and *op* is in $\{ = , \neq , >, \geq, <, \leq \}$, or
- $|P|$ *op* k where P is a path in the XML document tree, *op* is in $\{ = , \neq , >, \geq, <, \leq \}$, and k is a non-negative integer.

Definition 3. An *atomic node formula* compares a node property with a constant value or with the property of a different node. Atomic node formulas can be specified as follows:
- Comparison of values (element values identified by predicate *Value* and attribute values by predicate *AttrValue*).
- *Value*(N_1) *op* *Value*(N_2), where *op* is in $\{ = , \neq , >, \geq, <, \leq \}$ (applies only to numeric values).

- *Value(N) op k*, where *k* is an integer and *op* is in $\{ =, \neq, >, \geq, <, \leq \}$ (applies only to numeric values).
- *Value(N$_1$) rel Value(N$_2$)*, where *rel* is in $\{ =, \neq, substr, \dots \}$ (applies only to string values).
- *Value(N) rel string*, where *string* is any string and rel is in $\{ =, \neq, substr, \dots \}$ (applies only to string values).
- *AttrValue(N$_1$,attrName) op AttrValue(N$_2$,attrName)*, where *op* is in $\{ =, \neq, >, \geq, < , \leq \}$ (applies only to numeric values).
- *AttrValue(N,attrName) op k*, where *k* is an integer and *op* is in $\{ =, \neq, >, \geq, <, \leq \}$ (applies only to numeric values).
- *AttrValue(N$_1$,attrName) rel AttrValue(N$_2$,attrName)*, where *rel* is in $\{ =, \neq, substr, \dots \}$ (applies only to string values).
- *AttrValue(N,attrName) rel string*, where *string* is any string and rel is in $\{ =, \neq, substr, \dots \}$ (applies only to string values).
- Comparison of node meta properties
- *Degree(N) op k*, where *Degree(N)* denotes the number of children of *N* in the tree, *k* is a non-negative integer and *op* is in $\{ =, \neq, >, \geq, <, \leq \}$. Clearly, all leaf nodes have degree '*0*'.
- *Degree(N$_1$) op Degree(N$_2$)*, where *op* is in $\{ =, \neq, >, \geq, <, \leq \}$.
- *Order(N$_1$) op Order(N$_2$)*, where *op* is in $\{ =, \neq, >, \geq, <, \leq \}$ and *Order()* is not an attribute, but a function assigning a unique value to each node in the XML tree, according to a specific order (e.g., preorder).
- *Tag(N) rel string*, where *string* is any string and *rel* is in $\{ =, \neq, substr, \dots \}$.
- *Tag(N$_1$) rel Tag(N$_2$)*, where *rel* is in $\{ =, \neq, substr, \dots \}$.

Definition 4. A *node-relation* rule $NR(A_1:a_1, \dots, A_r:a_r)$ is represented by a Boolean *node formula*. A *node formula* is recursively defined from the set of *atomic distance formulas* and *atomic node formulas* by applying the standard conjunction and negation operators as well as quantification on nodes.

Existential quantification has the form: $\exists N \in P: F(N)$, where *N* is a node appearing in the path *P* of the XML tree and *F(N)* is a node formula. Since negation is allowed, universal quantification and disjunction are implicitly part of the language.

We now illustrate through some examples how the proposed language addresses the expressiveness requirements (1-4) listed above.

Example 4. The following matching rule *AttrValue(N$_1$,item)* = *"chip"* $\cap$ *AttrValue(N$_1$,item)* = *AttrValue(N$_2$,item)* is satisfied if the attribute *item* of node *N$_1$* has the same value *"chip"* as attribute *item* of node *N$_2$*. If we also want to check that the distance between these two nodes in the XML document is less than 3, the following language expression can be used in conjunction with the above: $|P(N_1)| + |P(N_2)| - 2 * |P(N_1) \cap P(N_2)| < 3$. This example shows how the language addresses the expressiveness requirement described at point 1 above.

Example 5. The language expression $\exists N \in P(N_1)$: $Tag(N) = <Classified> \cap \exists N' \in P(N_2)$: $Tag(N') = <Classified>$ can be used to check if in both paths leading to nodes N_1 and N_2 there is at least one node having the tag $<Classified>$. This example shows how the language addresses the expressiveness requirement described at point 2 above.

Example 6. The following matching rule

$\exists N \in Suffix_2 (P(N_1))$: $AttrValue(N,item)$ superstring "component"

is satisfied if either the parent node or the parent of the parent node of N_1 has a value for the attribute "*item*" which contains the string "*component*", as e.g., "*electronic-component*". Note that N_1 is identified by testing whether it contains one of the values in the controlled items. This example, together with the previous ones, shows how the language addresses the expressiveness requirement described at point 3 above.

Example 7. In order to check how the language addresses the expressiveness requirement described at point 4 above, consider the following language expression that could be used in an XML version of our example about the overriding constraint related to the "chocolate" "chip" occurrence: $Value(N_1) = $ "*chocolate*" $\cap Value(N_2) = $ "*chip*" $\cap Order(N_1) < Order(N_2) \cap \exists N \in Suffix_1 (P(N_1)) \cap \exists N' \in Suffix_1 (P(N_2)) \cap Order(N) = Order(N')$. Here, the first occurrence of the function $Order()$ is used to enforce document restriction only if node N_1 precedes node N_2 in the XML document. The second occurrence is used as a trick to state that nodes N and N', the parent nodes of N_1 and N_2 respectively, are actually the same node, i.e., N_1 and N_2 are siblings in the XML structure.

Note that paths in atomic distance formulas can be considered constants when a specific XML document is considered. This is different from nodes in atomic node formulas that can be both constants and variables. Indeed, they are constants if the nodes are among the ones corresponding to the values $a_1, \ldots, a_r$ in the controlled items, and variables otherwise. If they are variables they will appear in the node formula under quantification.

4   The Integration of a Learning Module

While the security officer in some cases may be able to explicitly provide both controlled items and associated matching rules, we believe there are a large number of documents to be restricted for which only more vague criteria are available. For this reason, our framework proposes the integration in the above architecture of a *Learning Module* that has the main goal of learning release constraints. In particular, in this paper we will show how the learning component can generate specific matching rules starting from controlled items, some domain knowledge, and a training set containing documents already marked as restricted or released.

In principle, given a sufficiently large training set of positive and negative examples we may ask a learning algorithm to derive controlled items and matching rules accordingly to the syntax described above. In practice, this is not a realistic requirement: the learning process, and, in particular, the extraction of features from the examples must be guided by some knowledge about the specific domain. One possibility is to start with a possible set of "critical" correlated keywords from the security officer and with a set of parameterized matching rules. For example, the security officer may consider the distance of two keywords in a document to be a relevant criterion, while the number of occurrences of keywords not to be a relevant one. In this case, the upper bound on the "distance" becomes a parameter to be tuned by the learning process.

The main issue is how to choose appropriate parameterized rules so that the algorithm may minimize the rate of mistakenly released and mistakenly restricted documents by tuning the parameters. In order to illustrate the general idea in the specific context of our matching rules, we give an example, by considering only cardinality rules. As we have observed in Section 3, the default and most conservative cardinality rule $NumVal \geq k$ is obtained by using $k=1$. The value of k may actually be used as a parameter in the learning process. For example, from the training set it may be observed that all correctly restricted documents contain at least 2 terms of the controlled items, while many mistakenly restricted ones contain only one. The value of k may then be raised to 2. Of course, there are several hypotheses on the document corpus and on the learning algorithm (including the size of the training set) that should hold to preserve a correct behavior of the system while reducing its mistakes.

In the context of security, it may be desirable to implement a learning process that preserves the following "conservativeness" property:

All documents that have been certified as restricted by the security officer will be restricted by the system.

Preserving this property implies that any derivation of new rules or refinement of existing rules must lead to a global set of release constraints that is still able to correctly classify documents that are known to be restricted.

Figure 2 depicts the Learning Module and its integration in the overall architecture, including a Monitoring Tool that will be discussed below.

4.1   The Learning Module

The learning module has two main functionalities. The first is *the derivation of release constraints for the initial set-up of the system.* As mentioned above, performing this task requires a training set of documents marked to be restricted or released, approved by the security officer; it also requires some domain knowledge, possibly in the form of controlled items and/or parametric rules. We impose that the rules obtained by the learning algorithm will preserve the conservativeness property, i.e., the system using these rules would correctly restrict at least all documents marked to be restricted in the training set. The algorithms and strategies involved in this task under specific assumptions are described in Section 5.

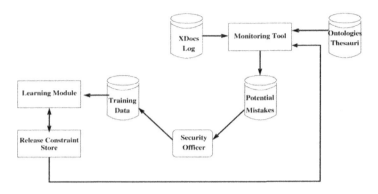

Figure 2. The Learning Module and the Monitoring Tool

The second functionality is *the refinement of the system behavior upon the identification during system operation of mistakenly released and mistakenly restricted documents*. This task is based on the assumption that the security officer monitors the system behavior and provides feedback to the learning module by dividing samples of the processed documents in four categories: correctly restricted (CRes), correctly released (CRel), mistakenly restricted (MRes), and mistakenly released (MRel). It can be considered a form of online learning since the process may automatically start once a large enough set of these samples becomes available.[2] There are essentially two approaches to perform this task: (i) Re-applying the learning process used in the initial set-up considering as the training set the new samples as well as all documents whose classification has been verified in the past by the security officer. When the set becomes too large, many strategies are possible, including, for example, the use of a sliding time window for the past, or of a "least recently used" strategy. The rules obtained through this process replace the previous ones. (ii) Refining the current rules using only the new set of CRes, CRel, MRes, and MRel documents. This is potentially a more efficient approach, since it avoids repeating the whole learning process, but details on how to implement such an incremental refinement are very dependent on the learning algorithm.

4.2   The Monitoring Tool

A critical system will have a huge number of documents flowing through it, and specific strategies must be devised to monitor its behavior in order to provide feedback to the learning module. The most trivial strategy consists of periodically extracting samples and forwarding them to the security officer, but it is likely to be unsatisfactory, since any significant frequency of sampling involves an unsustainable amount of work for the security officer.

---

[2] Actually, considering the conservativeness property, even a single example of mistakenly released document can be useful to refine the rules.

In our architecture we propose to introduce a monitoring tool that filters the documents based on a "similarity" metric so to drastically reduce the number of documents to be examined by the security officer. Note that in principle the tool should be applied both to restricted documents to identify potentially mistakenly restricted ones, and to released documents to identify potentially mistakenly released ones. However, while mistakenly restricted documents may have other ways to be recognized (e.g. feedback from users whose requests have been refused) and are less critical, the problem is serious for released ones. Also, each restricted document is associated with the release constraint (controlled items and matching rules) that has prevented its release. When the security officer examines the document this association can help recognizing the reason for the sensitivity and, in case of a mistaken restriction may lead to drop or explicitly modify a rule. Released documents on the other side have no attached information. Our focus is on tools to detect potentially mistakenly released documents.

The monitoring tool considers "similarity" of released documents to restricted ones based on the closeness of the document to the classification threshold. This technique is still based on learning and details really depend on the specific learning algorithm, but, intuitively, it works as follows: essential features of documents to be restricted and to be released can be represented by numerical values, and an n-dimensional boundary that separates the two types of documents can be found. Then, a document being examined has the same features computed and the closeness to this boundary can be evaluated. Intuitively, documents that are close to the boundary are similar both to restricted and released ones. The monitoring tool should rank the documents according to their closeness to the boundaries, so that the security officer can dynamically and asynchronously examine them. For the documents that are being released, this implies that a copy should be saved and forwarded to the security officer.

The monitoring tool also uses other techniques to identify potential MRel *documents*:
- The use of ontologies and thesauri to substitute words or structures with those that appear in controlled items.
- The explicit relaxation of some of the rules. For example, increase distance (for distance based condition), decrease cardinality, allow regular expression in the string literals, dropping rules by making them always satisfied (e.g., indefinite order, infinite distance).

Intuitively, the application of these techniques, as well as of the learning based one, should be guided by the goal of identifying a very small fraction of the released documents. This is both required due to the limited resources and, more importantly, by the implicit assumption that security officer policies are quite conservative: it is more likely that few restricted documents have been incorrectly released.

These components of the architecture operate asynchronously with respect to the main Release Constraint System.

5   Learning Keyword-Based Release Control Constraints

Learning for the purpose of obtaining specific release control constraints plays an essential role. As observed in previous sections, domain experts (possibly security officers) should guide the learning by giving relevant features that the learning process should focus on. In this section, we study, in more detail, such a *feature-based learning* when keywords-based release control constraints are considered.

In general, a feature-based learning requires that domain experts provide certain domain knowledge to the task of learning. The domain knowledge specifies what types of features are important for the task at hand. A learning mechanism is to identify the specific features, within the given types, that can be used to distinguish between different sets of documents.

We believe this approach is rather useful in practice. Indeed, in information retrieval techniques, features of texts are routinely used in deciding the relevance of documents. For example, text appearing in subject line, title, or abstract, may be more important than that appearing in the body of a document. However, the features used in information retrieval are usually "hard coded" into the information retrieval systems. This may be reasonable for documents that do not have much of structure. When a document is represented in XML, features of various types need to be considered.

Often, specific domains of applications determine the features that are important in XML documents. For example, in applications where documents are structured as a hierarchical tree (e.g., parts contain chapters, chapters contain sections, and section contain paragraphs), it is important to talk about contents belonging to a particular level of the hierarchy (e.g., two sections of the same chapter). Hence, it is important for the domain experts to specify certain 'generic' types of features that are relevant to the domain.

For release control, the above discussion about domain-specific features implies the following strategy for generating release control rules. Firstly, the domain experts specify certain type of features that they consider relevant. Secondly, the learning system discovers the conditions on the features for the release control purpose. In the following, we illustrate this approach for keyword-based release control.

5.1   Keyword-Based Features

We assume the controlled items are simply keywords, and each feature specifies a relationship based on particular ways of appearance of these keywords in a document. The "particular ways" of appearance is a type of feature given by a domain expert. We codify such features by using the notion of a *feature function*.

Definition 5. A *feature function* is a function f such that, given an XML document *Doc* and m nodes of *Doc*, it returns a tuple of n values, i.e., $f(Doc, N_1, \ldots, N_m) = (a_1, \ldots, a_n)$.

Note that the functions we define are on the nodes of XML documents. We still call them keyword-based since we will use the appearance of keywords to determine which nodes in the XML document to consider, as we will show later. Intuitively, the values returned by the feature function are values of parameters that may be automatically learned.

Example 8. The following are three example of features:

- Distance feature: $dist(Doc, N_1, N_2) = D$, where D is an integer parameter, and $dist(Doc, N_1, N_2)$ is defined as $|P(N_1)| + |P(N_2)| - 2 * |P(N_1) \cap P(N_2)|$. This feature extracts the distance between the two nodes when the document tree is viewed as a graph.
- Least common ancestor feature: $lca(Doc, N_1, N_2) = T$, where T is the tag of the node defined by $Suffix_1 (P(N_1) \cap P(N_2))$. Here T is a string and $P(N_i)$ is the path from the root of *Doc* to node N_i. This feature extracts the tag value of the lowest (in terms of the node level) common ancestor of the two given nodes.
- Ordering: $ocd(Doc, N_1, N_2) = rel$, where $Order(N_1) \; rel \; Order(N_2)$. Here, *rel* is one of the relational comparison symbols. This feature gives the order relationship between two nodes.

In the above examples, each feature function only returns one value (more specifically, a tuple with one value in it).

The above feature functions can naturally be used for specifying conditions on the appearance of keywords in XML documents. For example, given two keywords K_1 and K_2, we may want to check for their appearance within a certain distance in an XML document. This can be achieved by specifying a condition involving the distance of the nodes that "contain" K_1 and K_2, respectively. More formally, we define the notion of *occurrences of keywords* in an XML document as follows.

Definition 6. Given a set of keywords $\kappa = \{K_1, \ldots, K_n\}$ and a document *Doc*, an *m-occurrence of κ* in *Doc*, where m is an integer no greater than the number of elements in κ, is a partial mapping $occ()$ from κ to the nodes of *Doc* such that $Value(occ(K_i)) = K_i$ for each $i=1,\ldots, n$ if $occ(K_i)$ is defined, and the number of K_i with $occ(K_i)$ defined is exactly m. $occ()$ is said to be a *maximum* one if it is defined on the maximum number of keywords in κ among all the occurrences of κ in *Doc*.

The above definition may be generalized to allow mappings considering K_i, not only as the value of the XML element corresponding to the node $occ(K_i)$, as stated by the predicate *Value()* (see Section 3.2), but also as the value of any attribute of the element corresponding to $occ(K_i)$. To simplify the presentation, in the following we ignore this generalization.

Example 9. In the XML document represented in Figure 3, there are seven 2-occurrences of $\{$"A", "B", "K_3"$\}$. Note that in the XML tree representation, we only show the node values in the XML tree. Other information of the XML document is omitted. The labels within the nodes (within the circle) are meant to identify the nodes for presentation purpose, and are not part of the XML documents.

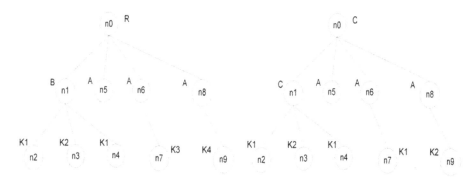

Figure 3. An XML document.   **Figure 4.** Another XML document.

Now we are ready to extract keyword-based features from XML documents. Assume the feature function takes the form $f(Doc, N_1, ..., N_m) = (a_1, ..., a_n)$. Then, the features extracted from the document via function f are represented by the set of n-tuples given as follows: $(a_1, ..., a_n)$ is a n-tuple of the set if and only if there exists an m-occurrence occ of K in Doc such that $f(Doc, occ(K_1), ..., occ(K_m)) = (a_1, ..., a_n)$.

Example 10. Given the distance feature function and the set of keywords $\{$"K_1", "K_2"$\}$, the set of features extracted from the XML document in Figure 3 is $\{(2)\}$. The set of features for the same keywords extracted from the XML document in Figure 4 is $\{(2), (4)\}$.

Together with a set of keywords (used as controlled items), a Boolean condition based on the features extracted via feature functions can be used as a release control constraint. More specifically, given a document, we extract the features using the feature functions, and then test the Boolean condition on the features. If anyone of the specific features satisfies the condition, we should block the release of the document.

Example 11. Suppose a release control constraint specifies the distance between keywords "K_1" and "K_2" to be less than 3. Then, none of the documents in Figures 3&4 can be released since each one contains at least one occurrence with distance 2. Suppose another release control constraint specifies the lowest common ancestor of keywords "K_1" and "K_2" to have value "B". Then, the document in Figure 3 cannot be released while the one in Figure 4 can.

5.2   Learning for Keyword-Based Release Control Constraints

A security officer can certainly set up a set of release control constraints by giving a set of keywords and a condition on the keyword-based features (extracted from a set of feature functions). In practice, however, it is more likely that system need to learn from a set of examples to establish the specific release control constraints. In this subsection, we will show how this may be done for keyword-based release control constraints.

As mentioned earlier, we assume that (1) a set of feature extraction functions are set up by domain experts as the likely types of features to be concerned by the release control constraints; (2) the security officer gives a collection of keyword sets to be controlled, and (3) a set of documents is provided as learning samples (i.e., the documents either cleared for release or restricted by the security officer). Given (1), (2) and (3) above, the task of learning is to give a set of release control constraints by specifying conditions on the feature values extracted by the feature functions. We now outline a method to do this. The key issue is to convert this learning problem to one where traditional learning algorithms can apply.

Assume κ is the set of keywords we are concerned with. For each feature function $f(Doc, N_1, ..., N_m) = (a_1, ..., a_n)$, we create the following attributes (as in a relational database schema): For each i, $i=1, ..., n$, and each subset $\{K_1, ..., K_m\}$ (of size m) of κ, we get an attribute name $f[a_i, K_1, ..., K_m]$. We use a relational schema of all such attributes. Furthermore, we add a document ID as an extra attribute to the relational schema.

Example 12. Consider the keyword set $\{K_1, K_2, K_3\}$ and the three features given in Example 8. Then we have the following 18 attributes (in addition to the document ID attribute):

$dist[D, K_1, K_2]$	$lca[T, K_1, K_2]$	$ocd[R, K_1, K_2]$
$dist[D, K_2, K_1]$	$lca[T, K_2, K_1]$	$ocd[R, K_2, K_1]$
$dist[D, K_1, K_3]$	$lca[T, K_1, K_3]$	$ocd[R, K_1, K_3]$
$dist[D, K_3, K_1]$	$lca[T, K_3, K_1]$	$ocd[R, K_3, K_1]$
$dist[D, K_2, K_3]$	$lca[T, K_2, K_3]$	$ocd[R, K_2, K_3]$
$dist[D, K_3, K_2]$	$lca[T, K_3, K_2]$	$ocd[R, K_3, K_2]$

Of course, certain relationships between the parameters may lead to a reduction of the number of attributes. For example, since the value for $dist[D, K_1, K_2]$ is the same as $dist[D, K_2, K_1]$, we can omit one if we already have the other. Another example is that if we know $ocd[R, K_1, K_2]$, then we implicitly know $ocd[R, K_2, K_1]$, and we can omit one of these two attributes. From this reasoning, we can reduce the number of attributes in the example to nine (in addition to the document ID attribute).

By using the training samples, we populate the relation defined by the above relational schema with feature tuples. More precisely, given an XML document *Doc*, a set of keywords κ, and a maximum occurrence *occ* of κ in *Doc*, we generate a tuple as follows: For attribute $f[a_i, K_1, ..., K_m]$, it gets a **null** value if the number of keywords *that occ* is defined on is less than m; otherwise, the attribute gets the corresponding value from $f(occ(K_1), ..., occ(K_m))$.

Example 13. Consider the keyword set $\kappa=\{K_1, K_2, K_3\}$ and the XML document in Figure 3. Consider the occurrence of κ in the document such that K_1 is mapped to n_2, K_2 to n_3 and K_3 to n_7. Then, the value for $dist[D, K_1, K_2]$ is 2, while the value for $ocd[R, K_2, K_3]$ is the relation " $<$ ".

In the above method, each occurrence of a set of keywords in an XML document provides a feature tuple to be added to the given relational schema. Given a set of documents and a set of keywords, we can obtain a set of feature tuples for each occurrence of keywords in each document.

The learning process requires an initial set of *positive* examples and an initial set of *negative* examples. In our context, positive examples are provided by feature tuples extracted from a set of documents that have been certified by the security officer to be restricted, while negative examples are provided by feature tuples extracted from a set of documents that have been certified for possible release.

Note, however, that there is an apparent difference in the semantics of the feature tuples in the above two sets. In the set of feature tuples extracted from documents certified to be "restricted", a document needs to be restricted even if only one tuple (among all those that belong to the same document) represents a "dangerous" relationship.

Example 14. Suppose we want to restrict a document from being released when the keywords "K_1" and "K_2" appear within distance 3. In this case, both XML documents in Figures 3&4 should be restricted. However, not all the distance features of "K_1" and "K_2" in Figure 4, namely 2 and 4, satisfy the restricting constraint.

By reducing the learning task to two sets of feature tuples as given above, we can now apply any traditional learning algorithm [Mit97, Qui96]. In general, the learning algorithm will produce a *classification* condition on the parameter values. That is, given a feature tuple in the relational schema derived as shown above, the classification condition gives either **restrict** or **release**. For each document, if any of its feature tuple results in the value **restrict**, then the document should not be released. This classification condition will be used as the matching rule in a release control constraint and the corresponding keywords will be the controlled items.

6   Related Work

The concept of information release control has been explicitly introduced recently in [Wie00, Mon01, RW01], but a general formal framework does not currently exist.

Some form of control over outgoing data has been performed since a long time in different contexts, but it has been mostly based on basic filtering tools, and heuristics have been directly coded into programs. An attempt to specify rules in a high level language is represented by *Felt* [Swa94], which, among its features, provides language statements to identify words, or parts of words in documents and to drop or substitute these words. Restricting rules are then compiled into a program for automatic matching. Despite we are not aware of any structured formal framework for release control as the one we are proposing, we should mention the very active research field of information filtering which also includes publication/subscription systems.

An information filtering system is an information system designed for unstructured or semistructured data [BC92], as opposed to typical database applications that work with highly structured data. With respect to the general information retrieval paradigm, in which a large body of data has to be searched against a specific user search criteria, in information filtering it is usually the case that there are a large number of specifications about information needs of a large number of people and/or tasks, and they all have to be matched against the same text data, in most cases dynamically produced and distributed by some data sources. Publication/subscription systems (see, e.g., [FJL+01] and [ASS+99]) are an instance of information filtering applications. For example, consider the task of sending to each user subscribing to a news service the subset of the daily news specified in his profile. The analogy with our work is quite clear: the set of release constraints can be considered a set of subscriptions, and any matching against the outgoing data leads to a specific action, which usually is preventing the release of the data. Despite this analogy, our goal is to deal with a more heterogeneous set of data that includes also structured data resulting from database queries.

Some work has been done specifically on XML documents filtering for publication/subscription systems [AF00, DFFT02, PFJ+01]. The XFilter project [AF00] is considering Xpath expressions as subscription specifications; these expressions are then converted into FSM (Finite State Machines) that react to XML parsing events. Algorithm performance is improved by using indexing techniques to limit the number of FSM to execute for a given document. While XFilter makes no attempt to eliminate redundant processing for similar queries, the YFilter system [DFFT02] combines multiple queries into a single NFA (Nondeterministic Finite Automaton) allowing a substantial reduction in the number of states needed to represent the set of user queries. The ideas in [FJL+01] are also used in an XML filtering system, Webfilter [PFJ+01], which also allows arbitrary XPath expressions as filtering preferences. Differently from [AF00, DFFT02], Webfilter adopts set oriented techniques including a dynamic clustering strategy to limit the number of subscriptions to consider at each XML event. In [PFJ+01], Webfilter is reported to be able to process substantially more subscriptions and XML documents per second than XFilter. We are considering the algorithms and techniques proposed in this area for their adaptation to implement the matching module of our architecture. However, it is still not clear if the algorithms can be adapted to our language for matching rules and if they are compatible with the specific requirements that a security application imposes.

Alternative approaches for the matching module are represented by continuous query techniques [CCC+02, CDTW00, MSHR02].

Our work is also related to what is commonly known as Internet filtering software. Filtering or blocking software restricts access to Internet content through a variety of means. It may scan a Web site's content based on keywords, phrases or strings of text. It may also restrict access based on the source of the information or through a subjective ratings system assigned by an anonymous third party. Mostly, this software has been focused on blocking pornographic content, and it has not been considered very successful until now, either for under-blocking or over-blocking Internet content. This is partly due to the way blocking criteria have been devised and partly from the inherent complexity of the task. Despite some aspects are very related, we are considering several issues about the treatment of structured and semi-structured data while the data considered by these systems is usually unstructured, or the structure it has it is totally unknown. Regarding our learning-based approach, the general techniques to learn the release constraints from a training set of positive and negative examples are well known [Qui96, Mit97]. Learning has been extensively applied in text categorization and text filtering [Seb02], but efforts to study and apply learning techniques for the categorization and filtering of XML documents have just recently started and pose many open questions. We plan to investigate further the problem of learning release constraints and of refining the constraints considering, in particular, recent statistical learning approaches [CST00].

Regarding our intention of integrating keyword-based techniques with text categorization algorithms, we will take into account the results of the Genoa Technology Integration Experiment [Mon01] performed as part of a DARPA project on boundary control. In the experiment keyword-based and NLP (Natural Language Processing) techniques were compared in their accuracy on a concrete experimental scenario; the experiment involved a corpus of heterogeneous documents that had to be controlled for the release of potentially sensitive information for terrorist attacks. (The scenario referred in particular to the Aum Shinrikyo Japanese cult that bombed the Japanese metro system with an anthrax pathogen.)

Release control is also clearly related to access control. An access control model provides a formalism to define policy rules regulating the access to certain data by certain users, and a mechanism to consistently apply the rules and enforce the global policy (see e.g. [JSSS01]). Access control models have mostly been proposed for relational databases, but they have been adapted to different data representations as well, like multimedia databases, object oriented databases and XML data. Information release control should not be seen as an alternative security approach to access control, since it has several complementary features. In addition to address insider attacks, one of them is certainly the ability to prevent the release of sensitive data that has been assembled using either glitches in the access control policy or inference/cooperative techniques that are difficult to take into account in the access control policy. Actually, the automatic derivation of release constraints from access control rules also provides a way to validate the access control policy. Moreover, access control rules usually operate at the level of database tables while release control can be very focused and work at the level of attribute values in the case of databases. Some work has been done on enhancing a mandatory access control system with monitoring database queries in order to avoid inferences that may lead users to obtain confidential data they are not supposed to get [BFJ00]. However our approach is different, since we plan to automatically derive the specification of appropriate release constraints from the database and metadata constraints that can be used for inference. In contrast, the approach in [BFJ00] keeps a history of all the queries users have made, and upon a new query it computes what can be discovered by the user with that information; the access is granted only if nothing in the resulting set is confidential. In this case complex inference must be performed at each user query.

Finally, a large amount of work has been done in the past decade on word sense disambiguation (see, e.g., [Les86]), and ontology-based reasoning (see, e.g., [GL02]) which are important issues for any content-based document management application and, in particular, for a more accurate release control. An example of use of word sense disambiguation and natural language processing in boundary control, limited to text documents, is the Genoa Technology Integration Experiment [Mon01] performed as part of a DARPA project on boundary control. In our case ontology-based reasoning is used to add relevant rules and/or feature functions over XML documents.

7   Conclusion

We argue that information release control is a new paradigm for information security that is complementary to access control. In this paper we presented a general architecture and formal framework for information release control, including a formal language to define release constraints for XML documents. We also discussed the role that learning techniques could play in the definition of release control constraints, illustrating how they can actually be applied for learning keyword-based release control constraints.

The above release control system can be useful in a traditional data system, such as database system, FTP directories, and web sites. More recent applications, such as web services, can also benefit from release control. Web services [New02] are an emerging paradigm for Internet computing heavily based on XML and on the SOAP protocol. Web services present to the network a standard way of interfacing with back-end software systems, such as DBMS, .NET, J2EE, CORBA objects, adapters to ERP packages, and others. While standards are currently under definition for authentication and authorization, as well as for encryption, controlling the information that is released through a web service to the general internet or to a restricted subset of cooperating processes will be one of the major issues that will also probably affect the success of the new paradigm. While the major objectives of the proposed project are not to develop a specific technology for web services, we envision a very interesting integration of the technologies that may emerge from our results into a web service architecture.

Content-based firewall is another interesting application of our release control system. Current firewall systems are mostly based on selecting incoming and outgoing packets based on source/destination IP and port numbers. Filtering software based on dirty-word checking or virus identification in some cases have been integrated. The content analysis is however quite primitive both in the definition of the filtering criteria and in the matching algorithms. We advocate an approach that incorporates the release control into firewall systems to allow more advanced monitoring on the contents that are released through the firewall.

Acknowledgements

This work was supported by the NSF under grant IIS-0242237. The work of Bettini was also partly supported by Italian MIUR (FIRB "Web-Minds" project N. RBNE01WEJT_005). The work of Wang was also partly supported by NSF Career Award 9875114. The authors would like to thank Nicolò Cesa-Bianchi of the University of Milan for insightful discussions on computational learning techniques.

References

[AF00] Mehmet Altinel and Michael J. Franklin. Efficient filtering of XML documents for selective dissemination of information. In *Proceedings of 26th International Conference on Very Large Data Bases*, pages 53—64, USA, 2000.

[ASS+99] Marcos K. Aguilera, Robert E. Strom, Daniel C. Sturman, Mark Astley, and Tushar D. Chandra. Matching events in a content-based subscription system. In *Proceedings of the Eighteenth Annual ACM Symposium on Principles of Distributed Computing (PODC)*, pages 53—62, May 1999.

[BC92] N. J. Belkin and W. B. Croft. Information Filtering and Information Retrieval: Two Sides of the Same Coin? *Communications of the ACM,* 35(12):29—38, December 1992.

[BFJ00] Alexander Brodsky, Csilla Farkas, Sushil Jajodia: Secure Databases: Constraints, Inference Channels, and Monitoring Disclosures. IEEE Trans. Knowl. Data Eng. 12(6): 900-919, 2000.

[CCC+02] Don Carney, Ugur Cetintemel, Mitch Cherniack, Christian Convey, Sangdon Lee, Greg Seidman, Michael Stonebraker, Nesime Tatbul, and Stan Zdonik. Monitoring streams – A new class of data management applications. In *Proceedings of the 28th International Conference on Very Large DataBases (VLDB)*, pages 215—226, 2002.

[CDTW00] Jianjun Chen, David J. DeWitt, Feng Tian, and Yuan Wang. NiagaraCQ: a scalable continuous query system for Internet databases. In *Proceedings of the 2000 ACM SIGMOD International Conference on Management of Data: May 16—18, 2000, Dallas, Texas*, pages 379—390, 2000.

[CST00] N. Cristianini and J. Shawe-Taylor. *An Introduction to Support Machines (and other kernel-based learning methods)*, Cambridge University Press, UK, 2000.

[DFFT02] Yanlei Diao, Peter Fischer, Michael Franklin, and Raymond To. Yfilter: Efficient and scalable filtering of xml documents. In *Proceedings of the International Conference on Data Engineering (ICDE)*, pages 341—342, 2002.

[FJL+01] Francoise Fabret, H. Arno Jacobsen, Francois Llirbat, Joao Pereira, Kenneth A. Ross, and Dennis Shasha. Filtering algorithms and implementation for very fast Publish/Subscribe systems. In *Proceedings of ACM International Conference on Management of Data (SIGMOD)*, pages 115—126, 2001.

[GL02] Michael Gruninger and Jintae Lee. Ontology: applications and design. *Communications of the ACM*, 45(2):39—41, February 2002.

[JSSS01] Sushil Jajodia, Pierangela Samarati, Maria Luisa Sapino, and V. S. Subrahmanian. Flexible support for multiple access control policies. *ACM Transactions on Database Systems*, 26(2):214—260, June 2001.

[Les86] Michael E. Lesk. Automated sense disambiguation using machine-readable dictionaries: How to tell a pinecone from an ice cream cone. In *Proceedings of the SIGDOC Conference*, 1986.

[Mit97] Tom M. Mitchell. *Machine Learning*. McGraw-Hill, 1997.

[Mon01] Eric Monteith. Genoa TIE, advanced boundary controller experiment. In *17th Annual Computer Security Applications Conference*. ACM, 2001.

[MSHR02] Samuel Madden, Mehul Shah, Joseph M. Hellerstein, and Vijayshankar Raman. Continuously adaptive continuous queries over streams. In *Proceedings of the 2002 ACM SIGMOD international conference on Management of data (SIGMOD)*, pages 49—60, 2002.

[New02] Eric Newcomer. *Understanding Web Services*. Addison Wesley, 2002.

[PFJ+01] Joao Pereira, Francoise Fabret, H. Arno Jacobsen, Francois Llirbat, and Dennis Shasha. Webfilter: A high-throughput XML-based publish and subscribe system. In *Proceedings of the 27th International Conference on Very Large Data Bases (VLDB)*, pages 723—725, September 2001.

[Qui96] J. R. Quinlan. Learning decision tree classifiers. *ACM Computing Surveys*, 28(1):71—72, March 1996.

[RW01] Arnon Rosenthal and Gio Wiederhold. Document release versus data access controls: Two sides of a coin? In *Proceedings of the Tenth International Conference on Information and Knowledge Management (CIKM)*, pages 544—546, November 5—10, 2001.

[Seb02] Fabrizio Sebastiani. Machine learning in automated text categorization. *ACM Computing Surveys*, 34(1):1—47, 2002.

[Swa94] V. Swarup. Automatic generation of high assurance security guard filters. In *Proc. 17th. NIST-NCSC National Computer Security Conference*, pages 123—141, 1994.

[Wie00] Gio Wiederhold. Protecting information when access is granted for collaboration. In *Proc. of Data and Application Security, Development and Directions, IFIP TC11/ WG11.3 Fourteenth Annual Working Conference on Database Security*, pages 1—14, 2000.

Enforcing Semantics-Aware Security in Multimedia Surveillance[*]

Naren Kodali[2], Csilla Farkas[3,4], and Duminda Wijesekera[1,2]

[1] Center for Secure Information Systems
[2] Dept of Info. Systems and Software Eng.,
George Mason University, Fairfax, VA 22030–4444
nkodali@gmu.edu, dwijesek@gmu.edu
[3] Information Security Laboratory
[4] Dept. of Computer Science and Engineering,
University of South Carolina, Columbia, SC-29208
farkas@cse.sc.edu

Abstract. Continuous audio-visual surveillance is utilized to ensure the physical safety of critical infrastructures such as airports, nuclear power plants and national laboratories. In order to do so, traditional surveillance systems place cameras, microphones and other sensory input devices in appropriate locations [Sch99]. These facilities are arranged in a hierarchy of physical zones reflecting the secrecy of the guarded information. Guards in these facilities carry clearances that permit them only in appropriate zones of the hierarchy, and monitor the facilities by using devices such as hand-held displays that send streaming media of the guarded zones possibly with some instructions. The main security constraint applicable to this model is that any guard can see streams emanating from locations with secrecy levels equal to or lower than theirs, but not higher. We show how to model these surveillance requirements using the synchronized multimedia integration language (SMIL) [Aya01] with appropriate security enhancements. Our solution consists of imposing a multi-level security model on SMIL documents to specify surveillance requirements. Our access control model ensures that a multimedia stream can only be displayed on a device if the security clearance of the display device dominates the security clearance of the monitored zone. Additionally, we pre-process a set of cover stories that can be released during emergency situations that allow using the services of guards with lower clearances without disclosing data with higher sensitive levels. For this, we create a view for each level, and show that these views are semantically coherent and comply with specified security polices.

1   Introduction

Physical structures such as air-ports, nuclear power plants and national laboratories are considered critical, and therefore are guarded continuously. Although the

---

[*] This work was partially supported by the National Science Foundation under grants CCS-0113515 and IIS-0237782.

S. Spaccapietra et al. (Eds.): Journal on Data Semantics II, LNCS 3360, pp. 199–221, 2004.

ultimate security providers are human guards, they are aided by physical surveillance instruments consisting of networked audio-visual devices such as cameras and microphones. Additionally, such facilities also have a hierarchical structure reflecting the levels of secrecy of the information contained in them. Accordingly, people accessing a zone carry appropriate clearances. For example, common areas such as ticket counters are accessible to all people, but baggage areas are accessible to an authorized subset only. Furthermore those that are allowed in the control towers are further restricted, reflecting the sensitivity of the control information. Thus audio-visual monitoring of these facilities must respect these sensitivities. For example, the guards that are only allowed in baggage area have no need to see the cameras monitoring the control towers. Consequently, there is a need to restrict the distribution of surveillance streams to only those guards with appropriate levels of clearances. Doing so using the *synchronized multimedia integration language (SMIL)* [Aya01] is the subject matter of this paper. Here we provide a framework to do so by using SMIL to specify the streaming media requirements, and a multi-level security (MLS) model for security aspects. Consequently, we decorate SMIL documents with security requirements so that appropriate MLS model is imposed. We further show how to utilize the services of guards with lower clearances to aid in emergencies that may occur in high security zones by showing appropriately constructed multimedia cover stories.

We use SMIL because of two choices. Firstly, most display devices are now SMIL compatible [Spy, Nok], and secondly, by using W3C standards and recommendations, our framework can be Web-enabled. Toolkit support to integrate XML compliant services across various platforms [PCV02, Nok, Bul98, EUMJ] are available commercially and freely. Therefore, our framework can be implemented with appropriate tools and ported to a wide range of general-purpose mobile multimedia devices such as those available in automobile navigation systems and hand-held devices.

Secondly, although SMIL is an XML-like language for specifying synchronized multimedia, unlike XML formatted textual documents, multimedia constructs have semantics that predates XML. Therefore, it is necessary to specify SMIL documents that capture those semantics while enforcing specified security policies. We address this issue by proposing a *Multi Level Secure Normal Form (mlsNF)* for multimedia documents. Accordingly, we create secure views appropriate at each level of our MLS model.

Thirdly, given the runtime delays of an operational platform, we show how to generate an executable appropriate for a candidate runtime, which we refer to as *a display normal form* of a SMIL document. We then encrypt media streams in display normal form and transmit them to intended recipients under normal and emergency operating conditions.

The rest of the paper is organized as follows. Section 2 introduces multimedia surveillance and a running example for the problem domain. Section 3 provides a summary of related work and Section 4 reviews SMIL, the XML-like language for multimedia. Section 5 describes the algorithm for transforming to the *Multi Level Secure Normal Form (mlsNF)*and Section 6 proves the correctness of the transformation algorithm. Section 7 addresses compile time issues and runtime activities including encryption and resource management. Section 8 concludes the paper.

2   Multimedia Surveillance

Physical safety of critical infrastructure such as airports, nuclear power plants and national laboratories require that they be continuously monitored for intrusive or suspicious activities. In order to so, traditional surveillance systems place cameras, microphones [Sch99] and other sensory input devices in strategic locations. Appropriate combinations of such continuously flowing information streams provide a clear understanding of the physical safety of the facility under surveillance. Mostly, secured facilities have several degrees of sensitivities, resulting in categorizing intended users according to their accessibility to physical locations. Similarly, guarding personnel are also categorized according to the sensitivity of the information they are authorized to receive under normal operating conditions. However, in response to unusual circumstances (e.g., emergencies) security personnel may be required to perform actions that are outside their normal duties leading to the release of data about the unauthorized areas. For example, in case of a fire in a high security area emergency workers who are unauthorized to access this area may still be required to obtain fire fighting materials. For this, they need to know what is the extent of the fire and what type of fire extinguisher to obtain. However, they should not be able to know the exact type of the material burning or any information about the burning area that is not directly necessary for their emergency duties. We address this problem by providing our multimedia surveillance system with a semantically rich, pre-orchestrated multimedia cover story repository, so that in emergencies cover stories can be released to lower security levels.

The main difference between a traditional MLS system and MLS for live surveillance feeds during day-to-day operations is the need to disseminate classified information continuously to appropriate personnel for the latter. We assume a multilevel security classification of physical areas depending on their geographical location and their corresponding surveillance data is considered to have the same classification. We develop a methodology to express multimedia compositions with their rich runtime semantics, techniques to enforce integrity and access control, and enable exploitation of cover stories to disseminate relevant material to unauthorized users during emergencies. In addition to enforcing MLS, we propose to record all sensory inputs obtained using the input devices, to be used for forensic analysis, as well as to improve the quality of cover stories.

Figure 1 shows a hypothetical research facility with varying levels of sensitivity. Assume that the area enclosed by the innermost rectangle ABCD contains weapons with highest degree of sensitivity and is accessible (and therefore guarded) by personnel with the highest level of clearance, say top secret (TS). The area between the rectangles PQRS and ABCD is classified at medium level of sensitivity and therefore requires personnel with secret (S) security clearances.

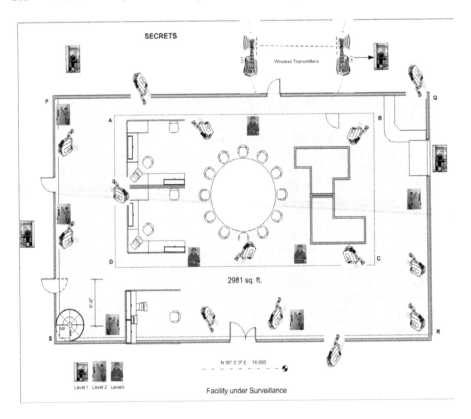

Fig. 1. A hypothetical facility under Surveillance

The area external to PQRS contains least sensitive material, and can be accessed by unclassified personnel, like visitors and reporters. We classify the areas into Top-Secret (TS), Secret (S) and Unclassified (UC) security levels with application domains, e.g., Dom as categories. Security labels form a lattice structure. For simplicity, we omit the application domain and use TS, S, and UC as security labels. The area inside ABCD is TS, the area inside of PQRS, but outside of ABCD is S, and the area outside PQRS is UC. Employees, guards, support services personnel, and general public have TS > S > UC clearances, where > corresponds to the dominance relation defined in MLS systems. As shown in Figure 1, an area with higher level of sensitivity is a sub-part of areas with all lower levels of sensitivities. Therefore, a guard with top-secret clearance may be used in the classified area, but not vice versa. For surveillance purposes, cameras (infrared and normal light) and other devices such as microphones are situated throughout the facility. Multimedia streams emanating from these devices are continuously used to monitor the facility. We propose a design where all multimedia data is transmitted to a centralized control facility and then directed to handheld devices of appropriate security personnel.

3   Related Work

A distributed architecture for multi-participant and interactive multimedia that enables multiple users to share media streams within a networked environment is presented in [Sch99]. In this architecture, multimedia streams originating from multiple sources can be combined to provide media clips that accommodate look-around capabilities. Multilevel security (MLS) has been widely studied to ensure data confidentiality, integrity, and availability [Osb]. MLS systems provide controlled information flow based on the security classification of the protection objects (e.g., data items) and subjects of the MLS system (e.g., applications running in behalf of a user). To provide information confidentiality, data is allowed to flow only from low security levels to higher security levels [Low99]. Information security policies in databases aim to protect the *confidentiality* (secrecy) and *integrity* of data, while ensuring *availability* of data. In Multilevel Secure (MLS) systems direct violations of data confidentiality are prevented by mandatory access control (MAC) mechanisms, such as those based on the Bell-LaPadula (BLP) [San93] model. Mandatory (or lattice-based) policies are expressed via security classification labels that are assigned to *subjects*, i.e., active computer system entities that can initiate requests for information, and to *objects*, i.e., passive computer system entities that are used to store information. Security labels are composed from two components: 1) a hierarchical component, e.g., *public* < *secret* < *top-secret*, and 2) a sub-set lattice compartment, e.g., $\{\} \subset \{navy\} \subset \{navy, military\}$ and $\{\} \subset \{military\} \subset \{navy, military\}$, however, there is no subset relation between $\{military\}$ and $\{navy\}$. Security labels are formed by combining the two components together, i.e., (top-secret, $\{navy\}$), (secret, $\{navy, military\}$), etc. Security labels form a mathematical lattice structure with a dominance relation among the labels. If no dominance relation exists among the labels, then they are called incompatible. MAC policies control read and write operations on the data objects based on the classification labels of the requested data objects and the classification label (also called clearance) of the subject requesting the operation. For simplicity, in this work we only use the hierarchical component of the security labels, i.e., *public* < *secret* < *top-secret*. However, our results hold on full lattice-based access control models.

Regulating access to XML formatted text documents has been actively researched in the past few years offering a multitude of solutions. Bertino et al. [BBC+00] have developed Author-X, a Java based system to secure XML documents that enforces access control policies at various granularities and corresponding user credentials. Author-X encodes security policies for a set of XML documents in an XML file referred to as the policy base containing both permissions and prohibitions. Damiani et al. [DdVPS00, DdVPS02] developed an access control model where the tree structure of XML documents is exploited using XPATH expressions to control access at different levels of granularity. The smallest protection granularity is an XPATH node, and security policies specify permissions or prohibitions to all descendent objects of a node.

Damiani et al. [DdV03] discuss feature protection of XML format images. Its primary focus is controlled dissemination of sensitive data within an image. They propose an access control model with complex filtering conditions. This model uses SVG to render the map of a physical facility. While this model could be used to represent our application, it is limited in flexibility and adaptability to certain issues related to physical security using MLS.

Bertino et al. [BHAE02] provides a security framework to model access control in video databases. They provide security granularity, where objects are sequences of frames or particular objects within frames. The access control model is based on the concepts of security objects, subjects, and permitted access modes, like viewing and editing. The proposed model is provides a general framework for the problem domain, but does not explain how access control objects to be released are formalized and enforced.

Stoica at al. [SF02] present cover stories for XML with the aim of hiding non-permitted data from the naive user. The work is motivated by the need to provide secure release of multilevel XML documents and corresponding DTD files in a semantically correct and inference free manner where security sensitivity is not monotonically increasing along all paths originating from the node. Substantial amounts of contemporary research addresses real-time moving object detection and tracking them from stationary and moving camera platforms [VCM], object pose estimation with respect to a geospatial site model, human gait analysis [VSA], recognizing simple multi-agent activities, real-time data dissemination, data logging and dynamic scene visualization. While they offer valuable directions to our research model, they are not a panacea to physical security.

None of the above approaches are completely satisfactory for multimedia surveillance . They primarily address textual documents and exploit the granular structure of XML documents. Multimedia for various reasons as stated has to be treated differently. Synchronization and integration of diverse events to produce sensible information is non-trivial when compared to textual data. The process of retrieval without losing the sense of continuity and synchronization needs better techniques and algorithms which all of the above models do not completely address. Kodali et al. [KW02, KWJ03, KFW03] propose models for multimedia access control for different security paradigms. A release control for SMIL formatted multimedia objects for pay-per-view movies on the Internet that enforces DAC is described in [KW02]. The cinematic structure consisting of acts, scenes, frames of an actual movies are written as a SMIL document without losing the sense of a story. Here access is restricted to the granularity of an *act* in a movie. A secure and progressively updatable SMIL document [KWJ03] is used to enforce RBAC and respond to traffic emergencies. In an emergency response situation, different roles played by recipients determine the media clips they receive.

In [KFW03] an MLS application for secure surveillance of physical facilities is described, where guards with different security classification in charge of the physical security of the building are provided live feeds matching their level in the security hierarchy. This paper is an extended version of [KFW03], in which multimedia surveillance is described with limited operational semantics.

4   SMIL

SMIL [Aya01, RHO99] is an extension to XML developed by W3C to allow multimedia components such as audio, video, text and images to be integrated and synchronized to form presentations [RvOHB99]. The distinguishing features of SMIL over XML are the syntactic constructs for timing and synchronization of streams with qualitative requirements commonly known as QoS. In addition, SMIL provides a syntax for spatial layout including constructs for non-textual and non-image media and hyperlink support. SMIL constructs for synchronizing media are ⟨seq⟩, ⟨excl⟩ and ⟨par⟩. They are used to hierarchically specify synchronized multimedia compositions. The ⟨seq⟩ element plays the child elements one after another in the specified sequential order. The ⟨excl⟩ construct specifies that its children are played one child at a time, but does not impose any order. The ⟨par⟩ element plays all children elements as a group, allowing parallel play out. For example, the SMIL specification ⟨par⟩⟨video src=camera1⟩⟨audio src = microphone1⟩⟨/par⟩ specify that media sources camera1 and microphone1 are played in parallel. In SMIL, the time period that a media clip is played out is referred to as its active duration. For parallel play to be meaningful, both sources must have equal active durations. When clips do not have same active durations, SMIL provides many constructs to make them equal. Some examples are begin (allows to begin components after a given amount of time), dur (controls the duration), end (specifies the ending time of the component with respect to the whole construct), *repeatCount* (allows a media clip to be repeated a maximum number of times). In addition, attributes such as *syncTolerance* and *syncMaster* controls runtime synchronization, where the former specifies the tolerable mis-synchronization (such as tolerable lip-synchronization delays) and the latter specifies a master-slave relationship between synchronized streams. In this paper, we consider only the basic forms of synchronization construct which means, we do not specify *syncMaster* and *syncTolerance*. Thus we assume that components of ⟨par⟩ have equal play out times and they begin and end at the same time.

An important construct that we use is ⟨switch⟩ allowing one to switch among many alternative compositions listed among its components. These alternatives are chosen based on the values taken by some specified attributes. For example, ⟨switch⟩ ⟨audio src="stereo.wav" systemBitrate⟩25⟩⟨audio src="mono.wav" systemBitrate ⟨ 25⟩⟨/switch⟩ plays stereo.wav when the SMIL defined attribute *systemBitrate* is at least 25 and mono.wav otherwise. We use this construct to specify our surveillance application. In order to do so, we define two custom attributes *customTestMode* that can take values "normal" and "emergency" and *customTestSecurity* that take any value from ("TS","S","UC"). The first attribute is used to indicate the operating mode that can be either normal or emergency and the second attribute indicates the security level of streams that can be top secret, secret or unclassified. SMIL also requires that every application-defined attribute (custom attribute in SMIL terminology) have a title and a default value. It further has a special flag *override* that makes the value *hidden* or *visible*. When override takes the value hidden, the player is not allowed to change the value of the custom attributes. That feature is useful in specifying security attributes that are not to be altered by SMIL players.

Surveillance requirements, such as those in the example given in the SMIL fragment below specifies which multimedia sources have to be displayed under the two operating conditions. We assume that the source document specifies the security label of each source and that MLS policies are used to ensure that guards are permitted to view only those multimedia sources that are dominated by their security clearances. For this, we preprocess a given MLS multimedia document and produce views that are permitted to be seen by guards for each security classification. Then, we separately encrypt and broadcast multimedia documents for each category, to the appropriate locations by efficient use of bandwidth. In order to achieve this objective, we first transform every SMIL document with proposed security and mode attributes to three SMIL documents, where all security labels in each document consists of solely one *customTestSecurity* attribute, namely the one that is appropriate to be seen by guards with the label value. We now formally state and prove that this can be done for an arbitrary SMIL document with our security labels.

```
<smil xmlns="http://www.w3.org/2001/SMIL20/Language">
<customAttributesMODE>
      <customTestMode="Normal" title="Normal Mode"
        defaultState="true" override="hidden"
       <customTestMode id="Emergency" title="Emergency Mode"
        defaultState="true" override="hidden"
<customAttributesMODE> <customAttributesSecurity>
      <customTestSecurity id="TS" title="Top-Secret"
        defaultState="true" override="hidden"/>
      <customTestSecurity id="S" title="Secret"
        defaultState="true" override="hidden"/>
      <customTestSecurity id="UC"  title="Unclassified"
        defaultState="true" override="hidden"/>
</customAttributesSecurity>
<body>
<switch>
//Classification is TS(Top-Secret)
<par customTestMODE= "Normal">
<video src="CameraTS1.rm" channel="video1" customTestSecurity="TS"/>
<audio src="CameraTS1.wav" customTestSecurity="TS" />
//Classification is S(Secret)
<video src="CameraS1.rm" channel="video1" customTestSecurity="S"/>
<audio src="CameraS2.wav" customTestSecurity="S"/>
//Classification is U(Unclassified)
<video src="CameraU1.rm" channel="video2" customTestSecurity="S"/>
<audio src="CameraU1.wav" customTestSecurity="S" /> </par>
```

```
<par customTestMODE= "Emergency">
//All 3 above together (Total of 6 feeds)
//Here are the secret cover stories
<par>
<video src="CoverstoryTS-to-S1.rm" channel="video1"
id="TS-to-Secret" customTestSecurity="S"/>
<audio src="CoverstoryTS-toS1.wav" customTestSecurity="S"/>
</par>
//Here are the unclassified cover stories
<par>
<video src="CoverstoryTS-to-U1.rm" channel="video1"
id="TS-toUC1" customTestSecurity="U"/>
<audio src="CoverstoryTS-to-U1.wav" customTestSecurity="U"/>
<video src="CoverstoryS-to-U1.rm" channel="video1" id="Secret-toUC1"
customTestSecurity="U"/>
<audio src="CoverstoryS-to-U1.wav" customTestSecurity="U"/>
</par>
//Followed by normal the TWO UC camera feeds.
</switch>
    </body>
</smil>
```

As the fragment shows, the document consists of two sections, where the first section defines the custom attribute *customTestMode* with values "Normal" and "Emergency". Because the second and the fourth lines of fragment specify that *customTestMode* is hidden, the value of this attribute corresponding to each stream cannot be reset later. The second part of the file consists of a switch statement consisting of collection of media streams connected by ⟨par⟩ constructs. Notice that there are two section inside the ⟨switch⟩ statement, where the first one begins with the line ⟨par customTestMODE= "Normal"⟩ and the second one begins with the line ⟨par customTestMODE= "Emergency"⟩. That specifies that the streams inside be shown under normal and emergency operating conditions. In this example, each area has a camera and a microphone to record audio and video streams to be transmitted to appropriate guards. They are named CameraTS1.rm, CamerU1.wav etc. The security classification of each source is identified by the application defined SMIL attribute customTestSecurity. For example, ⟨video src="CameraTS1.rm" channel="video1" customTestSecurity="TS"/⟩ specifies that the video source named CameraTS1.rm has the Top Secret security level. The intent being that this source is to be shown only to top-secret guards. As the second half of the document shows, there are three audio-visual cover stories named CoverstoryTS-to-S1.rm to CoverstoryS-to-UC1.wav are shown with the appropriate security level specified with the attribute customTestSecurity. The main composition is encoded using a ⟨switch⟩ statement that is to be switched based on the operating mode (normal or emergency).

5 MLS Normalform and the Translation Algorithm

In this section we define the Multi Level Secure Normal Form (mlsNF) and also provide the algorithm for transforming an arbitrary SMIL specification into its MLS normal form.

Definition 1 (MLS Normal Form) *We say that a SMIL specification S is in Multi Level Secure Normal Form (mlsNF) if it is of one of the following forms:*

1. *It is of the form $\langle$ par $\rangle$ Cts(S) Cs(S) Cu (S) Cud(S) Cod $\langle$ /par $\rangle$ where all attribute TestSecurity attributes in Cts(S), Cs(S), Cu(S) are respectively TS, S and U. In addition, Cud(S) has no attribute TestSecurity and Cod(S) has two different value set for attribute TestSecurity.*

2. *It is of the form $\langle$ par $\rangle$ Cts(S) Cs(S) Cu (S) Cud(S) Cod(S) $\langle$ /par $\rangle$ with one or two components of $\langle$ par $\rangle$ may be missing. Here Cts(S), Cs(S) and Cu(S), Cud(S) Cod(S) satisfy requirements stated above.*

3. *It is of the form Cts(S), Cs(S), Cu(S), Cud(S), Cod(S) where Cts(S), Cs(S), Cu(S), Cud(S) and Cod(S) satisfy requirements stated above. We say that Cts(S), and Cs(S) and Cu(S) are respectively the top secret, secret and unclassified views of the specification S. Cud(S) is the view with missing security classifications and Cod(S) is the view with contradictory security classifications.*

As stated in Definition 1, a SMIL specification in mlsNF is one that is parallel composition of at most three specifications, where each specification belongs to one security class, that are said to be the views corresponding to the respective security classes. Notice that in Definition 1, the latter two cases are degenerate cases of case 1 where one or more views of the specification become null. In attempting to create views from an arbitrary SMIL document, one encounters two undesirable situations. The first is the missing security classifications resulting in a non-null Cud(S). The other is the situation with contradictory security classification due to over specification. An example under specified SMIL specification is $\langle$ audio src= "myAudio.wav" $\rangle$, and an example contradictory specification is $\langle$ video src= "myMovie.rm" attributeTestSecurity=TS attributeTestSecurity=S $\rangle$. Thus, it is tempting to avoid such situations by applying completeness and conflict resolution policies [JSSS01] designed to be used in XML formatted and databases. Note, that completeness and conflict resolution polices were intended to be used for inheritance hierarchies. Because SMIL hierarchies are not due to inheritances and instead they are syntactic constructs for media synchronization, blindly applying such policies to resolve under and over specification of SMIL documents destroys the synchronized play out semantics of media streams. In this paper, we use the neutral policy of discarding under and over specified fragments Cud(S) and Cod(S) of a SMIL specification S.

The Algorithm 1 details the mechanics of conversion from an arbitrary SMIL specification into mlsNF. It describes how the rewrite should be done when we encounter different time containers, some of which are nested. The generated output would have atmost three parallel compositions each corresponding to a unique security level. The MLS paradigm has an unique property which allows subjects with a higher classification access to the view of the lower classified subjects. This algorithm takes this property into consideration when generating smilNF.

Algorithm 1 TOmlsNF (Conversion to MLS Normal form)

INPUT : Arbitrary SMIL fragment. Possible classifications Top-Secret, Secret, Unclassified.

OUTPUT : mlsNF

(s) is an arbitrary SMIL specification (as described in 4 with a possible Security classification.

if (s) is $\langle$ seq $\rangle$ $s_1 s_2$ $\langle$ /seq $\rangle$ **then**

C_{ts} (s) = $\langle$ seq $\rangle$ $\langle$ par $\rangle$ $C_{ts}(s_1)$ $\langle$ /par $\rangle$ $\langle$ par $\rangle$ $C_{ts}(s_2)$ $\langle$ /par $\rangle$ $\langle$ /seq $\rangle$

C_s (s) = $\langle$ seq $\rangle$ $\langle$ par $\rangle$ $C_s(s_1)$ $\langle$ /par $\rangle$ $\langle$ par $\rangle$ $C_s(s_2)$ $\langle$ /par $\rangle$ $\langle$ /seq $\rangle$

C_u (s) = $\langle$ seq $\rangle$ $\langle$ par $\rangle$ $C_u(s_1)$ $\langle$ /par $\rangle$ $\langle$ par $\rangle$ $C_u(s_2)$ $\langle$ /par $\rangle$ $\langle$ /seq $\rangle$

else if (s) is $\langle$ par $\rangle$ s_1 s_2 $\langle$ /par $\rangle$ **then**

C_{ts} (s) = $\langle$ par $\rangle$ $C_t s(s_1)$ $\langle$ /par $\rangle$ $\langle$ par $\rangle$ $C_t s(s_2)$ $\langle$ /par $\rangle$

C_s (s) = $\langle$ par $\rangle$ $C_s(s_1)$ $\langle$ /par $\rangle$ $\langle$ par $\rangle$ $C_s(s_2)$ $\langle$ /par $\rangle$

C_u (s) = $\langle$ par $\rangle$ $C_u(s_1)$ $\langle$ /par $\rangle$ $\langle$ par $\rangle$ $C_u(s_2)$ $\langle$ /par $\rangle$

end if

if either of $C_x(s_i)$ are empty for some x $\in$ {TS,S,U} and i $\in$ {1,2} **then**

$C_x(s_i)$ in the right hand sides above must be substituted by ϕ (S_i) where ϕ (s_i) is defined as $\langle$ audio or video src = empty $\rangle$

end if

If Security classification =Top-Secret, then C_{ts} (s) = (s)

If Security classification =Secret, then $C_{ts}(s) = \phi$,C_s (s) = (s)

If Security classification=Unclassified, then C_{ts} (s) = ϕ , $C_s(s) = \phi$, and C_u (s)= (s).

Then let mlsNF (s) = $\langle$ seq $\rangle$ $\langle$ par $\rangle$ C_{ts} $\langle$ /par $\rangle$ $\langle$ par $\rangle$ (s) C_s $\langle$ /par $\rangle$ $\langle$ par $\rangle$ (s) C_u (s) $\langle$ /par $\rangle$ $\langle$ /seq $\rangle$.

We now have to ensure that Algorithm 1 preserves semantics. That is, top secret, secret and unclassified viewers of a specification S will view Cts(S), Cs(S) and Cu(S) respectively. This proof is easy, provided that we have a formal operational semantics for SMIL. While providing such semantics is not difficult, it does not exist yet. Therefore, while we are working on it, we provide a rudimentary operational semantics for the purposes of showing that our algorithms work as expected.

5.1   Operational Semantics for SMIL

In this section, we provide a simple operational semantics for media streams and SMIL documents constructed using ⟨par⟩, ⟨seq⟩ and ⟨switch⟩ commands. The sole objective of this exercise is to show that Algorithm 1 transforms a SMIL document to a collection of other SMIL documents to respect this semantics. The latter is referred to as semantic equivalence [Mul87]. Following customary practices in programming language semantics, our operational semantics and the proof of semantic equivalence will be inductive in nature. It is worth noting that our semantics is only applicable to our application scenario and syntactic constructs, and its extension to other purposes and constructs form our ongoing work.

Definition 2 (Timed Display Instance) *We say that a quadruple (S, T-begin, T-end, Security Set) is a timed display instance provided that:*

1. *S is a basic media element with a finite active duration $\delta \geq 0$ and T-begin leq T-end are arithmetic expressions of a single real variable t satisfying T-end = T-begin + δ.*
2. *Security set a subset of TS, S, U consisting of attribute TestSecurity attribute values of S.*
3. *We say that a set of timed display instances is a timed display set provided that there is at least one timed display element with t as its T-begin value.*
4. *Taken as expressions containing the variable t, the smallest T-begin value of a timed display set is said to be the origin of the timed display set. We use the notation O(TDI) for the origin of the timed display set TDI.*
5. *Taken as expressions containing the variable t, the largest T-begin value of a timed display set is said to be the end of the timed display set. We use the notation E(TDI) for the end of the timed display set TDI.*

The following two elements tdi_1 and tdi_2 are examples of timed display instances.

1. tdi_1 = ((⟨video, src= "myVideo.rm", dur=5, attributeTestSecurity=TS ⟩, t, t+7, TS)
2. tdi_2 = ((⟨audio, src= "myAudio.rm", dur=10, attributeTestSecurity=U⟩, t+7, t+17, U)

Therefore, $\{tdi_1, tdi_2\}$ is timed display set with its origin t and end t+17. The intent here is to consider TDI= $\{tdi_1, tdi_2\}$ as a possible playout of the SMIL specification ⟨seq⟩ ⟨video, src= "myVideo.rm", dur=5, attributeTestSecurity=TS⟩, ⟨audio, src= "myAudio.rm", dur=10, attributeTestSecurity=U ⟩ ⟨/seq⟩ that begin at an arbitrary but thereafter fixed time t and ends at t+17. Now we describe some algebraic operations on timed display sets that are necessary to complete the definition of our operational semantics of SMIL. The first is that of origin substitution defined as follows.

Definition 3 (Algebra of Timed Display Sets: Substitution)   *Suppose TDS is a timed display set with the formal time variable t and s is any* *arithmetic expression possibly containing other real valued variables. Then TDS(s/t) is the notation for the timed display set obtained by syntactically substituting all timing values (that is T-begin and T-end values) t by s in all expressions of TDS.*

For the example TDI given prior to Definition 3, $TDI(2t+7/t)$ consists of $tdi_1(2t+7/t), tdi_2(2t+7/t)$ where $tdi_1(2t+7/t)$ and $tdi_2(2t+7/t)$ are defined as:

1. $tdi_1(2t+7/t) = (\langle video, src= "myVideo.rm", dur=5, attributeTestSecurity= TS\rangle, 2t+7, 2t+21, \{TS\})$
2. $tdi_2(2t+7/t) = (\langle audio, src= "myAudio.rm", dur=10, attributeTestSecurity= U\rangle, 2t+21, 2t+31, \{U\})$

The reason for having Definition 3 is that in order to provide formal semantics for the $\langle seq\rangle$ operator, it is necessary to shift the second child of the $\langle seq\rangle$ by the time duration of its first child and recursively repeat this procedure for all of $\langle seq\rangle$'s children. To exemplify the point, the first example the TDI= $\{tdi_1, tdi_2\}$ is infact $\{tdi_1\} \cup TDI'(t+7/t)\}$ where TDI' is given by $tdi' = (\langle audio, src = "myAudio.rm", dur=10, attributeTestSecurity = U\rangle, t, t+10, \{U\})$. We are now ready to obtain operational semantics for SMIL specifications, provide the following assumptions are valid.

Definition 4 (Basis Mapping) *Suppose M is the set of basic media elements of S. Then any mapping [[ ]] from M to a set of Timed Display Instances TDI is said to be a basis mapping for a denotation iff all T-begin elements of M have the same value t, where t is a real variable. Then we say that [[ ]] is a basis mapping parameterized by t.*

Lemma 1 (Existence of basis mappings). *Suppose M is a set of basic media streams with time durations. Then M has a basis mapping.*

Proof: For each media stream m= $\langle type, src= "...", dur=value, attributeTestSecurity= "..." type\rangle$, in M, let [[M]] map to (m, t, t+value, Att Values). Then [[ ]] is a basis mapping.
We now use a basis mapping to define operational semantics of any SMIL specification S as follows.

Definition 5 (Operational Semantics for SMIL) *Suppose S is a SMIL specification and [[ ]] is a basis mapping for the basic media elements B of S with the formal parameter t. Then we inductively extend [[ ]] to S as follows.*
   1) [[Null]] = Φ
   2) [[$\langle seq\rangle$ S1 S2$\langle /seq\rangle$]] = [[S1]] U [[S2]](end([[S1]])/t)
   3) [[$\langle par\rangle$ S1 S2$\langle /par\rangle$]] = [[S1]] U [[S2]].
   4) [[$\langle switch\rangle$ S1 S2 $\langle /switch\rangle$]] = [[S1]] if S1 satisfies the attribute of the switch. = [[S2]] otherwise if S2 satisfies the attribute of the switch. = Φ otherwise.

We now say that the extended mapping [[ ]] is a semantic mapping parameterized by t. It is our position that the informal definition given by the SMIL
specification is captured by our operational semantics, provided we are able to
evaluate the attribute of the switch. This can be easily formalized using customary practices of program language semantics, and is therefore omitted here for
brevity. We now formally state and prove the semantic equivalence of Algorithm
1. That shows that rewritten specification has the same operational semantics
as the original that we offer as the correctness argument for the rewrite.

6   Correctness of the Translation Algorithm

Theorem 1 (Correctness of Algorithm 1) *Suppose that S is a SMIL spec-*
ification and [[ ]] is a semantic mapping parameterized by t. Then [[S]] = [[ml-
sNF(S)]].

Proof: As stated earlier, this proof also proceeds by induction on the structure
of S. Thus, for the sake of brevity, we show one base case and one inductive case.
Example Base Case:
Suppose S is ⟨ type src=" ", dur=n, attributeTestSecurity="S" type ⟩. Then,
by Algorithm 1,

```
Cts(S) = Null, Cs(S) = S, Cu(S) = Null, Cud(S) = Null and Cod(S) =
Null. Therefore, [[<par>Cts(S) Cs(S) Cu(S) Cud(S) Cod(S) </par>]]=
[[<par>Null S Null Null Null</par>]] = [[Null]] U [[S]] U [[Null]]
U [[Null]] U [[Null]] = [[S]]. Hence [[mlsNF(S)]] = [[S]].
```

Example Inductive Case:
Suppose S is ⟨seq⟩ S1 S2⟨/seq⟩. Then, from Algorithm 1,

```
[[mlsNF(S)]] =[[<par>Cts(S) Cs(S) Cu(S) Cud(S) Cod(S) </par>]] =
[[Cts(S)]] U [[Cs(S)]] U [[Cu(S)]] U [[Cud(S)]] U [[Cod(S)]] =
[[<seq>Cts(S1) Cts(S2)</seq>]] U [[<seq>Cs(S1) Cs(S2)</seq>]] U
[[<seq>Cu(S1) Cu(S2)</seq>]] U [[<seq>Cud(S1) Cud(S2)</seq>]] U
[[<seq>Cod(S1) Cod(S2)</seq>]]
    =
    [[Cts(S1)]] U [[Cts(S2)]](end([[Cts(S1)]])/t) U[[Cs(S1)]]
    U [[Cs(S2)]] (end([[Cs(S1)]])/t)
    U [[Cu(S1)]] U [[Cu(S2)]](end([[Cu(S1)]])/t) U[[Cud(S1)]]
    U [[Cud(S2)]] (end([[Cud(S1)]])/t)
    U [[Cod(S1)]] U [[Cod(S2)]](end([[Cod(S1)]])/t)
```

Conversely,

```
[[S]]    = [[<seq> S1 S2 </seq>]] = [[S1]] U
[[S2]](end(S1)/t)
= [[Cts(S1)]] U [[Cs(S1)]] U[[Cu(S1)]] [[Cud(S1)]] U [[Cod(S1)]]
U( [[Cts(S2)]] U [[Cs(S2)]] U[[Cu(S2)]] [[Cud(S2)]] U [[Cod(S2)]])
(end(S1)/t)
```

by the inductive assumption.

But notice that

```
([[Cts(S2)]] U [[Cs(S2)]] U[[Cu(S2)]] [[Cud(S2)]]U
[[Cod(S2)]]) (end(S1)/t)
     =
[[Cts(S2)]](end([[Cts(S1)]])/t) U
[[Cs(S2)]](end([[Cs(S1)]])/t) U [[Cu(S2)]](end([[Cu(S1)]])/t) U
[[Cud(S2)]](end([[Cud(S1)]])/t) U [[Cod(S1)]] U
[[Cod(S2)]](end([[Cod(S1)]])/t)
```

Therefore $[[\mathrm{mlsNF}(S)]] = [[S]]$, thereby justifying the inductive case.

6.1 Representing Secure Views in SMIL

On rewriting the SMIL fragment in Section 4 into the MLS Normal form we create different views for each of the following cases represented as a separate SMIL document. In the SMIL fragment represented below , we have the format of such a specification denoting the entire structure of a "Top-Secret" view in the normal mode and a "Secret" view in the emergency mode.

```
<smil xmlns="http://www.w3.org/2001/SMIL20/Language">
<customAttributesMODE>
     ---
<customAttributesSecurity>

<seq>
<switch>
<par customTestMode="Normal" customTestSecurity = "TS">
 <par> <video src="Tsamera1.rm" channel="video1" dur="45s"/>
       <audio src="TSCamera1.wav"   />
 </par>
 <par> <video src="TSCamera2.rm" channel="video1" />
       <audio src="TSCamera2.wav"/> </par> </par>
<par customTestMode ="Normal" customTestSecurity = "S">
XXXXXXXXXX //Normal Form View for Normal Mode "S" Class
</par>
<par customTestMode ="Normal" customTestSecurity = "UC">
XXXXXXXXXX //Normal Form View Normal Mode "UC" Class
</par>
<par customTestMode ="Emergency" customTestSecurity = "TS">
XXXXXXXXXX //Normal Form View for Normal Mode "TS" Class
</par>
<par customTestMode ="Emergency" customTestSecurity = "S">
 <video src="SCamera1.rm" channel="video2" dur="25s"/>
 <audio src="SCamera1.wav"   /> </par>
<par> <video src="Scamera2.rm" channel="video2"/>
      <audio src="Scamera2.wav"   /> </par>
<par>
<video src="CoverstoryTS1.rm"  channel="video1" id="TSCoverstory1"/>
```

```
<audio src="CoverstoryTS1.wav" />
</par>
<par>
<video src="CoverstoryTS1.rm" channel="video1" id="TSCoverstory1"/>
<audio src="CoverstoryTS1.wav"   />
</par>
<par customTestMode ="Emergency" customTestSecurity = "UC">
 XXXXXXXX//Normal Form View for Emergency Mode "UC" Class
</par> </switch> </seq>
```

Each view will be made into a SMIL document and named as follows ModeNClassTS.smil, ModeEClassTS.smil, ModeNClassS.smil, ModeEClassS.smil, ModeNClassUC.smil, ModeEClassUC.smil depending on it mode and classification attributes.

7   Runtime Operations

In the most general case, a SMIL specification in mlsNF is of the form ⟨par⟩ Cts Cs Cu Cod Cud ⟨/par⟩ where Cts Cs Cu Cod and Cud respectively have top secret, secret, unclassified, over specified and under specified security levels. How one resolves under specification and over specification is a matter of policy, and is not addressed in this paper. Independently, Cts, Cs, Cu are to be shown to guards with top secret, secret, and unclassified clearances. In addition, in order to respond to emergencies, these specifications have a mode switch encode using a custom attribute *attributeTestMode*. As observed in Figure 2, this attribute is to be evaluated at the beginning of a ⟨switch⟩ statement. That is unsatisfactory for intended purposes, after this switch statement is executed, the operating mode could vary many times. Because the ⟨switch⟩ is evaluated only once, the SMIL specification is now oblivious to such changes in application situations. In this section, we show how to rewrite a SMIL document with one ⟨switch⟩ statement for changing a mode to that one that makes the *attributeTestMode* be evaluated at regular intervals. Although in theory any system could switch its operating mode in an arbitrarily small time intervals, practical considerations limits this interval to a minimum. This minimum switching granularity may depend upon many parameters such as hardware, software and the inherent delays in of switching on firefighting and other emergency related equipment. Therefore, given a switching delay D, we rewrite the given SMIL document so that the mode attribute *attributeTestMode* re-evaluated every D time units. How that is done is discussed in the next section.

7.1   Informal Display Normal Form

The following SMIL specification given below, has the same structure as the fragment considered in Section 4. If we want to break up this specification so that the *attributeTestMode* is tested each D units of time and the switch reevaluated, then the fragment S1 can be translated as shown in S2.

```
S1 =<switch> <par  attributeTestMode= "normal"> XX </par> <par
attributeTestMode= "emergency"></par> </switch>
```

```
S2 = <par dur=D, repeatCount="indefinite"><switch> <par
attributeTestMode="normal"> XX</par> <par
attributeTestMode="emergency">YY </par> </switch> </par>
```

Notice that the outer ⟨par⟩ construct specifies that enclosing specification be executed for duration of D time units and repeated indefinitely. However, the outer ⟨par⟩ construct has only one element, namely the switch. Therefore, the ⟨switch⟩ construct is executed for infinitely many times, and each time the *attributeTestMode* is tested. Given a SMIL specification with the *attributeTest-Mode* specified in the form where the switch is reevaluated every D time units is said to be in display normal form for the attribute *attributeTestMode* and time duration D. We can now informally say that every SMIL document where the *attributeTestMode* is used in the stated form can be translated into its display normal form. We stress the informal nature of our argument because of our commitment to limited operational semantics. However these semantics can be enhanced so that this construction will preserve semantic equivalence.

7.2 Operational Semantics for Making Display Normal Form Semantically Equivalent

In this section, we briefly show how our operational semantics of SMIL can be enhanced so that any SMIL construction with a specified structure and its display normal form are semantically equivalent. First, we close timed display sets under finite concatenations and re-interpret SMIL semantics with respect to them.

Definition 6 (Algebra of TDS: Downward Closure and Concatenation)
Suppose $tdi_1 = (<type\ src="xx",\ ..dur=d1,\ attributeTestSecurity="y",\ T\text{-}begin1, T\text{-}end1>,\ \{y\})$ *and* $tdi_2 = (<type\ src="xx",\ ..dur=d2,\ attributeTest\text{-}Security="y",\ T\text{-}begin2,\ T\text{-}end2>,\ \{y\})$ *are two timed display units with the same source, attributeTestSecurity values, security components satisfying* $T\text{-}end1 = T\text{-}begin2.$

1. *Then we say that* $tdi_3 = (\langle type\ src="xx",\ ..dur=d1,\ attributeTestSecurity ="y",\ T\text{-}begin1, T\text{-}end2\rangle,\ \{y\})$ *is the concatenation of* tdi_1 *and* tdi_2. *We denote the concatenation of* tdi_1 *and* tdi_2 *by* $tdi_1; tdi_2$.
2. *We say that a timed display set TDS is concatenation closed if* $tdi_1, tdi_2 \in TDS \Rightarrow tdi_1; tdi_2 \in TDS$.
3. *We say that a timed display set TDS is downward closed if* $. = (\langle type\ src="xx",\ ..dur=d1,\ attributeTestSecurity="y",\ T\text{-}begin1, T\text{-}end1\rangle,\ \{y\}) \in TDS$, *then* $= (\langle type\ src="xx",\ ..dur=d1,\ attributeTestSecurity="y", T\text{-}begin1', T\text{-}end1'\rangle, \{y\}) \in TDS$ *for any* $T\text{-}begin' > T\text{-}begin$ *and* $T\text{-}end' < t\text{-}end$.

According to Definition 6, downward closure allows any timed display set to include all segments of already included media streams. Concatenation closure allows piecing together successive segments of the same stream to obtain longer streams.

Lemma 2 (Minimal Concatenation Downward Closure of TDS: CD Closure).

Given a timed display set TDS, the concatenation closure of TDS, TDS* is defined as follows:

1. $TDS^0 = \{(< type, src"x", attTestValue=Y>, t, t, \{Y\}) \mid (¡type, src"x", attTest-Value = Y>, t_1, t_2, \{Y\}) \in TDS$ and $t_1 \leq t \leq t_2\}$
2. $TDS^1 = TDS$
3. $TDS^{n+1} = TDS^n ; TDS$
4. $TDS^* = \cup \{TDS^n \mid 0 \leq n\}$
5. $TDS^\wedge = \{(¡type, src"x", attTestValue=Y ¿, t_1, t_2, \{Y\}) \mid (¡type, src"x", attTest-Value = Y>, t_3, t_4, \{Y\}) \in TDS$ and $t_1 \geq t_3$ and $t_4 \leq t_2\}$

Then, $(TDS^*)^\wedge$ is the minimal timed display set containing TDS that is both concatenation and downward closed.

Proof: Omitted

We now enhance the semantics of SMIL by using CD closure sets of base sets. Hence, we strengthen definition 5 as follows.

Definition 7 (Enhanced Semantics for SMIL) *Suppose S is a SMIL specification and [[ ]] is a basis mapping for the basic media elements B of S with the formal parameter t. Then we inductively extend [[ ]]+ to S as follows.*

1) $[[Null]]+ = \Phi.$
2) $[[S']]+ = ([[S']])^{*\wedge}$ *for all basic media streams S' of S.*
3) $[[< seq > S1\ S2 < /seq >]]+ = ([[S1]]+\ U\ [[S2]]+(end([[S1]]+)/t))^{*\wedge}$
4) $[[<par> S1\ S2</par>]]+ = [[S1]]+\ U\ [[S2]]+.$
5) $[[<switch> S1\ S2 </switch>]]+ = [[S1]]+$ *if S1 satisfies the attribute of the switch.* $= [[S2]]+$ *otherwise if S2 satisfies the attribute of the switch.* $= \Phi$ *otherwise.*

We now say that the enhanced mapping [[ ]]+ is a semantic mapping parameterized by t. Now we show how this semantics preserves the display normal form. Notice that the difficulty of the semantics given in definition 5 was with respect to piecing together successive segments of the same stream. By taking concatenations, this problem was solved in definition 5. Downward closures were taken to permit taking all subintervals of permitted streams.

Lemma 3 (Equivalence of Display Normal Form).

The two specifications S1 and S2 have the same semantics.

Informal Proof First observe that if S1 is the specification given on the left and S2 is the specification given on the right, then tdi $\in$ [[S1]]+ iff tdi^n

$\in [[S2]]+$. The reason being that S2 executes S1 arbitrarily many times. But, $[[S2]]+$ is concatenation and downward closed. Therefore, $tdi^n \in [[S2]]+$ iff tdi $\in [[S2]]+$. The reader will now see that downward closure was required in order to obtain $tdi \in [[S2]]+$ from $tdi^n \in [[S2]]+$.

7.3   Dynamic Runtime Activity

As explained, any given SMIL specification S for surveillance is statically translated into its MLS normal form mlsNF(S). Then, when the runtime provides D, mlsNF(S) is translated into its display normal form, say DNF(mlsNF(S),D). Then the runtime takes each the set of streams within the switch that has duration of D, evaluates the switch, and depending upon the mode encrypts and transmits either the streams corresponding to normal operating mode or those that correspond to the emergency operating mode. The SMIL fragment below shows the display normal form for the *Secret View*

```
<smil xmlns="http://www.w3.org/2001/SMIL20/Language"> <head>
<customAttributesMODE>
      <customTestMode="Normal" title="Normal Mode"
        defaultState="true" override="hidden"
        uid="ControllerChoice" />
       <customTestMode id="Emergency" title="Emergency Mode"
        defaultState="false" override="hidden"
        uid="ControllerChoice" />
</customAttributesMODE>
<customAttributesSecClass>
      <customTestsecClass id="TS" title="Top-Secret"
        defaultState="true" override="hidden"/>
<customTestsecClass id="S" title="Secret"
        defaultState="true" override="hidden"/>
<customTestsecClass id="UC"  title="Unlassfied"
        defaultState="trye" override="hidden"/>
</customAttributesSecClass> <body>
    <switch>
<ref src="ModeNClassS.smil" customTestMode ="Normal"
customTestsecClass ="S" /> <ref src="ModeEClassS.smil"
customTestMode ="Emergency" customTestsecClass ="S" />

<ref src="ModeEClassUC.smil" customTestMode ="Emergency"
customTestsecClass ="UC" />
    </switch>
  </body>
</smil>
```

Similarly views for all classification in both the Normal and the Emergency modes can be created. The mode evaluation procedures for setting of the *mode value* associated with a `customTestMODE` is as follows:

1. The initial setting is taken from the value of the `defaultState` attribute, if present. If no default state is explicitly defined, a value of false is used.
2. The URI (Controller Choice) defined by the uid attribute is checked to see if a persistent value has been defined for the custom test attribute with the associated id (Normal, Emergency). If such a value is present, it is used instead of the default state defined in the document (if any). Otherwise, the existing initial state is maintained.
3. As with predefined system test attributes, this evaluation will occur in an implementation-defined manner. The value will be (re) evaluated dynamically.

7.4   Quality of Service(QoS) and Encryption Issues

The Service Level Agreement(SLA) determines the specifications and restrictions that have to be communicated between the client and the server in order to maintain good quality [WS96]. The requirements of the processors and memory (primary and secondary), and other technicalities such as tolerable delay, loss, pixels have to be negotiated prior or sometimes during the transfer process. HQML [GNY+01] proposes an XML based language for the exchange of processor characteristics. The most important characteristic is the amount of buffer, in terms of memory that the recipient device should have in order to maintain continuity. These specifications would be represented within the SMIL document, so that the recipient device will first prepare or disqualify itself for a reception. In the proposed model, the QoS parameters are generally negotiated prior to the display. They could be set as custom defined attributes that have to resolve to true for the display to happen. We can use some of the standard attributes of the switch statement `systemRequired`, `systemScreenDepth`, and `systemScreenSize` to enforce regulation. The SMIL fragment depicted above shows the QoS Negotiation TAGS in accordance with HQML [GNY+01] and [WS96]and the Encryption tags applied to the display normal form of the secret view to achieve fidelity and confidentiality

```
<smil>
  <App name = "Surveillance Facility#3">
    <Configuration id = "Level1Guard">
          <UserLevelQoS> high </UserLevelQoS>
            <UserFocus> memory </UserFocus>
      </Configuration>
      <Configuration id = "Level2Guard">
              <MemUnit mem = "Mbytes"> 5MB </mem>
              <UserLevelQoS> Average </UserLevelQoS>
```

```
                    <UserFocus> Delay </UserFocus>
                    <Delayunit del = "Minutes"> 7 </del>
                    <SLAModel> Conform SLA </SLAModel>
        </Configuration>
        <Configuration id = "Level3Guard">
                <UserLevelQoS> high </UserLevelQoS>
                <UserFocus> clarity </UserFocus>
                <Clarityunit clar= "pixels/inch"> 200 </clar>
        </Configuration>
 </App> <customAttributes>
  //Mode and Security defined here
 <customAttributes>
    </head>

<body> <seq> <switch>
 <par>
 <media src=" ModeNClassTS.smil " customTest3 = "Normal"/>
 <EncryptedData xmlns='http://www.w3.org/2001/04/xmlenc#'>
 <CipherData>
     <CipherValue>123BAVA6</CipherValue>
 </CipherData>
 </EncryptedData>
 </par>
 <par>
 <media src=" ModeNClassS.smil " customTest3="Emergency"/>
 <EncryptedData xmlns='http://www.w3.org/2001/04/xmlenc#'>
 <CipherData>
    <CipherValue>65APR1</CipherValue>
 </CipherData>
 </EncryptedData>
    </par>
//Other SMIL views.
        </switch> </seq> </body>
</smil>
```

Mobile handheld viewing devices [EUMJ] that have embedded SMIL players are the recipients in our architecture. A smartcard, which enforces access control, is embedded into the display device [KW02, KFW03]. Each display device has a unique smartcard depending on the classification of the guard that utilizes it and his/her classification and any other rules set by the controller. A decryption key associated with the privileges of the guard is also embedded in the smartcard. When a display device receives an encrypted SMIL document, the smartcard decrypts the appropriate segment depending on the available key. We encrypt each view in the document as shown the SMIL fragment with a unique Symmetric Key using the standard XML encryption specification. An inbuilt Cryptix

Parser [KW02] that is programmed in firmware (or in software) to handle the decryption process would enable selective decryption of the appropriate view based on the access privileges as defined in the smartcard. With encryption, we guarantee that nobody tampers the stream in transit even if there is mediate stream acquisition.

8   Conclusions

We provided a framework for audio-video surveillance of multi-level secured facilities during normal and pre-envisioned emergencies. We did so by enhancing SMIL specifications with security decorations that satisfy MLS security constraints during normal operations and provide controlled declassification during emergencies while maintaining the integrity and confidentiality. Then we showed how to transform such a SMIL composition to its MLS normal form that preserve runtime semantics intended by SMIL constructs, and how to create SMIL views compliant with MLS requirements. Given the delay characteristics of a runtime, we showed how to transform a SMIL document in MLS normal form so that the operating mode can be switched with a minimal delay while respecting runtime semantics. Our ongoing work extends this basic framework to incorporate richer multimedia semantics and diverse security requirements such as non-alterable media evidence and two way multimedia channels.

References

[Aya01]   Jeff Ayars. *Synchronized Multimedia Integration Language.* W3C Recommendation, 2001. http://www.w3.org/TR/2001/REC-smil20-20010807.

[BBC+00]   Elisa Bertino, M. Braun, Silvana Castano, Elena Ferrari, and Marco Mesiti. Author-x: A java-based system for XML data protection. In *IFIP Workshop on Database Security*, pages 15–26, 2000.

[BHAE02]   Elisa Bertino, Moustafa Hammad, Walid Aref, and Ahmed Elmagarmid. An access control model for video database systems. In *Conferece on Information and Knowledge Management*, 2002.

[Bul98]   David Bulterman. Grins: A graphical interface for creating and playing smil documents. In *Proc. of Seventh Int'l World Wide Web Conf. (WWW7)*. Elsevier Science, New York, April 1998.

[DdV03]   Ernesto Damiani and Sabrina De Capitani di Vimercati. Securing xml based multimedia content. In *18th IFIP International Information Security Conference*, 2003.

[DdVPS00] Ernesto Damiani, Sabrina De Capitani di Vimercati, Stefano Paraboschi, and Pierangela Samarati. Securing XML documents. *Lecture Notes in Computer Science*, 1777:121–122, 2000.

[DdVPS02] Ernesto Damiani, Sabrina De Capitani di Vimercati, Stefano Paraboschi, and Pierangela Samarati. A fine grained access control system for xml documents. *ACM Transactions on Information and System Security*, 5, 2002.

[EUMJ]   E. Ekudden, U.Horn, M.Melander, and J.Olin. On-demand mobile media- a rich service experience for mobile users.

[GNY+01]   Xiaohui Gu, Klara Nahrstedt, Wanghong Yuan, Duangdao Wichadakul, and Dongyan Xu. An XML-based quality of service enabling language for the web, 2001.

[JSSS01]   Sushil Jajodia, Pierangela Samarati, Maria Luisa Sapino, and V. S. Subrahmanian. Flexible support for multiple access control policies. *ACM Trans. Database Syst.*, 26(2):214–260, 2001.

[KFW03]   Naren Kodali, Csilla Farkas, and Duminda Wijesekera. Enforcing integrity in multimedia surveillance. In *IFIP 11.5 Working Conference on Integrity and Internal Control in Information Systems*, 2003.

[KW02]   Naren Kodali and Duminda Wijesekera. Regulating access to SMIL formatted pay-per-view movies. In *2002 ACM Workshop on XML Security*, 2002.

[KWJ03]   Naren Kodali, Duminda Wijesekera, and J.B.Michael. SPUTERS: a secure traffic surveillance and emergency response architecture. In *submission to the Journal of Intelligent Transportaion Systems*, 2003.

[Low99]   Gavin Lowe. Defining information flow, 1999.

[Mul87]   Ketan Mulmuley. *Full abstraction and semantic equivalence*. MIT Press, 1987.

[Nok]   Mobile Internet Toolkit: Nokia. www.nokia.com.

[Osb]   Sylvia Osborn. Mandatory access control and role-based access control revisited. pages 31–40.

[PCV02]   Kari Pihkala, Pablo Cesar, and Petri Vuorimaa. Cross platform smil player. In *International Conference on Communications, Internet and Information Technology*, 2002.

[RHO99]   L. Rutledge, L. Hardman, and J. Ossenbruggen. The use of smil: Multimedia research currently applied on a global scale, 1999.

[RvOHB99]   Lloyd Rutledge, Jacco van Ossenbruggen, Lynda Hardman, and Dick C. A. Bulterman. Anticipating SMIL 2.0: the developing cooperative infrastructure for multimedia on the Web. *Computer Networks (Amsterdam, Netherlands: 1999)*, 31(11–16):1421–1430, 1999.

[San93]   Ravi S. Sandhu. Lattice-based access control models. *IEEE Computer*, 26(11):9–19, 1993.

[Sch99]   B. K. Schmidt. An architecture for distributed, interactive, multi-stream, multi-participant audio and video. In *Technical Report No CSL-TR-99-781, Stanford Computer Science Department*, 1999.

[SF02]   Andrei Stoica and Csilla Farkas. Secure XML views. In *Proc IFIP 11.3 Working Conference on Database Security*, 2002.

[Spy]   Spymake. Integrated surveillance tools http://www.spymakeronline.com/.

[VCM]   Mobile VCMS. Field data collection system http://www.acrcorp.com.

[VSA]   VSAM. Video surveillance and monitoring webpage at http://www-2.cs.cmu.edu/ vsam/.

[WS96]   Duminda Wijesekera and Jaideep Srivastava. Quality of service QoS metrics for continuous media. *Multimedia Tools and Applications*, 3(2):127–166, 1996.

Author Index

Lecture Notes in Computer Science

For information about Vols. 1–3259

please contact your bookseller or Springer